# The Economics of Aging
## Second Edition

James H. Schulz

Florence Heller Graduate School
Brandeis University

Wadsworth Publishing Company, Inc.
Belmont, California

Sociology Editor: Curt Peoples
Production Editor: Scott Lowe
Designer: Vita Otrubova-Hayes
Copy Editor: Alice Rosenthal

Printed in the United States of America
1 2 3 4 5 6 7 8 9 10———84 83 82 81 80

Library of Congress Cataloging in Publication Data
Schulz, James H.
    The economics of aging

    Includes bibliography and index
        1. Old age pensions—United States.    2. Retirement income—United
States.    3. Aged—United States—Economic conditions.    I. Title.
HD7106. U5S33    1980        362.6'0973        79-18079
ISBN 0-534-00772-4

# Preface

The enthusiastic response to the first edition has been gratifying. It has encouraged me to try even harder in the second edition to provide noneconomists greater access to the important but often highly technical economics literature dealing with the issues of aging.

Major portions of the book have been changed and updated. More attention has been given to the political and economic implications of population trends. The impact of the new 1977 mandatory retirement law is examined. The major changes resulting from the 1977 social security amendments are discussed. New information is included on the growing impact of private pensions. Increased attention is given to the special pension problems of women. Finally, a glossary has been added to assist readers unfamiliar with key terms used throughout the book.

Economic destitution among the aged has been a recognized national problem for almost half a century; yet economists have virtually ignored the problem. Over the years only a handful of economists have given much attention to the economic issues associated with a growing aged population and the fact that a substantial proportion of the United States population has shifted out of the labor force.

Policy makers and the elderly themselves generally agree that economic security in old age is one of the most important problems needing solution. Yet, as in other areas of knowledge, misconceptions abound. Most aged are not poor; they are not the group most seriously hurt by inflation; they have not been *forced* to retire.

We do not know the answers to all the questions raised concerning the economic situation of the aged. However, this book attempts to present a wide range of existing knowledge, which permits a more sophisticated view of the many issues and which, in some cases, challenges the conventional wisdom.

Much of the earlier work in this area by economists and government agencies has focused on documenting the relatively poor economic status of the aged and problems associated with the social security system. Now, with dramatic declines in labor-force participation by older workers and equally dramatic, and related, increases in economic support programs for the elderly, many other major issues have arisen. Just a few of these are:

1. The economic implications of demographic shifts in the age structure of our population.
2. The structural employment problems of older workers in an economic milieu of age discrimination, rapid technological change, and frequent geographic shifts (national and international) by business.
3. The economic consequences and the distributional implications of the "early retirement" phenomenon.
4. The impact of inflation on the elderly and the development of appropriate indexing mechanisms.
5. The inter- and intra-generational equity of pension systems.
6. The impact of pensions on saving and investment.
7. The economic implications of a $200 billion private pension industry.
8. Appropriate economic policies toward the elderly in adopting public assistance and tax-reform programs.
9. How to design a quality health-delivery system without skyrocketing costs.

Fortunately, coincident with the expanding number of issues to be confronted, we have witnessed in recent years a significant rise in aging information, data, research, and programs. Our knowledge of the economic problems and alternative solutions is changing very rapidly.

To date, however, there has been no comprehensive review of what we know and where we are with regard to the economics of aging. The available knowledge and statistics are scattered in widely diverse places—many quite obscure. One major objective of this book is to bring much of this information together for the first time.

I have tried to cover a wide range of technical topics in a relatively nontechnical and concise manner. Inevitably a lot of the complexities and much of the existing literature could not be discussed. However, I have recommended at the end of each chapter the additional reading that in my judgment would be most useful for those readers seeking to extend their knowledge on particular issues. Again, however, I have tried to avoid highly technical works.

Some readers may be surprised by the proportion of the book devoted to pension issues (four chapters). To me, however, the key to understanding the current and future economic status of the aged is an understanding of private and public pension programs. Therefore, I have devoted considerable space in the book to describing these programs and, more importantly, to discussing their economic impact on the younger and older populations.

I first became interested in the economics of aging when some years ago I had the opportunity to ask one of the most knowledgeable persons in the aging field, Clark Tibbitts, "What have economists contributed to our knowledge about growing old?" His answer and challenge to a young graduate student who was then searching for a dissertation topic—"Why don't you find out?"—triggered a sequence of events of which this book is a product. It is appropriate then that the book begins again with an introduction by Clark Tibbitts, a person who has dedicated a major portion of his life to improving the social and economic welfare of older persons.

To the many people who read all or part of this book prior to publication and provided me with suggested changes, corrections, and useful insights, I express my sincere thanks:

First edition:
Vern Bengtson, Chief, Laboratory for Social Organization and Behavior, University of Southern California;
Robert Binstock, Director, Program in the Economics and Politics of Aging, Brandeis University;
William Birdsall, School of Social Work, University of Michigan;
Colin Campbell, Professor of Economics, Dartmouth College;
Wilbur J. Cohen, Dean, School of Education, University of Michigan;
Alan Fox, Office of Research and Statistics, Social Security Administration;
Walter Kolodrubetz, Office of Policy Planning and Research, Department of Labor;
Juanita Kreps, Secretary of Commerce;
Donald Landay, Bureau of Labor Statistics, Department of Labor (deceased);
Patience Lauriat, formerly Office of Research and Statistics, Social Security Administration;
Dan McGill, Chairman and Research Director, Pension Research Council, University of Pennsylvania;
Elizabeth Meier, President's Commission on Pension Policy;
Harold Orbach, Department of Sociology, Kansas State University;
George Rohrlich, Professor of Economics and Social Policy, Temple University;

Charles Schottland, Professor of Law and Social Welfare, Brandeis University;

Harold Sheppard, American Institute for Research;

Alfred Skolnik, Office of Research and Statistics, Social Security Administration (deceased);

Gayle Thompson, Office of Research and Statistics, Social Security Administration;

Lawrence Thompson, Acting Associate Commissioner, Social Security Administration;

Clark Tibbitts, Special Assistant to the Commissioner on Aging;

Harry Weitz, former Chief, Pension Section, Statistics Canada;

Yung-Ping Chen, Department of Economics, University of California, Los Angeles.

Second edition:

Letitia L. Alston, Texas A & M University

Richard S. Foster, Special Assistant to the Chief Actuary, Social Security Administration

Marilyn L. Flynn, University of Illinois, Urbana/Champaign

Susan Grad, Office of Research and Statistics, Social Security Administration

Linda Graham, Wichita State University

Dorothy R. Kittner, U.S. Bureau of Labor Statistics

Mark Krain, University of Arkansas, Little Rock

Regina O'Grady, Program in the Economics and Politics of Aging, Brandeis University

Harold Orbach, Kansas State University

Sara E. Rix, American Institute for Research

Marc Rosenblum, Advisory Board, *Aging and Work*

Harold Sheppard, American Institute for Research

John Snee, Office of Program Evaluation and Planning, Social Security Administration

I also wish to thank the Social Security Administration for making various unpublished statistics available for this book. And, finally, my sincere thanks to Margaret Stubbs for her research and typing assistance.

James H. Schulz
Waltham, Massachusetts

# Contents

# Introduction

The need for a revised edition of *The Economics of Aging* only a few years after the appearance of the pioneering original edition is a clear measure of the dynamic nature of the subject matter with which the book is concerned. The broad areas addressed are: trends in middle-aged and older worker labor force participation and retirement; levels, sources, and adequacy of income during the later stages of life; and the evolution, achievements, and shortcomings of public and private pension systems. Continuing change in all of these areas is indicative of the importance of the economics of aging to all who are living in, or are concerned with, the circumstances of their later lives as well as the policies and programs of numerous societal institutions in the public and private sector.

In preparing the extensive revisions for this new edition of *The Economics of Aging*, Professor Schulz has made extensive use of new legislation in the areas of employment and provision for retirement income, of reported experience relative to the new legislation, of new sources of statistical data, and of the growing body of knowledge from research. The number of authorities cited and the currentness and comprehensiveness of the revised bibliography attest to the scholarly approach applied to the revision of the entire book.

The new edition makes its appearance during what promises to be a critical and probably extended period of uncertainty and retrenchment in the nation's economic development, the effects of which are already limiting the effort to meet the needs of the older population. Foremost among the changes are: recognized limits to supplies of non-renewable energy; permanent and costly measures to restrict air, water, and ground pollution from manufacturing and agricultural processes and automobiles; persistent inflation; a sharply reduced rate of increase in the gross national product and disposable income, and the insistence of developing nations on having a larger share of the world's resources.

Parallel to these changes is the continuing increase in the older (and especially in the oldest) population which, following a very small increase during the mid-1900s, will rise to a net annual increase on the order of 1.2 million by 2025. However, following the large increase in the retired population will come a relatively stable proportion in the 18 to 64 year age group, which provides most of the support for the aging and retired. Largely as a consequence of these changes, the proportion of the Federal budget devoted to older people is expected to increase from 20 percent to 40 percent over the next thirty years.

The timeliness of *The Economics of Aging* is attested by the surge of public awareness and concern with the circumstances of the older population, and of the resources allocated to them following the last decennial White House Conference on Aging; a nationwide interest in gerontology on the part of college and university faculty and students; the desire of personnel employed in the field to improve their gerontological knowledge and skills; and the rapid expansion of courses and curricula responsive to the demand for trained policy makers, planners, program developers and administrators, researchers, and teachers in the field.

The availability of this textbook dealing with the economic aspects of aging substantially contributes to the subject matter of aging. The use of *The Economics of Aging* enables educational institutions to acquaint students with the highly significant economic factors in aging, complementing the biomedical and psychosocial subject matter which has traditionally dominated gerontology. The rounding out of gerontological curricula anticipates the appearance of concentration majors and specialized degrees in gerontology.

The basic phenomena of aging—increasing numbers and proportions of people surviving longer and the vastly altered functions of middle-aged and older adults in social institutions—have had their principal origins in biomedical and economic research and other advancing technologies. The results of these developments have been measured in the continuing flow of life-prolonging knowledge and techniques, and in exponential increases over the last 65 to 70 years in productivity, disposable income, and uncommitted, or leisure time. These developments were made possible by our almost total reliance on inanimate energy and technologies in the production of goods and services. Understanding the origin and future of aging is determined, to a considerable degree, by a knowledge of these forces as well as of the forces which underlie the current period of economic uncertainty.

With respect to aging of the individual, economics is concerned with such matters as the expenditure of time over the middle and later stages of adulthood, particularly following the tapering off of parental and work roles; separation from the labor force; changes in amounts and sources of income and its effect on patterns of consumption, including the ability to purchase health and medical care, housing, other services, and the amenities of life. Economics within the context of aging illuminates other aspects of growing old, particularly the changes in income and employment status which affect family and intergenerational relationships, social status, and personal and social adjustment.

The allocation of national income and resources to older persons and their apportionment for health, housing, social recreation, education, and transportation comes within the purview of economics. So, too, do such matters as individual versus collective responsibility for meeting needs, the effect of providing for older people on the income and availability of goods and services for younger elements of the population, the role of pension reserves in capital investment, the impact of social security and private pension systems on savings practices of younger adults, the relative cost and effectiveness of providing retirement income through public versus private pension systems, and the influence of pension income on labor force participation. *The Economics of Aging* deals with all of these matters.

Professor Schulz opens the revised edition on a note of guarded optimism. He reports that, in spite of several residual inequities, a good deal of progress has been made in providing a livable income to the majority of older people. He suggests that one challenge for the future will be to maintain the progress that has been made in light of the demographic and economic changes now underway.

Another positive development has been the increase in flexibility with regard to personal decision making and timing of retirement. The underlying factors contributing to this development are early retirement provisions in public and private pension systems (which enable workers to retire prior to reaching the traditional eligibility age of 65 years), and new legislation which raises the minimum age that may be used in setting retirement policy to 70 years and eliminates age as a criterion for mandatory retirement of federal employees. More than half of these who retire do so before age 65 and nearly 3 million persons 65 years and over are employed. Furthermore, there is solid evidence that most of the retired are at least reasonably satisfied with their retirement status and are not interested in returning to the work force.

There is recent legislation designed to safeguard the rights of workers covered by private pensions and to guarantee the soundness of the social security system at least well into the next century. Such legislation may be a factor in the results of public opinion polls which report the willingness of adults of all ages to contribute to public and private pension systems in order to assure themselves of having retirement income. The polls, plus the absence of strong protest over the sharp rise in the social security tax may be interpreted as evidence of a general readiness to eliminate poverty in the older population.

Throughout the revised book Professor Schulz identifies numerous issues that provide an agenda for both the present and the future, and which challenge policy makers, program administrators, and researchers in the economics of aging field. A few of these issues are identified below:

> What measures can be devised to improve the incomes of unmarried older women, minority persons, and nonsteady workers? Should social security credit be given for the years women devote to unpaid homemaking? Should survivor benefits be mandated in private pension systems?

> What should be the levels of guaranteed minimum incomes during the later years? Should the poverty level be accepted as the minimum level? Or should the Bureau of Labor Statistics lower or intermediate budget levels be so recognized? Or should a fixed salary/wage replacement level be established?

> How can retirement incomes from assets and from private pensions be protected from inflation? Should constant purchasing power bonds be be issued by the Government for persons at low and middle-income levels? Is the reverse mortgage mechanism a viable method of enabling retired persons to make use of their nonliquid assets?

> Should incentives to early retirement be prohibited for those able to work, and inducements to remaining longer in the work force be provided in order to increase income and reduce payments of public and private pension systems? How can the costs of disability pension payments be controlled and equity maintained?

> What criteria can be developed to substitute for chronological age as a criterion for policy and decision making in employment and retirement?

> Should systems of counseling, occupational retraining, and preparation for aging be fostered by the government in educational institutions?

Knowledge of the principal economic elements of aging, particularly of income-support systems and their individual and social ramifications, is essential preparation for those who would participate in societal decision making. It is also necessary for coping with the circumstances of later life, and is a condition for successful careers in many of the gerontological occupations.

The economic and economic-related issues identified by Professor Schulz can be resolved successfully only through a process which involves all those who choose to participate. Clearly, such participation can be useful only if it is based on knowledge of the subject matter involved.

From the individual or personal point of view, virtually every member of society has a stake in the resolution of these issues. All currently employed workers will leave the work force at some time, and will have a period of twenty to thirty years of retirement. Thus, almost all young and middle-aged people may expect to become beneficiaries of a public and/or private pension system. The adequacy of that system will be a major determinant of their life style for up to one-fourth or one-third of their lifetime.

Finally, those who are preparing for employment or who already are employed in policy development, planning, and program administration on behalf of older people will be called upon to demonstrate an increasingly systematic knowledge of aging, including the economic elements and their significance relative to the other elements.

Readers will be impressed with the amount of information Professor Schulz has provided, with the meticulous care with which it has been discussed, and with the painstaking effort he has made to make this complex subject intelligible for students, informed lay persons, and professionals in related fields who wish to be informed about the economics of aging.

Clark Tibbitts
Special Assistant to the Commissioner on Aging
Department of Health, Education, and Welfare

# Chapter One

## *Changing Populations and Retirement Expectations*

Not too many years ago it was relatively easy to write about the economic situation of the elderly population. All one needed to do was cite statistics that confirmed what everyone knew from either personal experience or observation. For years now everyone has known that most of the elderly have suffered from serious economic deprivation—that their incomes were inadequate, that inflation exacerbated the situation by reducing real incomes and eroding savings, and that the aged were one of the largest poverty groups in the country.

Today the situation is much more complex, due in large part to our nation's very positive response to the economic plight of the elderly. During the past few decades major breakthroughs have occurred in the development of private and public programs to deal with the economic problems of old age:

1. Over the past ten years, social security old age benefits have been increased by almost 100 percent, significantly faster than inflation over the same period.
2. Private pension programs have spread throughout industry and have grown rapidly—with dramatic increases in benefit levels.
3. Public health programs have been created—currently providing over $60 billion a year in benefits to older persons.
4. Property tax relief laws have been legislated in all our states.
5. Old age assistance has been abolished and a new Supplemental Security Income Program (SSI) has taken its place. This program roughly doubles the number of low income elderly eligible for income supplementation. And it raised benefit levels in twenty-four states above the previous levels of old age assistance—in some cases dramatically. In addition, a national food stamp program helps low income people of all ages.

1

Despite the economic problems that remain (which will be discussed later in this book), we must nevertheless not lose sight of the important economic gains that have been made. Dramatic changes have occurred in the levels of income provided older persons, especially from public and private pensions. Consequently, there has been a significant improvement in the general economic status of this group—traditionally viewed as poverty-stricken. In fact, researchers at the University of Wisconsin's Institute for Research on Poverty recently released poverty statistics that included sources of economic support usually omitted from government statistics (food stamps, Medicare, and housing subsidies). In contrast to the official aged poverty rate in 1976 of 13 percent, these estimates (Watts and Skidmore, 1977) suggest that in that year only about 5 percent of persons age 65 or older were living in poverty. The methodology used to make these new estimates is controversial, and hence not all agree with the results. The Wisconsin findings serve to dramatize, however, the undisputed progress that has been made in raising many from the ranks of the "most poor" to the ranks of the "near poor."*

So rapid and so great has been this improvement in the welfare of the aged that assessments of their condition have not kept apace with progress. Not only the general public but also many professionals concerned with the problems of the elderly have a serious misconception regarding the current economic situation of the aged. A study by Erdman Palmore (1977) reports that about one-half of the graduate students and faculty in the field of human development and aging at two prominent universities did not recognize as an *incorrect* statement the true-false quiz question: "The majority of old people have incomes below the poverty level (as defined by the federal government)." In contrast, these same students and faculty answered correctly about 90 percent of the other questions in the aging quiz covering twenty-four other areas of knowledge about older persons.

There is no doubt that many people are unaware of the rapidly improving economic status of the aged in America. Still fewer have thought about its implications for policy on the aging. Given, for example, the projected shortfall of the social security system in meeting its projected obligations (see Chapter 8), this news of a greatly improved economic situation for the aged is a development to be welcomed. As various ways of raising additional revenues for the system are considered, it is certainly heartening to hear that older people today are economically much better off than they were little more than a decade ago.

The decline in the seriousness of the elderly's economic problems

---

*Whether the progress is sufficient is a different question. We discuss, for example, the appropriateness of the official poverty index in the next chapter.

means that the task of helping the aged may not need to be as high on the social agenda as in prior years. In fact, given the rising costs of providing for the aged, some have begun to argue that we have already gone too far. Writing in the *Washington Post,* columnist David S. Broder (1973), for example, concludes that "the significant, semihidden story in the . . . federal budget is that America's public resources are increasingly being mortgaged for the use of a single group within our country: the elderly."

Robert J. Samuelson (1978) emphasizes the constraint the budget realities place on elected officials: "Put simply, the slow increase in the aged population, combined with the massive rise in assistance already promised the elderly, means that neither the President nor the Congress can afford to provide much new spending for anything else—unless they want to raise taxes or run permanently large budget deficits."

In 1978, Health, Education and Welfare Secretary Joseph A. Califano, Jr., became the first cabinet secretary to publicize the problem of rising federal expenditures for the elderly. He estimated that $112 billion was paid out that year by federal programs assisting the elderly. And he projected that these expenditures would rise from 24 percent of the federal budget in 1978 to 40 percent in the early part of the twenty-first century (Califano, 1979).

Have we done enough? To answer the question we can no longer generalize about the economic situation of all the aged as one group. Instead we must look at the multitude of programs for the elderly and analyze their impact on various subgroups of the elderly population. We must distinguish, for example, between the very old aged (the "vulnerable aged") and those just retiring, between widowed and married women, and between those with two private pensions and those with only a social security pension.

In the chapters to follow we will survey the major economic changes that have occurred among various groups of the aged. But before we do this, it is important to discuss the changes in retirement expectations that have occurred in American society and the important demographic shifts that are now occurring.

### The Right to Retire

As observed by Donahue, Orbach, and Pollak (1960), "retirement is a phenomenon of modern industrial society. . . . The older people of previous societies were not retired persons; there was no retirement role." A number of developments, however, changed this.

Even *before* public and private pension systems were widely established, large numbers of older persons were not in the labor force. As early as 1900, for example, almost one-third of all men age 65 and over were "retired," in large part because of health problems. Prior to the institution of **pension**\* systems, however, older persons not in the labor force had to rely on their own (often meager) resources, help from relatives, or public and private charity. Over the years recognition spread that complete reliance on these sources of old age support was unsatisfactory. *Public pensions were, in part, a reaction to the need of more rational support mechanisms for older persons unable to work.*

Industrialization created a new problem. In contrast to the farm, where people could almost always "work" (even if it was at reduced levels), industry was characterized by a large amount of job insecurity. Recurrent **recessions** and **depressions** and shifts in employment opportunities created competition for the available jobs. *Thus, another motivation for establishing pensions was to encourage older workers to leave the work force and create jobs for younger workers.*

But probably most important of all, industrial growth—fueled by rapid technological change—resulted in vast increases in economic output. As we discuss at length in Chapter 3, economic growth provides an expanding option for greater leisure with a simultaneous increase in living standards. That is, the rapid economic growth of the twentieth century made it possible to more easily support older people who could not (or did not wish to) work. Retirement became economically feasible.

Thus, we see the institutionalization of retirement arising as a result of and reaction to (a) the needs of large numbers of elderly unable to work, (b) short-run fluctuations in employment opportunities for both the young and the old, and (c) expanding economic resources over the long run. Pension programs were developed that "provided compensation based upon years of service rather than upon need per se. They were to emerge as an 'earned right' and were to become instrumental in defining a retirement status as appropriate for the older worker" (Friedman and Orbach, 1974).

### Changing Expectations

As just indicated, until recently retirement meant dependency—on relatives, friends, private charity, or government welfare. Indications are that many elderly tended to accept a subsistence lifestyle as the best that could be expected in old age. Attitudinal surveys have found, for example, that despite their relatively low economic status, very *high* proportions of

---

\*Many technical terms appearing in the text are defined or explained in a glossary at the back of the book. Terms in the glossary appear in boldface type the first time they appear in the text and, in the case of very important terms, at first appearance in subsequent chapters.

the elderly viewed their economic situation as satisfactory and not below their expectations.*

Predictably, those *approaching* old age viewed the period negatively. "The widespread opposition to retirement reported in studies during the 1940s and the early 1950s reflected an overwhelming concern over the consequences of serious deprivation associated with retirement" (Friedman and Orbach, 1974).

Retirement expectations are changing, however. In part, this has resulted from increases in living standards at all ages. More importantly, the development of pension programs and the continuous improvement in their provisions have given the elderly increasing independence and for the first time placed a comfortable standard of living within the reach of many. Increasing pension benefits and pension coverage seem to stimulate demands for still higher retirement incomes.

### Aging Populations

At the same time that retirement income expectations are changing, we are witnessing an aging of populations around the world. This phenomenon is relatively recent and restricted to a small but growing group of countries. Rosset (1964) classifies countries with 8 percent or more of their population age 65 or over as having aging populations. Hauser (1976) reports that in 1970 there were twenty-nine countries meeting that criterion.

Table 1 contrasts the 1970 demographic profile for the United States with other selected countries. In that year, the German Democratic Republic had the highest proportion of aged in the world—16 percent. Sweden had the highest **life expectancy** for men and (along with France, Norway, the Netherlands, and Iceland, which are not shown) the highest for women. Not surprisingly, the less-developed countries had dramatically different profiles.

Figures 1 and 2 show the marital status and living arrangements for the elderly in 1976. Most men are married; but given a longer life expectancy, many women become widowed. Hence, whereas men are usually heads of families, large numbers of women live alone or with nonrelatives.

In the United States the population age 65 and over increased more rapidly (20 percent) than the population as a whole (13 percent) during the 1960–1970 period. Yet, as Siegel (1976) points out, "the growth of this age

---

*See, for example, the report of Louis Harris and Associates listed in the Suggested Readings at the end of this chapter. For a conceptual framework that incorporates the notion of relative deprivation to help explain the perceived financial adequacy among the elderly, see Liang and Fairchild (1979).

*Table 1.* A Demographic Profile of the United States and Selected Countries, 1969–1971

| Country | Life Expectancy at Birth | | Birth Rate | Death Rate | Percent of Population | | |
| --- | --- | --- | --- | --- | --- | --- | --- |
| | Men | Women | | | Under 15 | 15–65 | 65 and Over |
| United States | 67 | 74 | 18 | 9 | 28 | 62 | 10 |
| German Democratic Republic | 69 | 74 | 14 | 14 | 23 | 61 | 16 |
| Sweden | 72 | 77 | 14 | 10 | 21 | 65 | 14 |
| Soviet Union | 65 | 74 | 18 | 8 | 31 | 61 | 8 |
| Mexico | 61 | 64 | 43 | 9 | 46 | 50 | 4 |
| India | 42 | 41 | 43 | 17 | 42 | 55 | 3 |
| Zambia | | 44 | 50 | 21 | 46 | 52 | 2 |
| More Developed Countries (Averages) | | 70 | 19 | 9 | 27 | 64 | 10 |
| Less Developed Countries (Averages) | | 50 | 41 | 16 | 41 | 55 | 3 |

Source: Based on data in Philip M. Hauser, "Aging and World-Wide Population Change," in R. H. Binstock and E. Shanas, *Handbook of Aging and the Social Sciences* (New York: Van Nostrand Reinhold, 1976), Tables 3 and 6. © 1976 by Litton Educational Publishing, Inc. Used by permission.

group during the 1960s was well below its growth rate during the 1950s (35 percent) and the preceding decades (35 to 37 percent for 1920 to 1950)." Given relatively stable mortality and net immigration rates (see Figure 21, p. 155), these fluctuations in growth since the Second World War have largely been due to fluctuations in the **fertility rate** (births per 1,000 women 15 to 44 years old). Figure 3 shows the changing fertility rate over the 1930–1976 period.

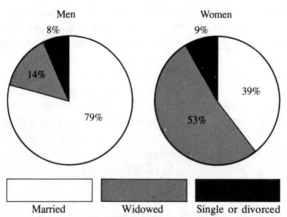

*Figure 1. 1976 Marital Status of Older Persons*

Source: National Clearing House on Aging, *Facts About Older Americans 1977* (Washington, D.C.: U.S. Department of HEW, 1977).

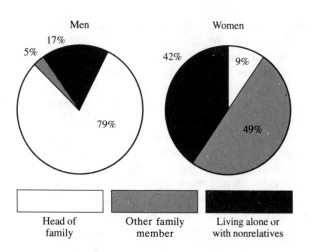

*Figure 2. 1976 Living
Arrangements of the Noninstitutional Aged*

Source: National Clearing House on Aging, *Facts About Older Americans 1977*
(Washington, D.C.: U.S. Department of HEW, 1977).

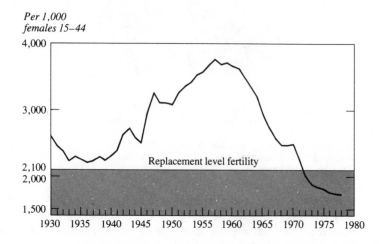

*Figure 3. Fertility Rate, 1930–1976*

Source: U.S. Bureau of the Census, "Estimates of the Population of the United
States and Components of Change: 1940 to 1976," *Current Population Reports,*
Series P-25, No. 706 (Washington, D.C.: U.S. Government Printing Office, 1977).

Looking to the future, we can expect a much slower increase in the 65 and over population for the next three decades; this results from the lower number of births during the 1920–1940 period. But early in the next century the number of elderly will rise sharply as those born during the postwar baby boom enter the retirement years. Thus, given current trends, the **median** age of the population will rise sharply—increasing from age 29 in 1977 to about age 37 in the year 2020 (Figure 4).

Perhaps as significant as the general demographic shifts occurring in the United States are the specific changes occurring among subgroups of the population. Among the aged, the female population has been growing (and will continue to grow) much more rapidly than the male population. The sex ratio of the elderly population in 1975 shows 4.1 million more women than men, or 100 women for every 65 men. By the year 2000, the difference is expected to grow to 6.5 million, or 100 women for every 69 men (Siegel, 1976).

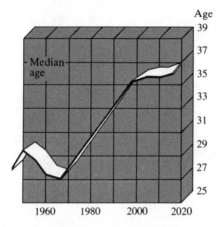

*Figure 4.   The Changing
Median Age of the Population*

Source: Reproduced from National Journal, *The Economics of Aging,* a National Journal Issues Book (Washington, D.C.: The Government Research Corporation, 1978). Used by permission.

Also, there is a progressive aging of the aging population itself. Between 1977 and 2000, those age 65 to 74 will increase by about 20 percent. "But take a look at what's going to happen to a group of Older Americans that *will* affect dramatically our individual lives and our government's commitments more than ever before: the population 80 and older, between 1977 and 2000. That age group will grow, not by 20 percent, but by 67 percent. . . . A smaller and smaller proportion of the very old who are in the greatest state of dependency will actually have any younger children who might otherwise be counted on to provide family based care" (Sheppard, 1978).*

### Dependency Ratios

An increase in the number of the aged causes concern among policy makers because this means an increase in the number of nonworkers who must be economically supported by the working population. Many people are now concerned about the increased competition that may arise among age groups as each strives for a larger share of the nation's output. For example, improving retirement income by increasing social security often heads the list of demands by the aged segment of the population; in contrast, this is a relatively unimportant priority for younger workers.

Given the various mechanisms for retirement income provision— social security, public assistance, private insurance, private charity, and/or personal savings—the fundamental economic fact remains that the part of national output consumed in any particular year by those *retired* is produced by the *working* population, regardless of the mix of mechanisms employed.** Figure 5 shows, for example, the proportion of total output estimated to be consumed by the aged in 1974. Some of this output was produced by persons over age 64 still in the labor force. But most of the aged, consuming about 10 percent of total output, did not participate in the production process.

To analyze the changing dependency ratio between workers and nonworkers, researchers commonly divide the population into those of *working age* (18–64), *young* dependents under 18, and *old* dependents 65 and over (see Clark, Kreps, and Spengler, 1978). These divisions, however, are only crude approximations of the relative numbers of persons in the two categories: dependents and workers. They are used so frequently because reliable data on future labor force participation are not readily available— given the difficulty of projecting trends for various age groups.

Using this approach, for example, Rejda and Shepler (1973) and Chen and Chu (1977) have studied the impact of the changing dependency ratio on the financing of the social security system. Both studies reach similar conclusions. They show that the changing age composition of the population "does not mean bankruptcy or insolvency of social security, but does

---

*This important point, along with other issues concerned with the impact of demographic changes on the family, is given expanded treatment in excellent articles by Shanas and Hauser (1974) and Tibbitts (1977). Demographic developments are much more complex than our brief comments in this section might suggest. For a good discussion of the various issues see Cutler and Harootyan (1975).

**While working, individuals store up claims to output produced after they stop working by acquiring financial assets (saving) and by the accrual of pension credits.

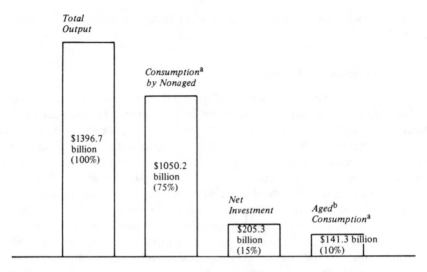

*Figure 5. Consumption
and Investment of National Output in 1974*

Source: Estimated using data in *Economic Report of the President* (Washington, D.C.: U.S. Government Printing Office, 1975).
[a]Includes government nontransfer expenditures apportioned on a per capita basis between aged and nonaged.
[b]Persons age 65 or more.

imply a shifting pattern of public expenditures for the two groups of dependents [young versus old]" (Chen and Chu, 1977).

One of the few studies that goes beyond the crude dependency measures is by Marc Rosenblum and is reported in Sheppard and Rix (1977). Table 2 shows Rosenblum's estimated dependency ratios for the 1975–2010 period. The data show that the labor force will rise much more rapidly than the nonworking segment of the population. This results from the fact that the rising number of aged is offset by the fall in the number of children in the lower ages. Sheppard and Rix caution, however, that Rosenblum's projections are only through the year 2010: "Labor-force projections for later years by Denis Johnston reveal that every 100 members of the labor force will be supporting 112 dependents by 2020 and 115 by 2040" (Sheppard and Rix, 1977). Even these higher ratios for 2020 and 2040, however, are lower than the ratio for 1975.

The projected changes in the dependency ratio indicate that we must continue to give attention to the changing numbers of *both* young and old. Unfortunately, little information exists on the extent to which the re-

Table 2.   Dependency Ratios Based on Labor Force Projections: 1975–2010

| Year | Total Noninstitutional Population (millions) | Total Labor Force (millions) | Nonlabor Force All Ages (millions) | Ratio[a] |
|------|------|------|------|------|
| 1975 | 211 | 95 | 116 | 123 |
| 1980 | 223 | 104 | 119 | 114 |
| 1990 | 245 | 117 | 129 | 110 |
| 2000 | 263 | 127 | 135 | 106 |
| 2010 | 279 | 137 | 141 | 103 |

Source: Harold L. Sheppard and Sara E. Rix, *The Graying of Working America—The Coming Crisis of Retirement-Age Policy* (New York: The Free Press, 1977), Table 3. Used by permission.
[a]Number of nonworkers per 100 workers, all ages (Series II U.S. Census Projections).

duced costs of fewer children might offset the rising costs of more retired persons. Robert Clark and Joseph Spengler (1978), using a broad measure of public support costs, find that government expenditures are three times greater for older dependents than for children. This is not surprising since, aside from education expenditures, most expenditures for children are made directly by parents—not, as in the case of the aged, through public expenditure or transfer programs. In contrast, Hilde Wander (1978) finds that in West Germany the total cost of rearing a child to 20 is one-fourth to one-third higher than that necessary to support someone 60 years old for the rest of his lifetime.

Even if the costs are less, the changing composition of the dependency ratio raises a number of major political questions as more must be paid out through the political tax–transfer process. Political scientist Robert Hudson argues that we can expect at least three political outcomes from these fiscal pressures: major new policy initiatives or appropriations for the aged beyond those provided for under existing legislation will meet with new and perhaps overwhelming resistance; agencies servicing the elderly will be subjected to more insistent demands for accountability; and, finally, the political influence of the aging and groups organized on their behalf will be put to a new and sterner test (Hudson, 1978).

### The Need for Individual and National Retirement Planning

Today those who have not yet reached the retirement period of life can look forward to that period without many of the fears that worried so many in the past. A wide variety of institutional mechanisms are now available to help individuals provide for their economic needs. In fact, almost all individuals are *required* to make substantial provision for retirement by mandatory participation in social security and other pension programs.

With the emergence of retirement as a normative expectation and the development of a variety of institutional arrangements affecting the terms and conditions of retirement, the economics of aging takes on a different perspective. As we shall see in the chapters to follow, the level of retirement living has generally improved but is still subject to a large degree of variation and also to individual discretion. More importantly, however, the level and adequacy of retirement living are influenced by the many uncertainties and risks that are associated with the institutional mechanisms we have created. Savings opportunities completely secure from the risks of inflation are generally not available. Private pension coverage varies greatly among industries and occupations, and job change may mean the loss of some or all of these pension rights. The ultimate level of social security benefits can be severely reduced by the misfortunes of structural unemployment or illness and by the obligations of child care—all of which keep individuals out of the regular labor force for long periods.

People can and should begin to look forward to the challenges and opportunities of retirement. But there is still a major need for individuals to think about and plan for retirement. In this book we look at various economic aspects of that planning. The concurrent rise in (a) the level of benefits to the aged, (b) retirement expectations, and (c) the number of aged as a proportion of the population also generates a need for more *national* planning in the area of the economics of aging.

In the chapters to follow we will look at the retirement preparation problem, both from an individual and national standpoint. We begin with chapters concerned with the economic status of the current elderly and the special problems of older workers. We then discuss the nature and magnitude of the economic retirement preparation task. Finally, the concluding chapters of the book discuss private and public pensions and the special and major role they play in providing income in retirement.

### Suggested Readings

Espenshade, Thomas J., and William J. Serow., Eds. *The Economic Consequences of Slowing Population Growth.* New York: Academic Press, 1978.

    A discussion of all major aspects of the changing demographic profile and its economic implications.

Fisher, David Hackett. *Growing Old in America.* Oxford: Oxford University Press, 1978.

    A skillful but controversial examination of the question: Have attitudes toward age changed in America during the past 400 years? The book includes a historical survey of developing economic support policy for the aged.

Friedman, Eugene A., and Harold L. Orbach. "Adjustment to Retirement." In Silvano Arieti, ed., *The Foundations of Psychiatry*. Vol. 1, *American Handbook of Psychiatry*, 2nd ed. New York: Basic Books, 1974, pp. 609–647.

    The authors discuss the emergence and institutionalization of retirement. They also provide a comprehensive review of research on the issue of adjustment to retirement. The authors conclude that most persons today have a generally positive attitude toward retirement as a future status and that as a separate sphere of life activity, work for most workers does not seem to take precedence over other life areas.

Harris, Louis, and Associates. *The Myth and Reality of Aging in America*. Washington, D.C.: The National Council on the Aging, 1975.

    A report on a representative national sample of 4,254 persons 18 years and over conducted in 1974. Topics covered are (a) public attitudes towards old age, (b) the public's image of "most" people over 65, (c) perceived social and economic contributions of the aged, (d) preparation for old age, (e) being old, (f) access to facilities, (g) the media's portrayal of the aged, and (h) the politics of old age.

National Journal. *The Economics of Aging*. A National Journal Issues Book. Washington, D.C.: The Government Research Corporation, 1978.

    A potpourri of topical articles on the economics and politics of aging, emphasizing the "graying of the federal budget."

Sheppard, Harold L., and Sara E. Rix. *The Graying of Working America—The Coming Crisis of Retirement-Age Policy*. New York: The Free Press, 1977.

    A book that attempts to push beyond the "conventional wisdom" in this area—emphasizing the potential problems and policy issues arising from demographic changes.

# Chapter Two

## The Economic Status of the Aged

*The treatment of old people in America, many of whom have a hard life behind them, is remarkable. . . . [This is illustrated by] the terrifying extent to which old people are left in poverty and destitution. . . . It cannot possible be the considered opinion of the majority of Americans that so many of those who in America are often called "senior citizens" should be left in misery, squalor, and often forbidding loneliness, unattended though they are in need of care. The situation is overripe for a radical reform of the old age security system.*

So wrote the well-known social commentator Gunnar Myrdal in his book *Challenge to Affluence* (1963). Myrdal was writing in the early 1960s. But as we noted in the preceding chapter, dramatic changes have occurred since then. In this chapter, therefore, we wish to assess in more detail the progress that has been made.

Prior to the 1960s there were relatively few data available to analyze the economic situation of the aged population in the United States. This situation changed dramatically in the early sixties as a result of the Social Security Administration's very comprehensive survey of the aged in 1962 (Epstein and Murray, 1967). Since then, a wide range of statistics has been published by the Social Security Administration, the Census Bureau, the Administration on Aging, the Department of Labor, and various private organizations. These data provide a variety of information on various aspects of the elderly's financial status.

Two important notes of caution are immediately in order, however. First, because it takes time to collect, check, analyze, and publish statistics, there is often a considerable lag in the availability of information. Throughout the chapter we present illustrative statistics—the latest that were available at the time of writing. Many readers, however, will want to seek the

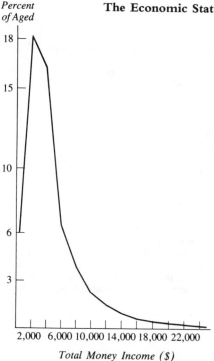

*Percent of Aged*

*Total Money Income ($)*

*Figure 6.   Percent of Persons Age 65
and Over with Various Amounts of Money Income,
1977*

Source: Based on data in U.S. Bureau of the Census, *Consumer Income,* Current Population Reports, No. 116 (Washington, D.C.: U.S. Government Printing Office, 1978).

newer data available. Second, all statistical information is subject to great abuse; unless users are very careful, they may misinterpret or misuse the available data. The discussion below, therefore, also attempts to deal with two important questions: What are the most useful kinds of data for evaluating the economic status of the aged, and what are the major problems in interpreting the data available?

## The Distribution of Aged Income

We begin our discussion of the elderly's economic status by looking at the income they receive. Income is not the only resource contributing to the economic welfare of the aged; later sections will look at a number of other important factors (for example, assets). But, as Mollie Orshansky has observed, "while money might not be everything, it is way ahead of whatever is in second place" (Irelan and Bond, 1976).

Figure 6 shows that in 1977 most elderly persons had incomes under

*Table 3.*  1977 Total Money Income[a] of Persons 65 and Over, by Sex

| Total Money Income | Men (%) | Women (%) |
|---|---|---|
| Less than $2,000 | 6 | 29 |
| $2,000–3,999 | 27 | 40 |
| 4,000–5,999 | 22 | 14 |
| 6,000–7,999 | 15 | 7 |
| 8,000–9,999 | 9 | 4 |
| 10,000–14,999 | 10 | 4 |
| 15,000–19,999 | 5 | 1 |
| 20,000–24,999 | 2 | b |
| 25,000 and Over | 4 | 1 |
| Total | 100 | 100 |

Source: U.S. Bureau of the Census, *Consumer Income.* Current Population Reports, No. 116 (Washington, D.C.: U.S. Government Printing Office, 1978).
[a]Money income includes salaries and wages; self-employment income; social insurance benefits; welfare payments; dividends, interest, and rents; pensions, alimony, and contributions from others; and unemployment, veterans', and workmen's compensation payments.
[b]Less than 1 percent.

$6,000 a year. Table 3 shows the difference in these incomes for men and women. As might be expected, the income of men is generally higher.

Of course, many of the women with low income are married to men with additional income. An alternative way to assess their status, therefore, is to look at family data. Table 4 provides the **median** incomes of men and women but also indicates the median income for families where the family head is age 65 or over. Table 4 also shows the median income of all *unrelated* aged, both men and women.

The income of families is significantly higher than the amount received by unrelated individuals, but it is still low when compared to data for all age groups. The 1977 median income of *all* families in the United States was about $16,000—nearly $7,000 higher than the median for aged families (Table 4).

If an aged person lives with his children or if the children live with their aged parent(s), should the two units be reported separately, or should the income be lumped together into one big family? It often makes a significant difference in the final results that are reported. There is a tendency to combine all the incomes of people living together. The result has been that a lot of aged poverty in the past has been hidden because the poorest aged—those who are unable to live by themselves—were submerged into the bigger and usually more prosperous family unit.

One might argue that if the aged are living with a family unit and the family unit is not itself poor then the aged standard of living is not likely to be poor. Using this perspective, one can argue further that there is no problem in such cases and that if you statistically separate the aged out

*Table 4.*   1977 Median Total Money Income and Percent with
Incomes Below $6,000

|  | *Median*[a] | *Percent with Income Below $6,000* |
|---|---|---|
| Men Age 65 and Over | $ 5,526 | 55 |
| Women Age 65 and Over | 3,088 | 83 |
| Families[b] Age 65 and Over | 9,110 | 26 |
| Families (All Ages) | 16,009 | 13 |
| Unrelated Aged Individuals | 3,829 | 75 |
| Unrelated Individuals (All Ages) | 5,907 | 51 |

Source: U.S. Bureau of the Census, *Consumer Income,* Current Population Reports, Series P-60, No. 116 (Washington, D.C.: U.S. Government Printing Office, 1978).
[a]See glossary for explanation of median versus mean statistics.
[b]Families where the age of the head is 65 and over.

(perhaps to try to justify higher pension benefits) you are basing the analysis on an artificial situation.

The opposing view, however, is that many of these people are not necessarily treated as members of the family. They are there by necessity, and often families do not permit them to share fully in the higher standard of living of the rest of the family. Or, even if the younger members of the family want them to share fully, many aged people are too independent to be willing to draw heavily upon the resources of the rest of the family. They would rather—even though they live within the family—live at a lower, perhaps subsistence, level.

Historically we know that as social security benefit levels have increased many aged persons have moved out of these families at the first opportunity and set up independent households. Statistically, as a result of these family units breaking up, new units headed by an aged person show up in the data. Since these new aged units almost always have very low income, the process tends to increase the reported incidence of poverty among the aged. We find, for example, that during certain periods the number of persons in poverty has declined among nonaged groups but has risen among the aged (partly as a result of the separation of the aged out of other families).

Thus, when the statistics show aged poverty increasing, it is not necessarily true that the situation is actually getting worse. In part the statistics are a reflection of things getting better. As pension benefits go up, some of the poor aged who prefer independent living are able to break out of other family units and thus become identifiable statistical units. But, again, it can be argued that they were always poor, and all that has changed is their living arrangements.

Figure 7 shows the sources of income for the elderly. While social security is the major source (39 percent), earnings (23 percent) and asset income (18 percent) make large contributions. We must remember, however, that various income sources are distributed unevenly among the subgroups of the aged population. Earnings go mostly to the nonretired; asset income goes mostly to a few high income elderly. In the next section we examine more closely these differences.

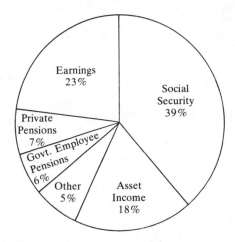

*Figure 7.   1976 Sources of Aged Money Income*

Source: Susan Grad and Karen Foster, *Income of the Population 65 and Older, 1976* (Washington, D.C.: Social Security Administration, 1979).

## The Aged Are Not a Homogeneous Group

The statistics given in the preceding section are useful but have a serious shortcoming: lumping all the aged population together seriously distorts the reality of the situation. It is common for writers and analysts to give only median incomes for all or large groups of the aged, but as we saw in Table 3, for example, there is a wide divergence in income among the aged.

Similar distortions result from grouping all the aged together and generalizing about their social problems. Most people who study old age and the process of aging (gerontology) are familiar with this aggregation problem in the social and psychological areas. There is no such thing as the collective aged; the aged are as diverse as the population itself, and this is just as true for economic status as it is for other areas.

If one views the aged as one homogeneous group, there is a tendency to try to develop for them one appropriate economic policy—just as in other areas we have tried to develop one appropriate housing policy and one appropriate health policy. We have learned over the years that such attempts almost always fail in diverse groups.

Unfortunately, much of the data published on a regular basis do not show the significant differences existing among the elderly. Probably the most frequently used economic data on the elderly are from the National Census and the Current Population Survey. But these published tabulations are generally for all (or large groups) of the aged. The most useful type of data for analysis and evaluation are those that break down the aged population into small subgroups. Unfortunately, in order to look more closely at the heterogeneous nature of the economics of aging, we must often use data that are less current.

*The Retired Versus the Nonretired*   Distributional data shown earlier in Table 3 are more representative than are means or medians alone, but many differences are still hidden. The first step toward further disaggregation of the data is very simple: separate the aged into at least two broad categories—the retired and the nonretired. Unfortunately, most of the data sources do not or cannot provide such a breakdown. They "do not" because often it simply does not occur to those presenting the data that this is an important distinction. They "cannot" because the questions asked in the survey providing the data do not always include the information necessary for judging whether a person is retired or not. Hence one sees data where the aged wage earners are grouped together with the non–wage earners. The earners, of course, tend to have much higher and more adequate incomes. When they are averaged together with the non–wage earners the total mean and median income for "the aged" is increased and makes the situation look much better than it actually is for retired people and much worse than it actually is for the employed.

If no one wants to segregate the retired from the nonretired, one immediately runs into the problem of how to define retirement for statistical purposes. Many aged persons work to supplement their pension and other retirement income. Is a person who is working twenty hours a week counted as a retired person or is he or she partially retired? If the latter, what does that mean?

Thus, even if we divide the aged population on the basis of retirement, it is not clear whether there should be two categories or more than two. A three-category tabulation, for example, might be full-time workers, part-time and unemployed workers, and the fully retired. In general, most discussions of the economic status of the aged do not even attempt to deal with this problem when presenting data. This omission is unfortunate since (as we will show) this is such an important issue in evaluating the economic well-being of elderly people.

One of the few sets of published data that distinguished between workers and nonworkers was the Social Security Administration's 1968 Survey of the Aged. Table 5 shows the differences in the distribution of income

Table 5.  Aged Income Distribution by Work Experience, 1967

| | Married Couples | | | | | | Nonmarried Persons | | | |
| | Both Worked | | One Worked | | Neither Worked[a] | | Worked[a] | | Did Not Work | |
| Total Money Income | 1967 | 1971 | 1967 | 1971 | 1967 | 1971 | 1967 | 1971 | 1967 | 1971 |
|---|---|---|---|---|---|---|---|---|---|---|---|
| Less Than $2,000 | 10 | 4 | 11 | 6 | 30 | 11 | 42 | 22 | 80 | 58 |
| $ 2,000–4,999 | 32 | 21 | 47 | 31 | 60 | 55 | 43 | 44 | 18 | 35 |
| 5,000–9,999 | 42 | 36 | 35 | 38 | 9 | 27 | 13 | 22 | 5 | 5 |
| 10,000–14,999 | 9 | 20 | 4 | 14 | 1 | 4 | 2 | 6 | b | 1 |
| 15,000 or More | 6 | 19 | 3 | 11 | 1 | 2 | 1 | 4 | b | 1 |
| Total Percent | 100[c] | 100 | 100 | 100 | 100 | 100 | 100 | 100 | 100 | 100 |

Source: Data for 1967 from Lenore E. Bixby et al., *Demographic and Economic Characteristics of the Aged* (Washington, D.C.: U.S. Government Printing Office, 1975), Table 2.8. Data for 1971 are unpublished data provided by the Social Security Administration from the March 1972 Current Population Survey.

[a]Couples with head 65 or older and nonmarried persons 65 or over.
[b]Less than 0.5.
[c]Totals may not add up to 100 due to rounding.

for aged couples and nonmarried persons when two, one, and zero persons worked. The distributions for working units are much higher. For example, about half of working couples in 1967 had incomes over $5,000, whereas about 10 percent of nonworking couples had incomes over that amount. Unpublished data provided by the Social Security Administration for 1971 are also shown in Table 5. While the income levels have improved greatly between 1967 and 1971, the differences between those working and those not working remain.

In recent years, the Census Bureau has begun to publish some data giving income by employment status of the family head. Although these tabulations are less differentiated than the social security data, they provide more recent information. Table 6 shows income by employment status for 1976.

*Table 6.*   1976 Money Income for Aged Families, by Work Experience of Head[a]

| Work Experience Last Year | Median Income | Less than $5,000 | $6,000– 9,999 | $10,000 or More | Total Percent |
|---|---|---|---|---|---|
| Head Did Not Work | $ 7,850 | 23 | 41 | 36 | 100 |
| Head Worked Part Time: | | | | | |
| 26 Weeks or Less | 8,300 | 18 | 41 | 41 | 100 |
| 27–52 Weeks | 10,669 | 9 | 37 | 54 | 100 |
| Head Worked Full Time: | | | | | |
| 26 Weeks or Less | 12,452 | 10 | 31 | 59 | 100 |
| 27–52 Weeks | 16,000[b] | 8 | 17 | 75 | 100 |

Source: U.S. Bureau of the Census, *Consumer Income,* Current Population Reports, Series P-60, No. 114 (Washington, D.C.: U.S. Government Printing Office, 1978).
[a]Head age 65 or more.
[b]An approximation.

*Different Age Groups*   A second major problem in analyzing data on the aged is that it often is not appropriate to group people together who differ in age by as much as fifteen or twenty years. Most statistics on the economic status of aged people group all persons age 65 and over together. Again, conclusions drawn from such data will be misleading. To begin with, it is important to realize that the needs of people at these two extremes of the retirement period are often quite different. For example, we do know that the very old tend to have expenditure patterns that are significantly different from people who have just retired, particularly in the areas of health care, recreation, clothing, and food.

If one wants to develop a budget for the aged, then, it is probably better to develop different budgets for at least two age groups (even though the range of ages chosen must be somewhat arbitrary). Not that you cannot find persons 85 and 90 years old who are as active and vigorous as someone 65 (or maybe 25). But on the average there seem to be enough distinctions for analytical purposes to warrant taking a range of ages into account in the presentation and analysis of economic data.

Another reason for separating the aged into various age groups is that the accustomed standard of living for the *very* old is usually quite different from that of the *newly* old. Each group grew up and worked during dissimilar periods. Each group's final earnings and the resulting levels of living prior to retirement are different. Given the lengths of time involved, these differences can be quite substantial. Thus, in evaluating the adequacy of income for aged people, one should allow for the fact that the *very* old themselves may have lower expectations about their standard of living than aged persons who retire a decade or two later.

There is, however, another factor that works in the opposite direction. Among the very old the incidence of exceptionally high expenditures for chronic illness and institutionalization rises dramatically. For those elderly persons who experience these problems, economic need can rise catastrophically.

Furthermore, the incomes of those who have recently retired are often much better than those who have been retired a long time—mainly because the former group's earnings are typically higher and pensions based upon them are consequently better. Also, the newer retirees are more likely to reap gains from the recent establishment of private pensions or improvements in old plans.

Finally, it becomes increasingly unsatisfactory to talk of only those people 65 and older as being aged—especially with the rise of early retirement in the United States. We know that to arbitrarily designate as old those who have reached a specific chronological age is a most inadequate way of approaching the problem of defining the aged. It takes no account of peoples' varying capacities for physical and mental activities and social involvement, among other things. We know that people age differently in terms of various characteristics.

The more serious economic problems of aging commonly arise from, or are aggravated by, the cessation of earnings following retirement. Thus it is important to study that part of the aged population having the most economic problems—those families where there are no regular workers. Increasingly this group includes people who are less than 65 years of age. If we look at persons younger than age 65, we can logically divide them into two groups: those younger than age 62 and those age 62 to 64. Age 62 seems to be an appropriate dividing point since at this age social security eligibility begins for everyone except widows (who can qualify at age 60).

Persons who retire before age 62 must rely on private pensions and/or their own assets and income from these assets. Data indicate that this group tends to be composed of both very high income people and very low income people—with very few in the middle (Kingson, 1979). That is, we find among this very early retirement group those people who *have* to retire early even though they do not have enough money and those people who *can* retire very early because they have sufficient economic resources to live satisfactorily.

Karen Schwab's (1976) analysis of early labor force withdrawal found that most of the men leaving early reported health-imposed work limitations. Figure 8 shows the proportion of men in 1969 age 58–63 no longer in the labor force by type of job, work limitations, and race. Of those with no work limitation, 63 percent had incomes over $5,000—in contrast to only 30 percent for the health-limited group.

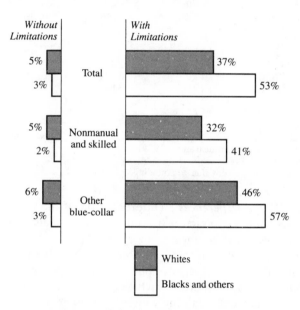

*Figure 8. Percent of Men Aged 58–63*
*Out of the Labor Force in 1969, by Type of Longest*
*Job, Health-Imposed Work Limitations, and Race*

Source: Lola M. Irelan et al., *Almost 65: Baseline Data from the Retirement History Study.* Research Report No. 49 (Washington, D.C.: Social Security Administration, 1976).

The age 62–64 group, normally referred to as the early retirement group, receives reduced social security benefits. Ever since the early retirement provisions under social security were first introduced (in 1956 for women and 1961 for men), more than half of the men and women starting to receive social security old age retirement benefits have opted for reduced benefits before age 65. The Social Security Administration reports in its

1975 *Annual Statistical Supplement* that, for example, 61 percent of the men and 80 percent of the women workers who *began* receiving social security old age benefits received reduced benefits.

Again, actual published economic data on various age groupings of the elderly population are sparse. Table 7 presents data for 1976 that illustrate the income differences between age groups by looking at young versus very old units.

*Table 7.*    1976 Money Income of Married Couples and Nonmarried Persons Age 55 and Older

| Age | Median Income[a] | Less than $5,000 | $5,000– 9,999 | $10,000 or More | Total Percent |
|---|---|---|---|---|---|
| 55–61 | $12,100 | 22 | 20 | 57 | 100[b] |
| 62–64 | 8,830 | 31 | 24 | 45 | 100 |
| 65–67 | 6,250 | 53 | 28 | 18 | 100 |
| 68–69 | 5,630 | 44 | 30 | 25 | 100 |
| 70–72 | 5,110 | 49 | 31 | 21 | 100 |
| 73 and Older | 3,920 | 62 | 25 | 13 | 100 |

Source: Susan Grad and Karen Foster, *Income of the Population 55 and Older, 1976* (Washington, D.C.: Social Security Administration, 1979).
[a]Rounded to the nearest $10.
[b]May not add up to 100 percent due to rounding.

*Black-White Differences*    Differentiation of the aged population by various socioeconomic characteristics must also be made. One of the best studies of black-white differences is by Julian Abbott (1977), who analyzes data for persons aged 60 and older in March 1972. Abbott finds that only a small proportion of the elderly population depends on public assistance payments but that this proportion includes a much larger percentage of the black elderly (30 percent) than the white (7 percent). The reverse is true for the receipt of income from assets: 13 percent for blacks and 53 percent for whites. The two groups, however, are about equal in the proportion receiving income from earnings (44 percent).

Figure 9 illustrates the similarities and differences in the shape of the income distribution curves for each racial group. Despite aggregate differences in money income, a sizable majority of individual black and white elderly units had similar incomes. Using a technical measure of the extent to which income distributions overlap, Abbott calculates an "index of integration" (i.e., overlap) equal to 0.74 and an "index of differentiation" equal to 0.26. These indices indicate that incomes for about three-fourths of black and white units were *not* different. Even within the lowest income groups, however, black and white units differed substantially in their sources of income.

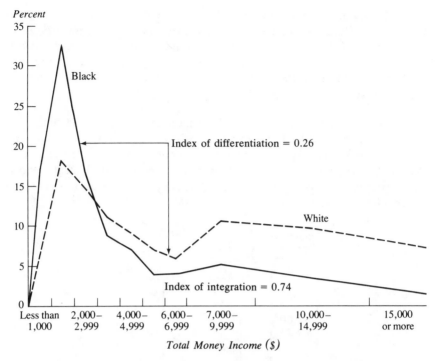

*Figure 9.    Percentage Distribution of Black and*
*White Elderly Units, by Total Money Income in 1971*

Source: Julian Abbott, "Socioeconomic Characteristics of the Elderly: Some
Black-White Differences," *Social Security Bulletin* 40 (July 1977): 16–42.

Abbott concludes, therefore, "that efforts to improve the income adequacy
of the elderly will have different effects on the two races. Benefit increases
in any of the retirement pensions would provide relatively less for blacks
because of their lower rate of coverage and their lower lifetime earnings. . . .
Blacks would benefit more from the improved, but means-tested, assistance
programs and from the continued availability of jobs for those still able to
work."

The plight of the minority aged has been characterized by some
writers as one of "double jeopardy" or "multiple hazards" (Jackson, 1970).
Data from a fairly large sample of middle-aged and aged blacks, Mexican
Americans, and whites living in Los Angeles County provide insight on this
issue. Dowd and Bengtson (1978) investigated differences across and within
ethnic categories. Their analysis supported the double jeopardy characterization—especially with regard to income and self-assessed health.

Similar findings are also reported by Shanas and Heineman (National Survey of the Black Aged, 1978). Almost twice as high a proportion of the black aged as of white say they need medical and dental care but have delayed treatment—primarily because of financial problems. And the black elderly more often than the white report their financial situation at interview time to be worse than it was when they were age 60.

*Dual Pensioners*    We discuss in later chapters the fact that a high proportion of wage and salary workers in private industry are *not* covered by private pensions. The result is that many people reaching retirement age have to rely solely on social security pensions. Figure 10 illustrates the income disparity between aged families with dual pensions and those receiving only social security.

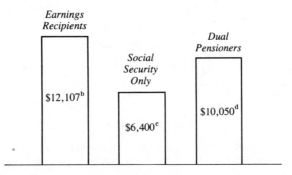

*Figure 10.    1976 Median Money Income of Aged Families with Earnings, Social Security Only, or Two Pensions*[a]

Source: U.S. Bureau of the Census, *Consumer Income,* Current Population Reports, No. 114 (Washington, D.C.: U.S. Government Printing Office, 1978).
[a]The second pensions are from either private or government employment.
[b]Total median income (i.e., earnings and all income other than earnings).
[c]Median shown is for families with social security and property income only.
[d]Median shown is for families with social security, another pension, and property income.

The median income of families with dual pensions was almost as high in 1976 as the income of the "most advantaged" aged—families with one or more members still working. However, those families with only pension income from social security typically had much lower income.

In later chapters we will discuss further this divergency of economic status among one- and two-pension families. One major policy issue currently being discussed is the extent to which government policy promotes a growing "pension elite" (i.e., dual pensioners with high pension income) while at the same time large numbers of aged have, essentially, only their social security income to rely on.

### The Impact of Taxation, Assets, and In-Kind Income

Thus far we have looked only at the distribution of money income among the aged. Three other factors have an important impact on the economic status of elderly people. First, there is the extent to which the income is actually available to meet current needs (what economists call *disposable income*); some of the income goes to government in taxes. Second, we need to assess the size, type, and distribution of assets held by older persons. And, finally, not all income is *money* income; sizable amounts of *in-kind* income are received by the elderly, improving their economic status.

*Taxation* Most income distribution statistics look at the pretax distribution of income. The aged, while they share in the advantageous tax provisions legislated for the general population, also have their own special loopholes to reduce the amount of taxes they must pay. The most important of the tax exemptions is the nontaxation of social security benefits. Payments into the social security system by employed workers are treated as taxable income during the year earned, but the untaxed benefits paid out are based on both worker *and employer* contributions and often exceed contributions (for a variety of other reasons discussed in later chapters). Also important is the special provision in the federal income tax law (and many state laws) that permits persons age 65 and over to double the amount of income deductible as "personal exemptions."

Property tax reductions are now granted in all states for elderly persons (Fairholm, 1978). The most common type of reduction (25 states in 1974) is a "circuit breaker." Tax relief under this mechanism is tied to need, as defined by taxpayers' income levels in relation to their property tax liabilities. The amount of relief declines (or phases out) as taxpayer income rises, using a formula that avoids a sharp drop in relief at some arbitrary income level. For example, the Vermont circuit breaker comes into play when the property tax burden exceeds 7 percent of household income; for Minnesota it is 6 percent; for many states it is 3 to 5 percent. These and other provisions of the circuit breaker vary from state to state. Income ceilings or rebate limits are different; some laws do not cover renters.

Another common method of property tax relief is the "homestead exemption." Under this mechanism, a state excludes before the tax rate is applied a portion of the assessed value of a single-family home from total assessed value. A few states allow deferral of property taxes until after an elderly owner dies or sells his residence, and a few freeze the tax rate at the rate in force when the aged person reaches a certain age, usually 63 or 65.

Favorable tax laws for the elderly—particularly the double exemption—tend to help the higher income elderly more than those with low income. Stanley Surrey (1973) has estimated that nearly half of the federal tax assistance goes to the few aged individuals with incomes above $10,000.

After-tax data are rarely published. Both the Social Security Administration and Census Bureau data are for money income before taxes. Pechman and Okner, in one of the few studies of its kind available, estimate effective tax rates for 1966. Table 8 shows the tax rates for various income groups classified by the age of the family head. The 1966 combined federal, state, and local tax rates were quite similar across the income spectrum, with the rates for both the lowest and the highest income families in both age groups being slightly higher. The tax rates for the elderly are lower for all income groups except the highest.

*Table 8.*  Effective Combined Federal, State, and Local Tax Rate[a] for the Nonaged and Aged, 1966

| Family's Rank from Lowest to Highest Income | Family Head | |
|---|---|---|
| | Under Age 65 (%) | Age 65 or Older (%) |
| Lowest Tenth[b] | 29.1 | 26.1 |
| Second Tenth | 26.0 | 23.4 |
| Third Tenth | 26.7 | 24.5 |
| Fourth Tenth | 26.2 | 24.1 |
| Fifth Tenth | 26.0 | 24.6 |
| Sixth Tenth | 25.8 | 24.1 |
| Seventh Tenth | 25.5 | 25.3 |
| Eighth Tenth | 25.6 | 25.1 |
| Ninth Tenth | 25.2 | 24.1 |
| Highest Tenth | 25.5 | 27.5 |

Source: Joseph A. Pechman and Benjamin A. Okner, *Who Bears the Tax Burden?* (Washington, D.C.: The Brookings Institution, © 1974), Table 5-5. Used by permission.
[a]Assumes corporate income and property taxes are passed on at least in part to consumers.
[b]Includes only units in the sixth to tenth percentiles.

Pechman and Okner point out, however, that the results of this type of analysis are quite sensitive to the assumptions made with regard to who actually pays various taxes, especially the corporate income and property taxes. While the tax rates remain similar for most income groups when alternative assumptions are used, this is not true for the highest and lowest groups. If it is assumed, for example, that corporate income and property taxes are paid by the owners of capital, Pechman and Okner find that the overall effective tax rate increases with income (i.e., is progressive).

*Assets*   In addition to current income, many of the aged own assets that provide housing, serve as a financial reserve for special or emergency needs, contribute directly to income through interest, dividends, and rents, and generally enhance the freedom with which they spend their available income. Most assets can be sold and thereby converted to money that can be used to buy goods and services. But one should distinguish between liquid assets and nonliquid assets. Fortunately, most published statistics on assets do make such a distinction.

*Liquid assets* are relatively easy to convert into goods and services or money (the most liquid of assets). These consist generally of cash, bank deposits, and corporate stocks and bonds. *Nonliquid assets* usually require more time to convert. The two major types of nonliquid assets are equity in housing and equity in a business.

Assets (or savings) are held by individuals because they perform a number of very useful economic functions. They are used as a precaution against unexpected happenings in the future. One puts money aside so that it can be drawn upon should the need arise. This saving might be viewed as self-insurance. Assets are also accumulated in anticipation of known or planned large expenditures in the future: because of a worsening illness one might anticipate going into a nursing home; or one might save in order to take a round-the-world retirement cruise. Still another reason for saving is to leave a legacy to one's children or to other people.

One of the most important reasons for saving is to smooth out the irregularities in the flow of income coming to an individual over his lifetime. People are becoming increasingly aware of the fact that (given current life expectancies) there is often a ten- to thirty-year period of living in retirement after earnings from work have stopped. Thus, individuals must decide how to deal financially with this nonwork period of life and whether to provide through asset accumulation economic resources to supplement pension income.

However, assets put aside as a precautionary measure or for anticipated major expenditures in old age are not available for meeting day-to-day needs. If you are worried, for example, about having high medical expenses that Medicare will not completely cover, if you expect that you might have to go into a nursing home, or if you anticipate that property taxes will increase dramatically in your area, you must accumulate additional assets to provide for daily living.

Similarly, if you have nonliquid assets such as housing, as long as you are determined to keep that housing and not sell the property, that asset is not convertible into income to be used for day-to-day living. In effect the asset is "locked in."

In fact, a high proportion of older people own a home or have an equity in it. About 80 percent of elderly couples live in an owned home compared to about 40 percent of nonmarried elderly persons. The amount of mortgage debt on those homes is usually very low; in fact, about four-fifths of elderly homeowners own their homes free of any mortgage. Thus we find that many older persons have a sizable asset accumulation, but often most of it is not available for day-to-day living expenses.

Until recently in the United States there was no available financial mechanism that would permit people to sell the equity in their home, get back money over a period of time, and still be able to live in the house. In contrast, in France a home annuity plan called *viager* has been in existence for many years, and the *Boston Globe* (December 3, 1978) reports that there are over 400,000 currently in existence. A *viager* arrangement is negotiated by the homeowner with a buyer and results in the buyer paying an agreed-upon down payment and a monthly payment to the owner for the rest of the owner's life (in return for the property at death). The amounts paid are mutually agreed upon—with the age and health status of the owner taken into account. The arrangement, to a certain extent, represents a gamble on the part of both parties. The buyer, however, can go to an insurance company and take out an actuarial insurance plan to help offset the payments promised in the resulting legal agreement.

Since January 1, 1979, the Federal Home Loan Bank Board (FHLBB) in the United States has allowed federally chartered savings and loan associations to offer *reverse annuity mortgages.* Under this mortgage, a homeowner may sell some equity in the house, receiving in return a fixed monthly sum based on a percentage of the current market value of the house. Reverse annuity mortgages are potentially available in all states, but each federal savings institution's program has to be approved by the FHLBB.

One must be cautious in drawing conclusions based on available asset data. The asset situation of some aged persons makes their economic status appear to be very good. It is often suggested that such assets should be prorated over the remaining expected lifetime of aged persons and added to income when assessing general status and needs. This can be, and in fact has been, done (Epstein and Murray, 1967; Weisbrod and Hansen, 1968). But the question arises as to how valid such a measure is—given precautionary considerations and the nonliquid nature of most of these assets.

Economists are correct in saying that if assets are totally neglected, assessment of the economic situation of the aged will be biased. Many national leaders, when they advocate improvements for the aged, conveniently forget about these assets—allowing matters to look worse than they really are.

Yet some studies (the most important ones by the Social Security Administration's Office of Research and Statistics) have found that prorating assets of the aged does not significantly improve the economic situation for many aged—especially those who are poor. There is a not insignificant minority of the aged for whom assets are important; but for most, taking assets into account does not make a great deal of difference. Moreover, if one looks just at the *liquid* assets of the aged, one finds that prorating these assets significantly improves the economic status of even fewer older persons.

Surveys to determine asset holdings of individuals have been undertaken very infrequently in the United States, and those attempted have been plagued by the problem that many people underreport their assets. Although surveys on the amounts and kinds of *income* also have underreporting problems, the amount of underreporting is greater when attempting to ascertain *assets*.

The most recent comprehensive information on the assets of the elderly is over a decade old. The 1968 Social Security Survey of the Aged presents detailed information on the assets of the elderly in 1967. Table 9 shows the proportion of elderly units holding various amounts of financial assets and equity in owned homes. What is most striking about this information is the large number of older families with relatively insignificant amounts of financial assets. About two-thirds of elderly couples and almost 80 percent of unrelated individuals had less than $5,000 in financial assets in 1967. In fact, 43 percent and 61 percent respectively had less than $1,000.

Some people have argued that the poor asset situation of past and current aged cohorts reflects in part the economic vicissitudes of past

*Table 9.*    Aged[a] Financial Assets and Homeowner Equity, 1967[b]

| | Financial Assets Only | | Equity in Home | |
| Asset Amount | Couples | Unrelated Individuals | Couples[c] | Unrelated Individuals[c] |
|---|---|---|---|---|
| None | 26 | 42 | [d] | [d] |
| $1–999 | 17 | 19 ⎫ | | |
| $1,000–2,999 | 15 | 11 ⎬ | 13 ⎫ | 18 |
| $3,000–4,999 | 8 | 6 ⎭ | ⎬ | |
| $5,000–9,999 | 12 | 9 ⎭ | 24 | 26 |
| $10,000–19,999 | 11 | 7 | 40 | 39 |
| $20,000 or More | 13 | 5 | 23 | 17 |
| Total Percent[e] | 100 | 100 | 100 | 100 |

Source: Based on data in Janet Murray, "Homeownership and Financial Assets: Findings from the 1968 Survey of the Aged," *Social Security Bulletin* 35 (August 1972): 3–23.
[a]Age 65 or older.
[b]Asset information does not include value of business and farm assets and equity in rental.
[c]Homeowners only.
[d]Not applicable.
[e]Totals may not add up to 100 due to rounding.

decades—especially the Great Depression and the post–World War II inflation—and that this situation might improve. Since the aged population is increasingly composed of those who worked and saved in the relatively prosperous years of the fifties and sixties, will not the future picture change?

Unfortunately, information to answer this question is almost nonexistent. Data from the Social Security Administration's Retirement History Study, however, provide 1969 asset statistics for a cohort of individuals approaching retirement. Table 10 contrasts the financial asset situation of the 1967 aged population with the picture for "preaged" persons aged 58 to 63 in 1969. The data show that there was little improvement in the financial asset status of this preretirement group as compared to the elderly. In fact, the two distributions are almost identical.

Also included in Table 10, to provide some historical perspective, is the financial asset situation for the elderly five years earlier (1962). Again, the data show that the distribution in that year is virtually identical with the 1967 situation.

*In-Kind Income*    In-kind income consists of goods or services available to the aged without expenditure or at least at a rate below the market value of the service. Medicare health benefits are one example. Another is subsidized housing. As a result of various special housing programs for the elderly, some aged persons pay for housing at a rate below the normal market price for such housing—a subsidy paid for by the government. However, unlike measuring money income (including pension and welfare transfers),

*Table 10.*    Financial Assets[a] of the Aged and a "Preretirement" Cohort

| Asset Amount | Survey Units with Head Age 58–63 in 1969[b] | Survey Units with Head Age 65 or More in 1967[b] | Survey Units with Head Age 65 or More in 1962 |
|---|---|---|---|
| None | 25 | 36 | 35 |
| $1–999 | 22 | 19 | 19 |
| $1,000–2,999 | 14 | 12 | 12 |
| $3,000–4,999 | 7 | 7 | 7 |
| $5,000–9,999 | 10 | 10 | 9 |
| $10,000–19,999 | 9 | 8⎫ | 18 |
| $20,000 or More | 12 | 8⎭ | |
| Total Percent[c] | 100 | 100 | 100 |

Source: Based on data in Lenore E. Bixby et al., *Demographic and Economic Characteristics of the Aged—The 1968 Social Security Survey* (Washington, D.C.: U.S. Government Printing Office, 1975) and Lola M. Irelan et al., *Almost 65: Baseline Data from the Retirement History Study* (Washington, D.C.: U.S. Government Printing Office, 1976).
[a]U.S. savings bonds, checking accounts, savings accounts, stocks, corporate bonds, mutual funds, and money owed by others.
[b]Tabulation of married couples and nonmarried individuals.
[c]Does not add up to 100 due to rounding.

measuring benefits from in-kind programs involves difficult conceptual issues. As Schmundt, Smolensky, and Stiefel (1975) have noted, the value that the recipients themselves place on some in-kind goods (such as medical services or housing) may well be substantially less than the market price.

According to the Congressional Research Service, (see U.S. House Select Committee on Aging, in the Suggested Readings for this chapter), there are 47 major federal programs benefiting the elderly over and above those providing direct money income. Two such programs are briefly discussed below: health services and food stamps.

One of the largest of the federal government's expenditures is to provide health care for the aged and certain other groups. The establishment of federal health insurance for the aged and disabled by amendment of the Social Security Act in 1965 resulted in a sharp decline in health expenses financed directly by the elderly.* In 1966 persons age 65 and over financed about 70 percent of their health care costs by either direct payment or private health insurance. In 1976, primarily as a result of Medicare, they financed about 32 percent of these costs privately—with federal and state government expenditures rising from about $2.5 billion in 1966 to $24 billion in 1976. Figure 11, for example, compares private and government expenditures for personal health costs in 1977. Younger age groups finance privately about three-quarters of their health costs, in contrast to about one-third for the elderly.

Moreover, in 1977 Congress extended the nation's food stamp program for four additional years. About one million persons age 60 and over benefit from this program, receiving coupons that can be used to purchase food in retail stores. Also, eligible persons over 60 who are disabled to the extent that they cannot prepare their own meals may use the stamps to purchase prepared meals as part of the "meals on wheels" program. Eligibility in both cases is subject to both income and asset tests.

The value of coupons received depends on both the income of recipients and the number of persons in a family. In 1979 an aged couple with assets of less than $3,000 (excluding their home) and a gross annual income of $4,000 was eligible for coupons with a value of about $300 per year. Benefits are updated every January and July to reflect changes in the prices of food as determined by the Bureau of Labor Statistics. A recent change in the law has eliminated the controversial "purchase requirement," which required food stamp recipients to use cash to purchase coupons worth more than the purchase price.

*Intrafamily Transfers*    Another issue to be considered is the impact of intrafamily transfers. Very little is known about the magnitude and nature

*See Chapter 6 for a more detailed discussion of Medicare and Medicaid.

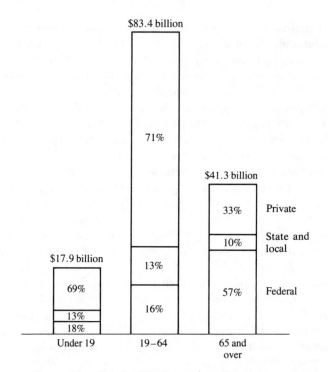

*Figure 11.   Fiscal 1977 Percentage Distribution of
Expenditures for Personal Health Care, by Source of
Funds and Age Group*

Source: Robert M. Gibson and Charles R. Fisher, "Age Differences in Health Care
Spending, Fiscal Year 1977," *Social Security Bulletin* 42 (January 1979): 3–16.

of transfers among family members (e.g., from children to parents or vice
versa). In the most recent study, Moon (1977) finds that intrafamily transfers altered the well-being of about 28 percent of aged families. However,
relatively large transfers flow both ways—with slightly more aged families
receiving assistance than assisting younger children.

### The Adequacy of Aged Income

In 1976 a task force of government experts reviewed ways of
measuring poverty more accurately. In their final report they emphasize the
fact that assessing income adequacy necessitates standards that are *relative*:

> *Poor persons living in the United States in the 1970s are rich in contrast to
> their counterparts in other times and places. They are not poor if by poor is
> meant the subsistence levels of living common in some other countries. Nor are*

*most poor like their counterparts in this country fifty or one hundred years ago. This country is concerned about poverty, its causes and correlates. It is willing to relieve the poverty of some of the poor, and it wants to measure the effectiveness of its efforts to do so. None of this can be done without some idea of who is to be considered poor and who is not. [Poverty Studies Task Force, 1976]*

In this section we look at various measures of adequacy in relation to the income of older persons. In early times, nations had little choice but to define basic needs in terms of survival. But for the more affluent nations of the world today, need becomes more relative and, hence, more difficult to measure.

The most popular measure of poverty in America today is the Social Security Administration's poverty index. Developed in the early 1960s, it gained prominence in the Johnson Administration's declared War on Poverty. The index continues to be widely used today, despite the fact that the Nixon Administration—very early in its first term—discouraged government agencies from using the index, arguing that because of conceptual and measurement problems it was a misleading and unreliable measure.

A succinct description of the Social Security Administration's poverty index was presented in 1967 testimony by Wilbur Cohen before the U.S. House Committee on Ways and Means (1967a):

> *The starting point for the SSA poverty index is the amount of money needed to purchase the food for a minimum adequate diet as determined by the Department of Agriculture. The food budget is the lowest that could be devised to supply all essential nutrients using food readily purchasable in the U.S. market (with customary regional variations). The poverty line is then calculated at three times the food budget (slightly smaller proportions for one- and two-person families) on the assumption—derived from studies of consumers—that a family that has spent a larger proportion of its income on food will be living at a very inadequate level. The food budgets and the derivative poverty income cutoff points are estimated in detail for families of differing size and composition (62 separate family types) with a farm/nonfarm differential for each type. This variation of the poverty measure in relation to family size and age of members is its most important distinguishing characteristic.*
>
> *Because the level of living implied by the poverty index is lower than we think most people would regard as an appropriate measure of adequacy of income for retired persons or disabled workers and their families or widows and children, we have also developed a slightly higher index. We call this the low income index, and it is definitely low income.*

It is an interesting fact that in actual practice the low income index has rarely been used for policy evaluation purposes. Instead the poverty index has almost exclusively dominated the discussions of how many nonaged and aged are in economic difficulty and what policies are needed to deal with these difficulties. It is important, therefore, to understand how the poverty index is calculated and its limitations.

*Calculating the Poverty Index*    Because of its wide use and importance, let us run through step by step the construction of this poverty measure. First, as was indicated in Cohen's statement above, an amount of
adequate food for the family unit is determined, and then the cost of that
food at prevailing prices is ascertained by pricing foods in retail stores.

For about thirty years the Department of Agriculture has produced
"food plans" that meet the nutritional standards set out by an organization
called the National Research Council. While these plans meet nutritional
standards, they also try to make the quantities and types of food chosen
compatible with the general preferences of American families, preferences
determined by food-consumption studies. It is not simply a matter of giving
poor people only beans. General eating habits are taken into account.

Thus, in constructing a food plan an attempt is made to respond to
the fact that people prefer meat to beans, although in terms of protein you
can get more or at least as much protein from beans as you can from meat.
The fact remains, however, that most of the protein in such plans is provided
by nonmeat products.

It is also important to note that the food plans were originally devised for emergency periods only and that no one is expected to have to live
over a long period of time on these very minimal food amounts. This implies
that these food diets would be detrimental to your health over an extended
period.

Finally, the Department of Agriculture makes no pretense of assum-
ing that all families can skillfully budget, or are willing to eat, the foods
specified in the plans. These assumptions need not be made, given the purpose of the plans. They were developed simply as a device to provide social
welfare agencies with a needs standard that was not completely subjective in
determining how much money poor people need to avoid serious malnutri-
tion.

The next step in developing the poverty measure is to construct food
budgets for different types of families. The poverty index is based on family
units with different combinations of the following characteristics:

1. Age of head over or under age 65.
2. Size of family (2 to 7 or more).
3. Farm and nonfarm.
4. Male and female head of household.
5. Number of related children under age 18.
6. "Unrelated" family units.

The final step is to multiply the cost of the various food plans by
three. As explained by the Social Security Administration:

*The Agriculture Department evaluated family food consumption and dietary
adequacy in a 1955 survey week and reported for all families of two or more—*

*farm and nonfarm—an expenditure for food approximating one-third of money income after taxes. Two-person nonfarm families used about 27 percent of their income for food and families with three or more persons about 35 percent. A later study made in 1960–61 by the Bureau of Labor Statistics found for urban families that nearly a fourth of a family's income (after taxes) went for food. There is less variation by size of family than might have been anticipated, ranging between 22 percent and 28 percent. . . . The earlier relationship based upon the Department of Agriculture's study was adopted as the basis for defining poverty—that is, an income less than three times the cost of the economy food plan for families of three or more persons. [U.S. House Committee on Ways and Means, 1967a]*

Thus we see that the "three" used to calculate the poverty level is based upon a survey of the ratio of food consumption to other expenditures of *all* families in the United States. Averaging all families, the Agriculture Department came out with an estimate of three. The Bureau of Labor Statistics' estimate of four was ignored by the Social Security Administration for unstated reasons.

*Poverty Index Statistics*    In 1979 the poverty index level for a non-farm, two-person family with head age 65 or more was approximately $4,200; the one-person level was about $3,500.

In 1977 (the latest year for which data were available) there were 3.2 million aged (or 14.1 percent of all the aged) with *money* income below the poverty level. Figure 12 shows the sharp decline that has occurred in the rate of poverty over the 1959–1977 period. But Table 11 also shows that there are wide differences in poverty rates among various subgroups of the elderly. For example, while the poverty rate for the white aged was 12 percent in 1977, it was 24 percent for the aged in families with a female head.

It is important to remember that the statistics discussed above are based on money income before paying taxes. "However, if in-kind income is included, taxes are taken out, and the Census data base is adjusted for underreporting of income, a very different picture emerges" (Congressional Budget Office, 1977b). Table 12 shows estimates published by the Congressional Budget Office for fiscal year 1976. Without social insurance benefits, it was estimated that 58 percent of the aged families would have been below the poverty level. With social insurance benefits, only 19 percent fell below the level. But when other income sources are added and estimates for in-kind income are included, the number below the poverty level drops dramatically to only 4 percent. The addition of money estimates for food stamps, Medicare, and Medicaid is the principal reason for this decline.

Thus, we see that poverty *as defined by the SSA poverty index* is very low. But remember, as indicated by the statistics in Table 4, many of the aged have moved from the ranks of the "poor" to join the ranks of the "near poor." Most aged still have money incomes below $6,000.

*Figure 12.    Percent of Aged with Money*
*Incomes Below the Poverty Level, 1959–1977*

Source: U.S. Bureau of the Census, *Consumer Income,* Current Population Reports, Series P–60, No. 116 (Washington, D.C.: U.S. Government Printing Office, 1978).

*Table 11.*    Poverty Rates: 1959, 1968, and 1977

|  | *1959* | *1968* | *1977* |
|---|---|---|---|
| All Persons in U.S. | 22% | 13% | 12% |
| All Persons Age 65 and Over | 35 | 25 | 14 |
| White Aged | 33 | 23 | 12 |
| Nonwhite Aged | 61 | 47 | 35 |
| Aged Persons in Families with Male Head | 30 | 18 | 9 |
| Aged Persons in Families with Female Head | 49 | 41 | 24 |
| Nonwhite Persons in Families with Female Head | 69 | 59 | 47 |

Source: Based on data in U.S. Bureau of the Census, *Consumer Income,* Current Population Reports, Series P–60, No. 116 (Washington, D.C.: U.S. Government Printing Office, 1978).

*Table 12.*    Families[a] Below the Poverty Level Under Alternative Income
Definitions, by Age, Fiscal Year 1976

| | Before Transfer[b] Income and Taxes | After Social Insurance[c] Added | After Other Transfers[b] Added | After In-Kind Income Added[d] |
|---|---|---|---|---|
| **Under Age 65** | | | | |
| Number in Thousands | 10,940 | 8,202 | 6,965 | 4,691 |
| Percent of Under 65 | 17.3 | 13.0 | 11.0 | 7.3 |
| **Age 65 and Over** | | | | |
| Number in Thousands | 9,297 | 2,977 | 2,107 | 646 |
| Percent of 65 and | | | | |
| Over | 57.7 | 18.5 | 13.1 | 4.0 |

Source: Congressional Budget Office, *Poverty Status of Families Under Alternative Definitions of Income,* Background Paper No. 17 (Washington, D.C.: U.S. Congress, 1977).
[a]Families are defined to include unrelated individuals as one-person families.
[b]Transfer programs include payments to individuals through social security, government pensions, unemployment insurance, and cash assistance such as AFDC and SSI.
[c]Social insurance as used here includes: social security, government pensions, and unemployment benefits.
[d]In-kind transfers estimated are food stamps, Medicare and Medicaid, housing assistance, and public expenditures for veterans' programs, health, and aid to education.

Also, remember that the SSA poverty index was set by government officials at an arbitrarily low level and has remained unchanged for nearly two decades, except to reflect price changes.

*How Good a Measure?*    The ratio of food to other expenditures is a key factor in constructing the poverty index. As we indicated above, a higher ratio based on Bureau of Labor Statistics data was not used when the index was first constructed. However, other data that have become available since 1955 also suggest that a higher ratio is appropriate. Tabulation of the 1965 Food Consumption Survey produced a 3.4:1 ratio. "More significantly, the Consumer Expenditure Surveys of 1960–61 and 1972–73 seem to indicate that the ratio exceeds 5:1" (Poverty Studies Task Force, 1976).

A related issue is the measurement of the minimum food requirements used to estimate food costs in the ratio. The current index uses a measure of adequate diet based on the Department of Agriculture's 1963 Economy Food Plan. In 1975 the Department of Agriculture replaced this food plan with a new Thrifty Food Plan. The Thrifty Food Plan reflects revised allowances for essential nutrients and newer data on family food selections.

Mollie Orshansky (1978) points out that the new food plan implies poverty income thresholds that are about 40 percent higher than current levels. "Shifting to the more realistic update . . . would just about double the number of aged poor to include nearly a third of all persons 65 or older, and the number either poor or near poor would embrace approximately two in every five" (Orshansky, 1978).

Another problem involves not counting low income persons as poor if they are institutionalized or living with relatives. In 1976 there were over a million "hidden poor" (mostly unmarried women) who were living with relatives because their low incomes did not permit independent living (Orshansky, 1978).

Thus, great caution must be used in assessing the poverty status of the elderly using the social security poverty index. As one major critic of the index has observed, "To tout a 'poverty line' based on a starvation diet and an outdated concept of a family's budget as an adequate measure of what is necessary to humanely survive is indefensible" (U.S. House Select Committee on Aging Staff, 1978).

*The Retired Couple's Budget*   The second major way of measuring the adequacy of aged income is the Bureau of Labor Statistics' Retired Couple's Budget: "The retired couple is defined as a husband age 65 or over and his wife. They are self-supporting, living independently in their own home, in reasonably good health, able to take care of themselves."

Actually there are three budgets—indicative of three different levels of living. The illustrative family is assumed to have, for each budget level, *average inventories* of clothing, house furnishings, major durables, and other equipment. The budgets pertain only to *urban* families with the specified characteristics. No budgets are available for rural families. The budgets are not intended to represent a minimum or subsistence level of living but rather a level described by the Bureau of Labor Statistics as "modest but adequate."

The history of this budget is interesting. Originally the Bureau of Labor Statistics had only one budget for a *nonaged* family of four persons, first developed in 1946–47. It was recognized quite early, however, that it was inappropriate to measure an older couple's needs in terms of the needs of a family of four. The younger family, for example, has extra expenses for the clothing and education of children.

Reacting to the different living situations of different families, the Social Security Administration developed concurrently with the Bureau of Labor Statistics' budget effort a separate budget for retired couples. In 1959 the Bureau of Labor Statistics revised the older couples' budget. This budget was then updated every three or four years to take account of price changes. But more importantly, the budget was periodically adjusted in an attempt to account for general increases in the standard of living. Thus, for example, in the 1959 budget *five out of six* aged families were assumed to have home telephones (which were used for local calls only). By 1966 the budgets assumed that *all* older couples needed to have phones and that provision for some long-distance calls was appropriate.

How are the budget changes in living standards determined? Most are based on "consumer expenditure surveys" of families with different incomes. As average income increases, average expenditures for different goods change. As described by the Bureau of Labor Statistics, the amount chosen for the budget is "the point on the income scale where families stop buying 'more and more' and start buying either 'better and better' or something else less essential to them."

By means of this technique a majority of changes in the budget level reflect changes in the real standard of living of individuals (rather than just price changes). Thus the Bureau of Labor Statistics' budget standard is not locked into a mechanism similar to the Social Security Administration's three-times-the-food-budget assumption. Once again, however, the assumptions made are somewhat arbitrary. In the words of the Bureau of Labor Statistics: "In general, the representative list of goods and services comprising the standard of budget reflects the collective judgment of families as to what is necessary and desirable to meet the conventional and social as well as the physical needs of families in the present decade."

In the autumn of 1971 the Bureau of Labor Statistics issued for the first time not one but three budget levels for an aged couple: a "lower," an "intermediate," and a "higher" budget. The development of alternative budgets was in part stimulated by the fact that some people were saying the Bureau of Labor Statistics' budget was too high for their purposes, while others were saying it was too low:

> It has been evident that no single budget at one specified level would meet all of the important needs. Throughout the decade of the 1940s, for example, state public assistance agencies appealed to BLS [Bureau of Labor Statistics] to develop a budget for a lower living standard or to suggest ways in which the moderate budget could be scaled down. . . . On the other hand, representatives of voluntary social and welfare agencies providing services to families with a special problem . . . frequently requested budget estimates for a standard higher than moderate to consider in determining eligibility or establishing a scale of fees paid for the services provided. [U.S. Bureau of Labor Statistics, 1967]

The last major revision in the Retired Couple's Budget was in 1969. Since then the budget has been updated annually by adjusting costs only for relevant changes in components of the Consumer Price Index. For the fall of 1977 the Bureau of Labor Statistics set the Retired Couple's Budget at $5,031 (lower level), $7,198 (intermediate level), and $10,711 (higher level) (U.S. Bureau of Labor Statistics, 1978). Unfortunately, one result of the new multiple budgets is that there is even more tendency toward arbitrary interpretation; we do not have one budget but three to choose from—

with no very explicit explanation as to why one should be used over the other.

*Maintaining Living Standards*   Today older workers are retiring at increasingly early ages (see Chapter 3). Following their departure from the labor force they are faced with the prospect of expenditure needs that do not decrease as much as many would like to believe. In the retirement period there are usually rising health expenditures, increased leisure activities, and increased need for supportive services. There is also a continuing need for the basic essentials of food and housing. Moreover, the retired quickly become aware of any rise in the living standards of nonretired families as these younger families share in the general, long-run economic growth of the country. Such increases no doubt generate a desire among many of the aged to "keep up."

It is this ability to keep up that we will focus on. In addition to the aged who find their income near or below the poverty level, there are other aged whose earnings during the working period allowed them to maintain a comfortable living standard but whose retirement incomes have dropped far below their preretirement levels.

In later chapters we discuss in great detail the extent to which pensions replace preretirement earnings and the use of replacement rates to assess pension income adequacy. In anticipation of that discussion, a few statistics from a study by the Social Security Administration (Fox, 1979) are given to show the magnitude of the problem. Of those couples who began receiving social security benefits in 1973–74, about 85 percent received social security benefits below the amount necessary to maintain their preretirement living standard. For about 30–40 percent, social security benefits alone were so low that in the absence of other income, living standards would have dropped dramatically. Some couples, however, also received public employee or private pension income. About half of these dual pension couples had total pension incomes high enough to enjoy a living standard close to their preretirement situation.

Thus, many of the aged have incomes above the poverty level but fail to achieve the adequacy levels specified by the older couple's budget. But even among the better-off elderly who meet the BLS standard, there are many who find themselves faced with a sharp decline in income over their preretirement levels and a consequent decline in their living standards. (We will have much more to say about this problem in chapters to come.)

### The Impact of Inflation

Economic instability, causing unemployment and inflation, creates insecurity for families and individuals of all ages because of the uncertainty of when and how it will strike. For those actually affected, inflation or unemployment can have a major impact on their economic situation by changing the real value of their wealth or affecting their earning power.

The phenomenon of inflation is without doubt one of the least understood of economic occurrences.* Almost everyone feels *harmed* by inflation; yet the truth is that some people and institutions *gain* from inflation. One person's loss is typically somebody else's gain. The result is a redistribution of wealth and income that can be both quite drastic and quite haphazard.

Inflation is a substantial sustained increase in the general level of prices. In any period the prices of some goods are declining; for example, calculator and computer prices have fallen dramatically over the past twenty years. When there is inflation, however, the quantity of goods and services with rising prices far outnumbers those with declining prices.

The most commonly employed measure of inflation is the Consumer Price Index (CPI). Until January 1978, the CPI measured changes in the prices of goods and services purchased by urban wage earners and clerical workers. In 1978, however, the Bureau of Labor Statistics began publication of a new version of the CPI for all urban consumers. This new **index** takes into account the expenditures not only of wage earners and clerical workers but also salaried professionals, technical and managerial workers, the self-employed, retirees, and the unemployed. This new index covers approximately 80 percent of the total noninstitutional civilian population—about twice the coverage of the old index.

The CPI is a weighted aggregative index with fixed weights; it seeks to represent the annual consumption patterns of various individuals. Consumption patterns are measured about every ten years by the Survey of Consumer Expenditures. Based on this survey, a "market basket" of about 400 goods and services is randomly selected and weighted. Prices for the CPI market basket are then obtained monthly, mostly by personal visits to a representative sample of nearly 18,000 stores and service establishments.

The CPI has a major effect on most Americans. Through its widespread use as an escalator of wages, pensions, and welfare benefits, about half of the population has *some* of its income pegged to the CPI (Shishkin, 1974). Moreover, virtually everyone is affected by its direct impact on aggregate economic policies instituted by the President, Congress, and the **Federal Reserve.**

While inflation affects people of all ages, we will restrict the discussion that follows to the older population. There are five principal ways older people can be affected adversely by inflation:

---

*We can go only briefly into the economics of inflation in this book. Readers interested in a relatively nontechnical but more extensive discussion of the issue should read Solow (1975).

1. If net creditors, assets that do not adjust in value for inflation will depreciate in value, reducing the net worth of individual or family.
2. If recipients of transfer (pensions, unemployment benefits, etc.) or other income, adjustments in these various income sources may lag behind inflation, reducing real income.
3. If employed, adjustments in earnings levels may lag behind inflation, reducing real wages.
4. If taxpayers, the real burden of federal and state income taxes may increase because the tax brackets in the laws are defined in *money* rather than *real* terms.
5. If inflation is concentrated among items such as food, which comprise a larger proportion of elderly persons' budgets, the older age group may be differentially affected—especially if indexes used to measure and adjust various sources of income do not correctly reflect aged buying patterns.

*Wealth*    With regard to the first item, the impact of inflation on the wealth position of the elderly, the evidence is most clear. As we indicated earlier in this chapter, substantial financial assets are held by the elderly, but these assets are highly concentrated in the possession of a relatively small number of the aged. On the other hand, tangible assets—such as homes, automobiles, and the like—are held by a large proportion of the aged population.

In general, the money value of tangible assets tends to increase with inflation, leaving the real value of this portion of the aged's wealth unaffected. But, apart from common stock and mutual funds, most *financial* assets do not adjust when the general level of prices changes. Persons holding bonds, checking accounts, savings accounts, and insurance policies find the real value of these assets falling with inflation; in contrast, persons with debts—such as an outstanding mortgage on a home—find the real value of these debts also falling (which is to their advantage).

A number of studies have investigated the effect of unanticipated inflation on the distribution of wealth among households. They have found that when households are grouped according to age of head, the largest decline in wealth occurs among families headed by elderly persons. In contrast, the largest *increase* in wealth occurs among the group aged 25 to 34. It is the minority of the aged with substantial nonadjusting financial assets who are most severely affected. That is, for those aged fortunate enough to have substantial savings, inflation is often a serious problem.

*Transfer Income*    With regard to the second item, lagging **transfer income,** again the impact is relatively clear, but in a way that will surprise some readers. Since persons living primarily on relatively fixed incomes are clearly hurt by rising prices and since the aged are so heavily dependent on pensions, the aged traditionally have been cited as the major group harmed by inflation. While this was a major problem for the aged in years past, recent developments have substantially moderated it. *The major source of retirement income, the social security program, now adjusts benefits automatically for inflation;* in 1979, for example, recipients received a 9.9 percent increase! Also, both the Supplemental Security Income (SSI) and food stamp programs for the aged poor automatically adjust their basic benefits for inflation. The three major income sources that do *not* adjust automatically are veterans' pensions, private pension benefits, and most supplemental state payments under SSI.* Also, the levels of allowable income determining eligibility for SSI, food stamps, and some Medicaid programs are not changed automatically. Thus the bulk of aged transfer income currently adjusts automatically for inflation with a relatively short lag.

*Earnings and Tax Brackets*    Both of these items share the common characteristic of being very difficult to predict with regard to inflationary impact. While earnings generally increase over time, partly in response to inflation, earnings in particular firms or industries may lag behind inflation. Some of the aged still working will find this to be a problem, but in general few are affected because not many of the elderly continue to work full time and because not all that do are employed in firms where earnings lag behind inflation.

Similarly, many aged do not pay income taxes because their incomes are low and social security income is tax exempt. Those who do, however, face two problems: some of the added income to compensate for inflation will be taxed away and, moreover, will be taxed away under progressive tax structures at progressively larger marginal rates.

*Expenditure Patterns and Cost-of-Living Indexes*    During inflationary periods, the prices of various goods change by different amounts. Since the expenditure patterns of individuals and families differ, any particular pattern of inflationary price increases will have a varying impact, depending on the particular expenditure patterns of the individuals. For example, if food and housing prices go up faster than other goods and services and if the aged spend a larger share of their income on food and housing, the result is a larger increase in prices paid by the aged than the nonaged.

Thus there is concern that the CPI used to measure inflation and adjust social security benefits does not reflect the aged's buying patterns. Certain organizations and individuals have advocated, for example, that a separate CPI for the elderly be established. Several studies have investigated the need for a separate index for the elderly. Hollister and Palmer (1972)

---

*We discuss later on in Chapter 7 the problem of inflation depreciating private pension benefits.

looked at the period 1947 to 1967; Theodore Torda (1972) reviewed the 1960–61 to mid-1972 period; and Thad Mirer (1974) studied the August 1971 to June 1974 period. The results of all three of these studies indicate that for the periods investigated, *the cost of living had not risen faster for the elderly than for other groups* and, thus, that the CPI did a good job of measuring inflation relative to the expenditure patterns of the elderly.

The 1970s, however, has been a period when food and housing price increases have been well above the average price changes for most goods and services. Since these two items weigh heavily in the expenditures of most aged, a persistent differential has appeared in recent years between the regular CPI and indices constructed by researchers to measure inflation for the aged poor (Borzilleri, 1978; King, 1976). Nevertheless, a study by Michael (1979), using expenditure data for nearly 12,000 households, found considerable differences among "homogeneous" households in the impact of inflation. When families were combined into homogeneous subgroups—by such characteristics as age, income, marital status, and education—variations in the impact of inflation were considerable in each group. Moreover, the within-group dispersion tended to be more important than the differences between groups.

Thus, how well the CPI measures changes in elderly living costs depends on *what* prices are rising or falling, *how rapidly* particular prices are changing, and the expenditure patterns of particular groups of the elderly. King (1976) observes that "although not conclusive, the evidence does suggest that use of special price indices for homogeneous' subgroups of the population will not necessarily be more equitable than use of the [regular] CPI. . . ."

### The Economic Status of the Elderly

We have tried to show in this chapter that attempts to assess the economic status of the elderly as one group are not very meaningful. Mindful of this danger of overgeneralizing about the aged, let us now summarize some of the major observations presented in preceding sections:

1. The economic status of the elderly has changed dramatically in recent years, primarily as a result of rising social security, private pension, and government employees' pension income.
2. Incomes of the aged tend to be lower than those of younger persons in the population—most aged persons have incomes below $6,000. The 1977 median income of all families in America was about $16,000—nearly $7,000 higher than the median for aged families.
3. The major source of elderly income is social security, but earnings still represent a large proportion of the total—going to the minority of aged still working.

4. Incomes of the elderly vary by employment status, age, marital status, race, and the number of pensions received.
5. Tax laws, assets, and in-kind income are all important factors in improving the economic status of the elderly.
6. Poverty among the aged, as measured by the SSA poverty index, has practically disappeared. Large numbers of the elderly, however, still suffer a large drop in living standard when they retire.
7. Contrary to popular belief, the aged have a large measure of protection from inflation. Those heavily dependent on financial assets and private pensions are most vulnerable.

## Suggested Readings

Bixby, Lenore E., W. W. Finegar, S. Grad, W. W. Kolodrubetz, P. Lauriat, and J. Murray. *Demographic and Economic Characteristics of the Aged.* Office of Research and Statistics, Research Report No. 45. Washington, D.C.: U.S. Government Printing Office, 1975.

    The "1968 Survey of the Aged." This survey was a follow-up to the 1963 Survey of the Aged (see Epstein and Murray below). Like its predecessor, it provides the most comprehensive data available on the aged population in 1967.

Epstein, Lenore A., and Janet H. Murray. *The Aged Population of the United States.* Office of Research and Statistics, Research Report No. 19. Washington, D.C.: U.S. Government Printing Office, 1967.

    The "1963 Survey of the Aged." This was the first comprehensive survey of the United States aged in 1962. It includes information not gathered in the census or other sample surveys and analysis of this data by the staff of the Social Security Administration.

Federal Council on the Aging. *The Impact of the Tax Structure on the Elderly.* Washington, D.C.: U.S. Government Printing Office, 1975.

    A review of various taxes as they apply to various subgroups of the elderly population.

Grad, Susan, and Karen Foster. *Income of the Population 55 and Older, 1976.* Washington, D.C.: Social Security Administration, 1979.

    Informative data on the economic status of the elderly—data not published on a regular basis.

Lamale, Helen H. "Measuring Retirees' Living Costs." *Aging and Work* (Fall 1978): 251–258.

    An explanation of the new revised Consumer Price Index and the Retired Couple's Budget. The author assesses the relative merits of different indices in measuring the impact of inflation on the elderly.

Moon, Marilyn. *The Measurement of Economic Welfare—Its Application to the Aged Poor.* New York: Academic Press, 1977.

    A good theoretical discussion of nonmoney factors affecting economic welfare. The book also presents empirical measures for the aged.

Poverty Studies Task Force. *The Measure of Poverty.* A Report to Congress as Mandated by the Education Amendments of 1974. Washington, D.C.: U.S. Department of Health, Education, and Welfare, 1976.

    "Must reading" for those who want a sophisticated understanding of issues involved in measuring poverty and collecting needed data.

*Social Security Bulletin.* Washington, D.C.: U.S. Government Printing Office (monthly).

   This journal reports changes in social security and other similar legislation and also publishes the results of research studies by the Social Security Administration (and SSA sponsored research projects), various survey findings, and international social security developments.

U.S. House Select Committee on Aging. *Federal Responsibility to the Elderly.* Washington, D.C.: U.S. Government Printing Office, 1977.

   A set of charts compiled by the Congressional Research Service listing the major federal programs benefiting the elderly in the areas of employment, health care, housing, income maintenance, social services, training and research, and transportation.

U.S. Senate Special Committee on Aging. *Developments in Aging.* Washington, D.C.: U.S. Government Printing Office (annually).

   This yearly report by the committee reviews a wide range of developments in aging, including economic aspects. An appendix contains reports from federal departments and agencies with specific activities affecting the elderly.

U.S. Senate Special Committee on Aging. *Economics of Aging: Toward a Full Share in Abundance.* Hearings: Parts 1–11 and various working papers. Washington, D.C.: U.S. Government Printing Office, 1969–1970.

   A collection of reports, working papers, and hearings covering a wide range of topics.

# Chapter Three

## *To Work or Not to Work*

Every individual during his lifetime makes important choices regarding the type and amount of work to be undertaken. The individual chooses some combination of work in the labor force (paid and volunteer), unpaid work in the nonmarket sector, and leisure. Economists emphasize the trade-off between work—which produces goods and services or results in income to buy the goods and services of others—and leisure—which in itself is something that people also find useful or valuable. Thus, more leisure is bought at the expense of fewer goods and services for the whole economy.

*Paid employment* results in the economic output—**gross national product**—measured by national income-accounting techniques and reported regularly by government statistics. *Nonmarket work,* for example homemaking, is not included in the nation income accounts but adds significantly to total output; Nordhaus and Tobin (1973) estimate that in 1965, for example, nonmarket work equaled 48 percent of gross national product. *Not working* translates into a given amount of leisure over the lifetime.

### The Work–Leisure Trade-off

Measuring work in terms of hours per week, we begin at a zero level in early childhood. At some point the individual might start a paper route, do some baby-sitting, or engage in some other part-time work. In the teen-age years, part-time work may increase, and some begin full-time work. Others go to college and "stop work." Through the middle years most men and about one-third of all women work in the labor force full time; most women also work in the nonmarket sector, and some work part time in the labor force. At age 65 (or, increasingly, earlier) work stops abruptly for many. This brief summary approximates the work pattern of the typical American worker today. Granted, of course, there are lots of variations to this pattern.

Juanita Kreps (1971) has written about the number of hours individuals in various other countries spend in the paid labor force:

> *The length of the workyear, determined by the number of hours worked per week and the number of weeks worked per year, must take into account not only average weekly hours but the amount of time allowed for annual vacations and holidays.... For the full-time factory worker in the various countries, very rough estimates can be made of the number of hours worked per year.... The range between Sweden's short and Switzerland's long workyear is thus more than 400 hours, or about 10 weeks annually. Of the three intermediate countries, the United States stands about midway between the two extremes set by Sweden and Switzerland, while Germany and the United Kingdom have workyears which more nearly approach that of Switzerland.*

Kreps and Spengler illustrate some of the options we face. Figure 13 presents their projections of the various possibilities of additional gross national product (GNP) and/or leisure available over a twenty-year period (1965–1985). As the various factors influencing economic growth (technological change, **investment,** rising quality of labor, etc.) increase productivity, new opportunities for increased leisure and/or increased consumption arise:

> *With regard to the possible future growth in leisure and its probable distribution ... at one extreme, assuming no change in working time, per capita gross national product could rise from $3,181 in 1965 to $5,802 in 1985, or by about 80 percent. At the other extreme, if one supposes that all growth is taken in leisure time except the amount necessary to keep per capita GNP constant at $3,181, the possible changes in working time would be as follows: the workweek could fall to 22 hours, or the workyear could be limited to 27 weeks per year, or retirement age could be lowered to 38 years, or almost half the labor force could be kept in retraining programs, or additional time available for education might well exceed our capacity to absorb such education. [Kreps and Spengler, 1966]*

If we took all the increased growth potential in the form of greater per capita output, Kreps and Spengler estimate that by the year 1985 we could almost double the level of per capita output achieved in 1965. This projection assumes that there are no "costs to growth," an assumption increasingly questioned by economists. Some of the growth, for example, will have to go into pollution control devices, sewage treatment plants, and defense (tanks and bombs); to say that this growth in output represents an increase in our standard of living is stretching a point.

Also the projections assume that the government encourages the potential growth by use of appropriate **monetary** and **fiscal policy** and that the assumptions about future changes in technology and the growth of capi-

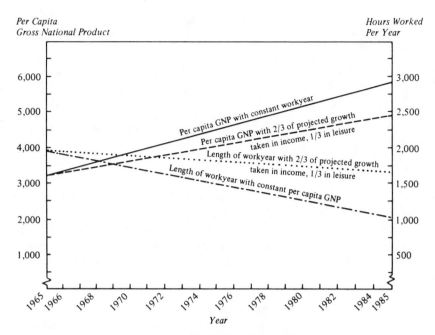

*Figure 13.   Alternative Uses of Economic Growth
Per Capita Gross National Product and Hours
Worked, 1965–1985*

Source: Juanita Kreps and Joseph Spengler, "The Leisure Component of Economic Growth," in National Commission on Technology, Automation and Economic Progress, *The Employment Impact of Technological Change,* Appendix Vol. II (Washington, D.C.: U.S. Government Printing Office, 1966), pp. 353–389.

tal based on past occurrences are correct. Accepting these qualifications, we can nevertheless see from Figure 13 that one major option available to the nation is a sizable increase in the future real standard of living of individuals in the society. Alternatively we can choose fewer goods and services but more leisure.

   *The Pattern of Leisure*   In addition to the choice between work (more output) and leisure, there is the question of when leisure is taken. The increases in leisure experienced early in this century came primarily in the form of shortened workweeks and longer vacations. In contrast, much of the new leisure in recent decades has been allocated to the end of the lifespan. Table 13 shows the changes in time allocation of the average twenty-year-old worker in the 1900–1968 period.

   Suppose that a country wants to hold constant the total amount of work and leisure over the lifespan but wishes to alter the way in which they are currently distributed. One procedure would be to determine at what

Table 13.    Proportion of Life Spent in Retirement

| Allocation (years) | 1900 | 1950 | 1968 |
|---|---|---|---|
| Work–Retirement Expectancy | 42.2 | 48.9 | 49.2 |
| Work Life Expectancy | 39.4 | 43.1 | 41.5 |
| Retirement Expectancy | 2.8 | 5.8 | 7.7 |
| Percent of Life in Retirement | 6.6 | 11.9 | 15.6 |

Source: Denis F. Johnston, "The Future of Work: Three Possible Alternatives," *Monthly Labor Review* (May 1972).

point in the life cycle it might be appropriate to taper off weekly hours of work, if the option were available. Providing more leisure by reducing hours of work means, however, that some people *must work more* at some other time—later or earlier in their lives. Realistically, providing increased leisure without a significant drop in lifetime income probably means working longer when older.

Why do many professionals advocate changes in our present mix of work and leisure? Why do some urge, for example, that we stop the trend toward earlier retirement? Many medical personnel are concerned about the rising trend toward "no work"; they claim that some people die earlier, partly as a result of the change from an active to a more sedentary lifestyle. Some social gerontologists argue that termination of work results in psychological problems connected with the loss of social role and adjustment to retirement realities.* Economists worry about the problems of financially supporting a growing retired population with its accompanying rise in public and private pension costs.

While gerontologists and advocates on behalf of the elderly have been almost unanimous in calling for more flexibility in retirement age policies, much of the movement has been in the opposite direction. For example, as we will show in later chapters, public and private pensions have been designed to encourage retirement to help deal with America's chronic unemployment problems. Professor Kreps has succinctly summarized the current situation:

> *Retirement, a relatively new lifestage, has quickly become a . . . device for balancing the number of job seekers with the demand for workers at going rates of pay. Insofar as retirement practice is used to drain workers from the labor force, a reversal of the downward pressure on retirement age would seem to be possible only if labor markets tighten. Extensions beyond the usual retirement*

---

*In the last section of this chapter we discuss mounting evidence that disputes this pessimistic view.

*age are granted when there is a demand for specific talents. Given current levels of unemployment, however, there is no incentive to prolong worklife in general; quite the contrary. As a result of worsening job prospects for youth, lower retirement age or reductions in working time through . . . union negotiations seem likely. Except for current concern for the solvency of the public and private pension funds, labor market conditions would probably signal moves to encourage retirement as early as sixty. [Kreps, 1977]*

Legislation passed in 1978 to prohibit mandatory retirement before age 70 is a step in the opposite direction. But, as we argue later in this chapter, the impact of this new law may be minimal (see pp. 67–70).

*Changing Labor Force Participation*    There is general agreement that one of the most important labor force developments of recent decades has been the dramatic rise in labor force withdrawals by older men. Figure 14 shows labor force participation in the United States by age for various groups of men and women over age 54 in 1976. The participation rate is highest for couples, where participation is defined as one or both partners working. In recent years there has been a very sharp drop in participation

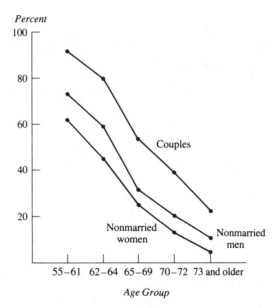

*Figure 14.    1976 Labor Force
Participation Rates of Persons Age 55 and Over*

Source: Susan Grad and Karen Foster, *Income of the Population 55 and Older, 1976* (Washington, D.C.: Social Security Administration, 1979).

*Table 14.*   Changing Labor Force Participation of Women

| Year | Labor Force Participation Rate of Women Age 16 and Over (percent) | Labor Force Participation Rate of Married Women with Employed Husbands (percent) |
|---|---|---|
| 1930 | 24[a] | — |
| 1940 | 28[a] | 15[b] |
| 1945 | 36[a] | 22[b] |
| 1950 | 34 | 24 |
| 1955 | 36 | 28 |
| 1960 | 38 | 31 |
| 1965 | 39 | 37 |
| 1970 | 43 | 44 |
| 1975 | 46 | 49 |
| 1976 | 47 | 50 |
| 1978 | 50 | — |

Source: U.S. Bureau of the Census, *Historical Statistics of the United States, Colonial Times to 1970* (Washington, D.C.: U.S. Government Printing Office, 1975); U.S. Bureau of Labor Statistics, *Handbook of Labor Statistics, 1977* (Washington, D.C.: U.S. Government Printing Office, 1978); and U.S. Bureau of Labor Statistics, Report 544, "Employment in Perspective: Working Women" (Washington, D.C.: Department of Labor, 1978).
[a]Aged 14 and over.
[b]Married women, husband present.

during the later years. Withdrawals cluster around the eligibility ages for initial (age 62) and regular (age 65) social security pension benefits. As a consequence, the labor force participation rate for males over 64 has dropped from 57 percent in 1955 to only 20 percent in 1977. But perhaps even more striking is the decline in participation at earlier ages. The labor force participation rate for men age 60 to 64 continues to fall (Rones, 1978):

| Year | Age 60 to 64 |
|---|---|
| 1957 | 82.5 |
| 1962 | 80.2 |
| 1967 | 77.6 |
| 1972 | 72.5 |
| 1977 | 62.9 |

In contrast, the proportion of females in the labor force has risen sharply in almost all age groups, with an overall increase from 26 percent in 1940 to over 50 percent in 1978 (see Table 14). Regarding older women, the labor force participation rate of women age 55–64 rose from 27 percent in 1950 to 41 percent in 1974. For those women over age 65 participation has remained relatively constant over the past three decades with some slight drop in recent years to slightly below 10 percent.

For both men and women, part-time work is most common among the very young and the very old. About half of employed persons over age 64 work part time (in 1978, 48 percent of men and 59 percent of women). Almost all the older persons working part time do so by preference. Some seek to supplement other income sources—primarily pension income. Others are forced by health limitations to cut back on worktime. Some prefer a gradual withdrawal to an abrupt stop. And finally, there are, no doubt, many who want more leisure but still value highly the various social and monetary benefits arising from some amount of labor force attachment.

Given the high dropout of workers before or at age 65, who are the people who continue working? A National Council on Aging survey of persons age 65 and over who were working in 1974 found that these persons were employed in the full range of occupations, but that some occupations "were more amenable" to continued work than were others. Table 15 contrasts the occupational distribution of those over age 65 with two younger age groups. As compared with younger ages, the data show that four occupational categories have higher proportions of over-65 workers: (a) managers and proprietors, (b) sales workers, (c) service workers, and (d) agricultural workers. These are the areas where there is a large degree of self-employment and part-time job opportunities and where fewer jobs are affected by mandatory retirement rules.

Table 16 shows considerable variation among nations in the proportion of people working after age 65. Compared with other industrialized countries, United States labor force participation by the aged falls in the middle range.

*Table 15.*  Occupational Distribution of Various Age Groups of Workers in 1974

| | | Age | | |
| Occupation | Total | 18–54 | 55–64 | 65 and Over |
|---|---|---|---|---|
| Professional | 19 | 20 | 13 | 10 |
| Manager, Official, Proprietor | 11 | 11 | 11 | 18 |
| Clerical Worker | 13 | 13 | 10 | 8 |
| Sales Worker | 6 | 6 | 5 | 10 |
| Skilled Craftsman, Foreman | 22 | 23 | 19 | 11 |
| Operative, Unskilled Laborer | 15 | 15 | 18 | 15 |
| Service Worker | 10 | 9 | 15 | 17 |
| Farmer, Farm Manager, Laborer | 3 | 2 | 6 | 8 |
| Other | 1 | 1 | 3 | 3 |

Source: Elizabeth L. Meier, "Over 65: Expectations and Realities of Work and Retirement," *Industrial Gerontology* 2 (Spring 1975): 95–109. Used by permission.

*Table 16.*   Percent of Persons Age 65 and Over Who Are Economically Active

| | |
|---|---|
| Australia | 11.7 |
| Austria | 4.9 |
| Belgium | 6.3 |
| Canada | 17.2 |
| Democratic Republic of Germany | 2.3 |
| Denmark | 18.9 |
| England/Wales | 11.4 |
| Federal Republic of Germany | 11.7 |
| Finland | 7.5 |
| France | 17.1 |
| Greece | 26.5 |
| Ireland | 26.2 |
| Italy | 12.9 |
| Japan | 34.9 |
| Netherlands | 7.3 |
| Northern Ireland | 11.5 |
| Norway | 21.2 |
| Portugal | 29.5 |
| Scotland | 11.3 |
| Spain | 11.2 |
| Sweden | 8.6 |
| Switzerland | 18.9 |
| United States | 16.2 |
| U.S.S.R. | 16.9 males[a] |
| | 5.8 females[a] |
| Yugoslavia | 30.6 |

Sources: Richard H. Rowland, "Withdrawal from the Work Force among Persons of Retirement Age in the USSR: 1959–1970," *Industrial Gerontology* (Spring 1975); *United Nations Demographic Yearbook* (New York: United Nations, 1972, 1973); *1973 Year Book of Labour Statistics* (Geneva: International Labour Office, 1973); Paul Fisher, "Labor Force Participation of the Aged and the Social Security System in Nine Countries," *Industrial Gerontology* (Winter 1975).
[a]Age 60 and over.

## Economic Problems of Older Workers

In recent years there has been increasing recognition that a variety of special economic problems confront middle-aged and older workers: (a) age discrimination in hiring, (b) job obsolescence, (c) changing job-performance capabilities, necessitating job change (or job redesign), and (d) adverse institutional structures (such as mandatory retirement). In addition, older workers, while often protected by seniority against job loss, generally find themselves almost as vulnerable as younger workers to plant shutdowns and many of the dislocations arising from mergers and government spending cutbacks. Not only do these problems create immediate difficulties for workers and their families, but they often have an economic impact on their situation during the retirement years. Long-term unemployment, for example, makes saving difficult if not impossible. Moreover, periods of unemployment often result in lower pension benefits in retirement.

These special employment problems associated with aging are part of a larger set of factors influencing individuals in their decisions to work or not to work. In this regard, economists talk about labor force participation and seek to understand the choices made in the relative amounts of time allocated between work and leisure, the latter including home work and volunteer work as well as leisure. In contrast to the retirement preparation discussed in the next chapter, we will emphasize in this section the institutional pressures and constraints placed on individuals in their determination of *when* to retire. We begin with a discussion of some of the economic problems confronting older workers and end with a discussion of the retirement decision.

An important distinction in terminology must be kept in mind here. Throughout most of the book when we talk about the aged or older persons, we are usually referring to those over age 65. In this chapter we talk about older workers but are not focusing exclusively, or even primarily, on persons over age 65. Rather, the major focus of this chapter is on workers who have reached middle age and those approaching retirement age (generally, the 45–65 age group).

*Work Problems*   As shown in Table 17, unemployment rates decline sharply with age but tend to be slightly higher in the later years than in the middle ones. Insulated from unemployment by job-dismissal customs and formal seniority rules, older workers are not as likely to lose their jobs. With changing consumer expenditure patterns, however, many established industries have experienced a stagnation or gradual decline in employment opportunities. In contracting or closing businesses even senior jobholders are adversely affected. Declines, for example, in the cotton and woolen textile, agriculture, railroad, and shoe industries have encouraged or forced millions of workers to seek alternative jobs. Older workers confronted by a job change often find themselves faced with a variety of problems.

There has been a clear bias in private and public employment policy against older workers. They have been discriminated against in job hiring. Work and job structures have been made relatively inflexible, making mid-career adjustments very difficult. Various policies have encouraged or forced

*Table 17.*   Unemployment Rates by Sex and Age for 1977 (Percent)

|       | 16–17 | 18–19 | 20–24 | 25–34 | 35–44 | 45–54 | 55–64 | Over 64 |
|-------|-------|-------|-------|-------|-------|-------|-------|---------|
| Men   | 17.6  | 13.0  | 9.3   | 5.0   | 3.1   | 3.0   | 3.3   | 4.9     |
| Women | 18.2  | 14.2  | 9.3   | 6.7   | 5.3   | 5.0   | 4.4   | 4.9     |

Source: *Employment and Training Report of the President* (Washington, D.C.: U.S. Government Printing Office, 1978), Table A-20.

workers to retire and then have discouraged or prevented them from returning to the work force.

In 1965 the nation was made aware of the extent and nature of
discrimination toward older workers through a report issued by the Department of Labor. This report documented that at that time more than 50 percent of all available job openings were closed to applicants over age 55
because of employers' policies *not* to hire any person over that age.
Moreover, about 25 percent of the job openings were closed to applicants
over age 45.

Since its passage in 1967, the federal Age Discrimination in
Employment Act has attempted to protect individuals from age discrimination in hiring, discharge, compensation, and other terms of employment.
This law originally covered (with some exceptions) persons between the ages
of 40 and 65 but was amended in 1978 to include workers up to age 69. As
a result, the more blatant signs of discrimination—such as newspaper ads
restricting jobs to younger persons—have declined significantly.

It is difficult to determine, though, the extent to which actual discrimination has in fact lessened, for little comprehensive evidence exists on
the matter. Data on older worker unemployment, however, may be one important indicator that serious problems still exist. Studies show that while
unemployment is relatively low among men age 45–65, men in this age
group who become unemployed typically remain unemployed much longer
than younger workers.

This longer average duration of unemployment is not all caused by
age discrimination, however. Often older workers lack the necessary skills to
qualify for available jobs or are not living in areas where job opportunities
exist. Competing for jobs in the growing electronics and computer industries, for example, is difficult for many older workers. Many skills developed
in the old established industries cannot be readily used in the "new technology" industries. And no large-scale programs exist in the United States to
provide these older workers with the required newer skills.

Moreover, the problems arising from this incompatibility of skills
have been aggravated by shifts in industries from their locations in the
Northeast, Middle Atlantic, and North Central states to the Southeast,
Southwest, and West. Many older workers with usable skills have been left
behind with little hope for suitable new employment.

With the growth of **private pensions** has come the recognition that
this fringe benefit in the pay package represents another possible factor contributing to the reemployment problems of older workers. Management may
be reluctant to hire older workers because it is usually more costly to provide such workers with a specified pension benefit. This higher cost results
primarily from two factors: (a) a shorter work history over which employer
pension contributions must be made and thus lower investment income aris-

ing from the pension contributions, and (b) a declining probability with age of employee withdrawal (job turnover) between hiring and retirement. That is, the later the age of job entry, the shorter the period over which contributions can be made, the shorter the period over which interest is earned on pension funds, and the less likely the worker will die or leave the plan before qualifying for any benefit. "Very definitely, then, most employers with pension plans have added costs if they hire older workers. If anything the differential has increased in the last decade, making it relatively even more costly to employ the experienced jobseeker" (Taggart, 1973).

Finally, evidence indicates that older workers have difficulty finding new jobs because of their "job seeking" behavior and the lower priority given to them by various manpower agencies. Sobel and Wilcock (1963) in a study of 4,000 job seekers found that older workers displayed less willingness (a) to change types of work methods or methods of looking for work, (b) to engage in job retraining, (c) to adjust salary expectations, and (d) to move to areas of higher employment opportunity. Sheppard and Belitsky (1966) in a study of 500 workers in one locality found that older workers were also "more restrictive" in their job search techniques and less persistent in their activities.

Older workers often get lower priority from government agencies set up to aid the unemployed. A 1973–74 study by the National Institute of Industrial Gerontology reaffirms earlier findings of the Sheppard and Belitsky study: there are no age differences in the proportion of unemployed persons seeking job assistance from the employment service but there is differential treatment by age. Figure 15 shows by age group the proportion of various employment service applicants receiving employment services, referral to a job, and placement in a job. Significantly fewer older workers were (a) tested, counseled, or enrolled in training,* (b) referred to employers for job interviews, or (c) actually placed in a job. Likewise, while older workers constitute a large proportion of the long-term unemployed, they have always been an almost insignificant proportion of the persons trained under the various manpower training programs operated or financed by federal and state governments.

*The Retirement Decision* In view of traditional work-oriented values in the United States and the importance of income derived from work, retirement is one of the most important decisions made by persons in our society. Aging in general and the retirement decision in particular, however, involve more complex choices than just deciding between more or less income. The amount of income and assets available is certainly one of the

---

*Similar but more recent findings on counseling and testing are reported by Pursell and Torrence (1979).

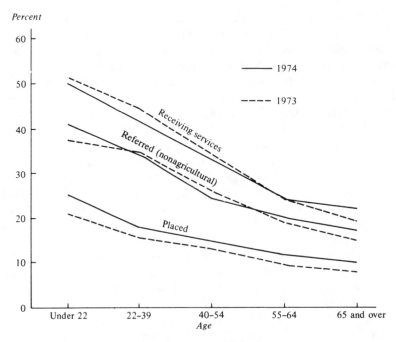

*Figure 15.    Action Taken:*
*Employment Service Applicants by Age*

Source: Elizabeth M. Heidbreder and M. D. Batten, *ESARS II—A Comparative View of Services to Age Groups,* Facts and Trends No. 4 (Washington, D.C.: National Council on Aging, 1974). Used by permission.

major considerations in deciding when to retire, but there are other *personal considerations.* For example, the individual must consider his health and evaluate the physical and emotional difficulties of continued employment on a specific job vis-à-vis the benefits and problems of alternative employment or of leaving the work force.

Various *institutional realities* also affect the individual's retirement decision—factors that, in part, are beyond the person's own control. Included among these factors are such things as (a) the provisions of public and private pension plans, (b) changing pension levels and eligibility ages, (c) prospects for earnings levels, (d) job security and available employment opportunities, and (e) the institutional setting prescribed by work rules and government legislation.

Prior to 1962, men could not get social security benefits before age 65. In that year, the law was changed to allow men the same option granted to women in a 1956 amendment—early retirement at ages 62 through 64 with actuarially reduced benefits. The result was an immediate and major increase in the number of men opting for early retirement. Figure 16 shows the separation rates in 1970 for men age 55 to 73. It is clear that the social security eligibility age has a major impact on the willingness of workers to retire, despite the relatively low level of benefits paid.

Some workers apparently retire before age 65 because they can afford to, often supplementing their reduced social security benefits with a private pension or other income. There is another group of workers who have already stopped working before the initial social security age of 62. The Social Security Administration's Survey of New Entitled Beneficiaries provides important new information on this group of workers. "Forty-one percent of the nonworking men entitled [becoming beneficiaries] at age 62 had been out of work for six months or more; 33 percent had not worked for at least a year; and 17 percent had been out of work three or more years" (Reno, 1971).

Deterioration of health is one of the most important factors encouraging early retirement. Some persons are unable to continue working because of disabling illness. Even those persons who, despite health prob-

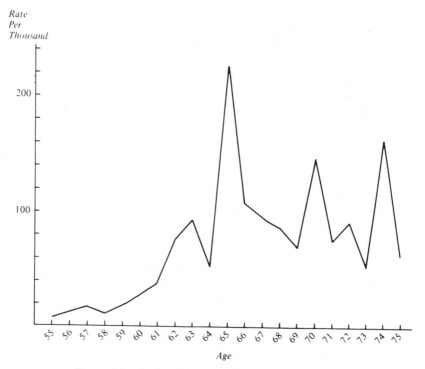

*Figure 16.    Male Retirement Separation Rates, 1970*

Source: Unpublished data, U.S. Bureau of Labor Statistics.

lems, could continue to work in their current job, or perhaps in a less demanding one, may decide to retire at age 62—given the alternative income from a pension now available.

Many studies have documented the importance of health in the retirement decision. A recent one (Parnes et al., 1974; Andrisani, 1977) is a 1966–1971 national longitudinal study of men initially age 45 to 59. The survey found that, other things being equal, men with health problems in 1966 were twice as likely to have retired between 1966 and 1971 as those who were free of health limitations.

This survey is of particular interest to us because it measured the influence of health problems *before* retirement on *subsequent* withdrawal from the work force. Most other studies have asked people *after* they retire why they retired, and consequently it has not been entirely clear whether the high proportion who cite health reasons are, in fact, giving what they consider to be a more socially acceptable reason for retirement. Joseph Quinn (1975), for example, reports that in the Social Security Longitudinal Retirement History Survey, 11 percent of the men and 18 percent of the women reporting good health and "no health limitations" gave (in another part of the survey) health as a prime motivation for their *early* retirement.

Studies have shown that the social security retirement test in the United States also has a strong negative influence on the willingness of the elderly to continue working. The debate over this provision of the social security law has been intense.*

In contrast to practice in the United States, some countries encourage work beyond age 65. For example, workers in certain countries are not penalized by loss of, or a reduction in, social security benefits if they continue to work. Others, like the United States, impose retirement tests, which limit the amount of work persons can engage in (or amount of earnings received) and still be eligible for all or part of their social security pension benefits. Table 18 shows that the number of noncommunist, industrial countries without a social security retirement test is quite large—about 50 percent. When you reach age 65 in Sweden, for example, you get your benefits whether you work or not. Recently Norway introduced a flexible retirement test that permits persons age 67 to 69 who wish to continue working on a less than full-time basis to claim a partial pension if the sum of pension and earnings does not exceed 80 percent of former earnings. Sweden now has a partial retirement scheme that permits workers between the ages of 60 and 65 to scale down their hours and simultaneously receive partial social security benefits. And both West Germany and Belgium have special retirement provisions for long-term unemployed older workers.

---

*See Chapter 6 for additional discussion of the retirement test.

*Table 18.*   Prevalence of Retirement Tests in Social Security Systems, 1973

| | Work Limitations While Collecting Benefits | | |
| --- | --- | --- | --- |
| | No Limitations on Work | Partial Limitations On Work[a] | No Work Allowed |
| Noncommunist | | | |
| Industrial Nations | 10 | 8 | 2 |
| Communist Nations | 1 | 7 | 3 |
| Developing Nations | 11 | 9 | 36 |
| Total | 22 | 24 | 41 |

Source: Based on data in Elizabeth Kreitler Kirkpatrick, "The Retirement Test: An International Study," *Social Security Bulletin* 37 (July 1973): 3–16.
[a]Some countries eliminate the test at a certain age, usually 65 or 70 for men (and often earlier for women).

## Mandatory Versus Flexible Retirement Options

*There used to be a stigma to going out. He was over the hill. But now it's a looked-for status. Those retirement parties, they used to be sad affairs. They are darn happy affairs now. The peer pressure is for early retirement.*

The above observation (Flint, 1977) is by Victor M. Zink, Director of Employee Benefits at General Motors Corporation. Early retirement is increasing, and workers' attitudes toward retirement seem to be changing dramatically. The statistics show the average age of retirement dropping rapidly in many companies—down at General Motors from age 70 in 1950 to the current age of 58. Barfield and Morgan (1978a) report that twice as many workers today want to retire early as did fifteen years ago.

At the same time, many recent gerontological studies show retirement to be less traumatic than was initially perceived (Shanas et al., 1968; Cottrell and Atchley, 1969; Atchley, 1971; Streib and Schneider, 1971). Atchley (1976) observes, for example, that "the general trends very definitely contradict the myth that retirement causes illness. . . . It appears that retirement is a welcome change for couples in good health who enjoy middle or upper socioeconomic status." Barfield and Morgan (1978b) reach a similar conclusion but state it in a different way. Analyzing data from two surveys taken at the beginning and end of the last decade, they derive "a view of the dissatisfied retiree as one whose health problems contribute significantly to leaving the labor force and whose retirement income is low, but not extremely so."

Paradoxically, as retirement ages decline and retirement living is becoming increasingly popular, public policy has taken a big step toward allowing workers to continue longer on their jobs. Bills amending the Age Discrimination in Employment Act swept through Congress in 1977. The House passed legislation abolishing mandatory retirement with only four dissenting votes. The Senate quickly followed with only seven dissenting votes.

The resulting new law extends protection against age discrimination to nonfederal employees up to age 69 and eliminates the upper age limit entirely for most federal workers. Mandatory retirement rules (including those associated with pension plans) are now banned before age 70 except for tenured college professors and executives with large pensions. Professors are exempt until July 1, 1982. Executives or persons in "high policymaking positions" are exempted if entitled to employer-financed private retirement benefits of at least $27,000 annually.

What was the impact of the now illegal mandatory retirement provisions? How many older persons want to work? Will the continued employment of older workers interfere with the employment opportunities of younger workers? It is to these issues that we now turn.

*Mandatory Retirement Practices*    During the past few decades, mandatory retirement rules were introduced by a large number of organizations in both the private and public sectors. The most comprehensive study of the prevalence and nature of retirement age rules is a 1961 Cornell University sample survey (Slavick, 1966) of industrial firms in the United States with fifty or more employees. Perhaps the study's most important finding was that industrial establishments without pension or profit-sharing plans overwhelmingly had flexible retirement policies (over 95 percent of establishments without pension plans, about two-thirds of those with only profit-sharing plans). Among all establishments with formal pension plans, the majority (60 percent) had a flexible age policy with no upper age limit. The remainder (40 percent) had either (a) compulsory retirement at the "normal retirement age" or at an age later than the "normal retirement age," or (b) some combination of retirement age flexibility and compulsion.

But this surprisingly high incidence of *flexible* retirement rules is strongly related to establishment size. For example, 68 percent of the establishments with fifty to ninety-nine employees had flexible rules as compared to only 30 percent of establishments with five hundred or more. In fact, of six independent variables investigated, the Cornell study found that only "size of [entire] company" and the "retirement benefit" showed any significant association with the existence of flexible retirement age policy.

If mandatory retirement was more prevalent in large firms than in smaller ones, what proportion of workers were subject to such rules? Since the extent of mandatory retirement was measured by the Cornell study in 1961, the prevalence of such practices has increased. A survey of wage and salary workers 45–59 years of age in 1966 (U.S. Manpower Administration, 1970) found 46 percent who faced compulsory retirement in their place of employment. Again, as in the earlier Cornell study, workers in firms without private pension plans were not as likely to be subject to such rules.

Thus, about half the wage and salary workers were subject to possible mandatory job termination at some age maximum. How many, however, were *actually terminated* as a result of such rules?

A partial answer to the question is provided by data found in the Social Security Administration's Survey of New Beneficiaries. In an analysis of the questionnaires completed by *men* age 62–65 who were not working at the time of the survey, the Social Security Administration reports that 12 percent indicated that compulsory retirement was "the most important reason for leaving their last job." And among social security beneficiaries entitled at age 66 or older, it was found that only 10 percent of the nonworking men and women surveyed said they left their last jobs because of a "compulsory retirement age" (4 percent) or because they had "reached retirement age" (6 percent). These findings indicate that the overwhelming number of retired workers were not directly affected by mandatory retirement rules.

To understand more clearly why so few workers' jobs were actually terminated by mandatory retirement rules, it is useful to break down the retirement population into categories. First of all, many workers were not subject to mandatory retirement rules because they worked for establishments without such provisions. And, of course, all self-employed persons were unaffected by such provisions.

Next, it is important to realize that many workers potentially subject to such rules left establishments *before* reaching the age maximum. Early retirement has become a normal occurrence in recent years, while retirement at or after the normal retirement age has become less common. Furthermore, as Streib and Schneider (1971) have recently documented, "not *all* persons subject to retirement at a certain chronological age are reluctant to retire; some welcome the step." And, of those who do *not* want to retire, a certain proportion are encouraged by health or physical condition to "accept" mandatory retirement and do not try to reenter the work force. Finally, some of those able and willing to work do, in fact, seek and find new jobs on a part-time or full-time basis. Figure 17 illustrates these various alternatives.

The percentage estimates shown in Figure 17 are based on a 1968–70 survey of social security beneficiaries and exclude those not covered by social security (e.g., federal and certain state and local government workers). The data show that about two out of five males (aged 65 or less) *who reach a compulsory retirement age* are able and willing to work but are not working. As the figure shows, however, these workers represent less than 10 percent of the total cohort of retired males.

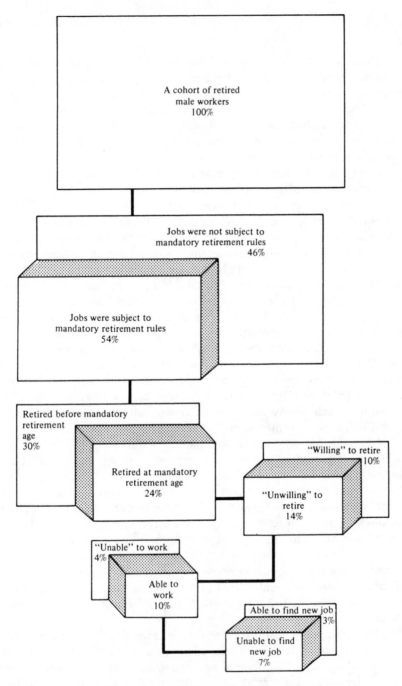

*Figure 17. The Incidence of Mandatory Retirement*

Source: James H. Schultz, "The Economics of Mandatory Retirement," *Industrial Gerontology,* Vol. 1, New Series (Winter 1974): 1–10. Used by permission.

*The Economics of Mandatory Retirement*    Each year, then, before 1977, there was a small but significant number of workers forced to retire who would have preferred to continue working. What are the economic implications of this fact? This question can be looked at from the perspective of the firm, the worker, and the nation as a whole.

Whether the firm gains economically from arbitrarily terminating older workers at some specified age depends in large part on the productivity and earning levels of those terminated versus (a) those of workers hired as replacements (in the case of constant or expanding output) or (b) those of other employees of the firm who would be otherwise terminated (in the case of contracting output). The question is not easy to answer because of the great difficulty in measuring the productivity of particular workers.

It is often asserted that mandatory retirement increases the **productivity** of a business. Dan McGill, for example, states in his pension book that one of the most important reasons why private pensions with mandatory retirement provisions were introduced was the desire of management to increase levels of work force productivity. He argues that private pensions permit "the employer to remove overage employees from the payroll in an orderly fashion, without fear of adverse employee and public reaction, and to replace them with younger, presumably more efficient workers" (McGill, 1975).

The evidence on the question of whether retiring older workers raises productivity indicates that one should be cautious about generalizing. The results of a relatively large number of research studies bearing on this issue are available, but the findings are far from conclusive.

> *Collectively, leading studies on various aspects of the effects of aging document the conclusion that chronological age alone is a poor indication of working ability. Health, mental and physical capacities, work attitudes and job performance are individual traits at any age. Indeed, measures of traits in different age groups usually show many of the older workers to be superior to the average for the younger group and many of the younger inferior to the average for the older group. [Emphasis added] [U.S. Department of Labor, 1965]*

> *Studies under actual working conditions show older workers performing as well as the younger if not better on most, but not all, measures. . . . Age patterns of actual performance do not necessarily reflect the comparative capacities of all older persons versus younger people, but are traceable in part to labor market conditions and to selective processes that may, for example, retain in their jobs the competent older workers, promote the superior . . . or recruit [the] younger . . . of entirely different types. [Riley and Foner, 1968]*

> *There are large individual differences in intellectual capacity, cognitive performance and personality among persons 65 years of age and older. Substantial variations in the biological-experiential demands of occupational tasks also exist.*

*It is therefore difficult to subscribe to the view that a fixed age exists at which
performance in all occupations falls below "expected" standards of achievement.*
*[Baugher, 1978]*

Factors working against older workers are (a) their on-average *formal* education deficit compared to younger workers (which may or may not
be offset by their greater on-the-job experience), (b) their greater risk of
chronic illness and the possibility of declining physical and mental capacity,
and (c) some degree of work assignment inflexibility due to the interaction
of work rules, seniority systems, and pay scales. Although it is probably
reasonable to assert that most employers recognize that the productivity of
some of their older employees is as high or higher than that of younger
workers, these employers also argue that it is difficult (and costly) to identify
such workers. Thus, they argue, mandatory retirement rules provide a practical administrative procedure that is objective, impersonal, and impartial
and avoids charges of discrimination, favoritism, or bias in the termination
process.

A 1974 national opinion survey conducted by Louis Harris and Associates for the National Council on the Aging collected interesting information on the public's mixed reaction to this issue:

*The public 18–64 and the public 65 and over were somewhat ambivalent
about their attitudes toward mandatory retirement. Eighty-six percent (both
groups) felt: "Nobody should be forced to retire because of age, if he wants to
continue working and is still able to do a good job." About three-fifths agreed
that "most people can continue to perform as well on the job as they did when
they were younger." On the other hand, almost half (48 percent) of the 18–64
group and more than half (54 percent) of those 65 and over agreed that "since
many people are ready to retire at 65 years of age, and it's hard to make exceptions for those who are not ready, it makes sense to have a fixed retirement age
for everyone." [Meier, 1975]*

There has been an important initial effort to develop techniques for
providing management with relatively objective ways of assessing workers'
capabilities. In Canada, Dr. Leon Koyl has developed functional criteria to
measure mental and physical fitness for various jobs. Koyl's system has been
applied successfully for almost two decades by deHavilland Aircraft, Ltd., in
Toronto, Canada. More recently, a demonstration project based upon the
Koyl system was carried out in Portland, Maine, by the National Council on
the Aging. This project reported favorable results for the system as a job
placement instrument for workers over 40 (Batten, 1973).

Without operational measures of fitness, employers are faced with
choosing among three options: (a) terminating workers arbitrarily at a
specific age, (b) allowing workers to decide when to retire, or (c) undertak-
ing relatively expensive activities for "sorting out" the insufficiently productive older workers. More importantly, the employer must justify these ter-

mination decisions so that general worker morale will not be adversely affected. Historically, employers have been reluctant to terminate workers solely on the basis of age—especially given past levels of social security old age pensions. But with the establishment of supplementary private pension plans, management (especially in larger firms) apparently felt such practices were much less inequitable. With the passage of new legislation delaying the age at which private management can impose mandatory retirement, there is likely to be renewed interest in techniques of measuring performance (see, for example, Walker and Lupton, 1978).

### Do the Aged Want to Work?

A Louis Harris poll in 1974 was devoted to "the myth and reality of aging in America." One of the most widely publicized findings from that survey relates to the number of older persons wanting employment. For example, *Newsweek,* in a cover story on "The Graying of America," reported the Harris poll finding that "nearly a third of the nation's over-65 retirees said if they could they still would be working" (February 28, 1977, p. 52).* When this finding is cited it is almost invariably (as in the *Newsweek* story) a part of a discussion examining the importance of work to the aged and the problems caused by mandatory retirement. Yet earlier in this chapter we presented data for the late sixties that indicated less than 10 percent of those approaching retirement were forced to retire because of mandatory retirement provisions. Are the two findings compatible?

What most discussions of the Harris survey fail to report are the answers to a related question asked in the survey. Those older persons not working who said they would like to work were asked, "What's keeping you from working?" The answers broke down as follows (National Council on the Aging, 1975):

| | |
|---|---|
| Poor health | 57% |
| Too old | 28 |
| No work available; lack of job opportunities | 15 |
| Lack of transportation | 10 |
| Other interests | 8 |
| Would lose pension benefits or pay too much in taxes if worked | 4 |

As we discussed previously, the high number of people giving health as a reason for not working is difficult to interpret; some people may use this

*Another Harris poll in 1979 reporting on the high proportion of people desiring to work in old age also received national publicity. The same qualifications discussed in the text apply to this newer survey.

answer as an excuse in place of less socially accepted reasons. What is clear, however, is that there is not one but a wide range of reasons why people who "would like to work" do not work. Thus, when those aged who were retired or unemployed were asked if they would come back to work or take on a new job that "suited them well," only 11 percent responded that they would definitely consider it. Moreover, only 12 percent of the retirees reported in the survey that they had some skills they would like to use but that no one would give them a chance to use the skills.

Another relevant and interesting set of findings is reported by Dena K. Motley (1978) from the Social Security Administration's Retirement History Study. Motley investigated men and women age 62 to 67 in 1973 who had retired since 1969. She measured their availability for work through survey questions on attitudes about work and their need for income. Again, the study found that very few retirees were available: "It appears that no more than 12 percent of such retirees would be very likely or even able to return to work. . . . Twenty-four percent of the respondents constitute an ambivalent group whose members might return to work if the drawing power of their need for more income were strong enough to override a disinclination for work or if a preference for employment were strong enough to prevail over the comfort of an adequate retirement income."

Finally, returning to the example of General Motors Corporation, we find statistics that dramatically illustrate the early ages at which employees now *elect to retire*. General Motors reports the age distribution of workers who retired in 1976 (Morris, 1977):

| Age | Percent |
|-----|---------|
| Under 55 | 29 |
| 55–64 | 60 |
| 65–67 | 9 |
| 68 (mandatory retirement) | 2 |

Thus, we see that only 2 percent of all GM retirees were workers who chose to remain until the mandatory retirement age. What is perhaps more surprising, however, is the large proportion of workers leaving before age 55 (29 percent!)—made possible by the special "thirty years and out" pension provision in labor contracts throughout the automobile industry. The experience of General Motors and the other car manufacturers has been that rank and file workers have continually pushed for liberalized early retirement options. An enthusiastic response by workers to pension provisions that allow early retirement is not surprising, therefore, but in many cases the magnitude of that response has been higher than expected.

With so many workers in *all* industries retiring "voluntarily" at increasingly early ages, the historic decline in the role of earnings from work to provide economic support in old age will continue.* The importance of pension income in providing that support will continue to increase. And the costs of supporting people in retirement will also increase. In Chapters 5, 6, and 7 we look at public and private pensions and the key role they play in the economics of aging. In Chapter 8 we discuss pension financing and the problem created by the declining retirement ages discussed in this chapter.

## Suggested Readings

*Aging and Work* (quarterly).

Formerly called *Industrial Gerontology,* this journal focuses on the interrelationships of work and age for middle aged and older workers, as well as the problems and prospects of retirement. Some of the nation's leading authorities on aging from government, industry, and academia contribute to this, the only journal concerned exclusively with the problems of middle aged and older workers.

Boglietti, G. "Discrimination Against Older Workers and the Promotion of Equality of Opportunity." *International Labour Review* 110 (October 1974): 351–365.

A review of older worker problems in various countries throughout the world and a summary of the International Labour Office's action in this problem area.

Kirkpatrick, Elizabeth Kreitler. "The Retirement Test: An International Study." *Social Security Bulletin* 37 (July 1973): 3–16.

Based on a survey of more than a hundred countries, this article describes and discusses the wide variety of rules regarding the receipt of social security benefits when persons, otherwise eligible, work.

Kreps, Juanita. *Lifetime Allocation of Work and Income.* Durham, N.C.: Duke University Press, 1971.

A series of essays that discuss various aspects of work and leisure over the lifespan.

O'Meara, J. Roger. *Retirement: Reward or Rejection?* New York: The Conference Board, Inc., 1977.

A report that attempts to provide guidelines—in terms of priorities and emphasis—that might serve as a checklist for company retirement programs.

Rhine, Shirley H. *Older Workers and Retirement.* New York: The Conference Board, Inc., 1978.

A succinct and very readable review of older worker characteristics, demographic shifts, labor force participation, the older unemployed, and mandatory retirement.

Rones, Philip L. "Older Men—The Choice Between Work and Retirement." *Monthly Labor Review* 101 (November 1978): 3–10.

A concise discussion of issues covered in this chapter, with recent detailed data on the percent of industry and occupational employment by age.

---

*There is increasing speculation that a growing awareness of the effect of high inflation rates on private pensions will discourage early retirement (see, for example, Ross, 1978).

Also presented is an index of the representation of older workers in each major industry and occupation.

Sheppard, Harold. "Work and Retirement." In Robert H. Binstock and Ethel Shanas, eds., *The Handbook of Aging and the Social Sciences.* New York: Van Nostrand Reinhold, 1976.

A survey of the research in this area by one of the leading authorities in the industrial gerontology field.

U.S. House Select Committee on Aging. *Mandatory Retirement: The Social and Human Cost of Enforced Idleness.* Washington, D.C.: U.S. Government Printing Office, 1977.

The report was written to justify the need for the 1977 mandatory retirement legislation.

Winter, Dorothy. *Help Yourself to a Job—A Guide for Retirees.* Boston: Beacon Press, 1976.

Practical suggestions on where to look for jobs, how to apply, and how to get assistance.

# Chapter Four

## *Providing Retirement Income*

We now turn from employment problems and the retirement decision to the issues of financial provision for retirement. There are various ways in which individuals can provide income in the retirement years, when normal income received from work declines or stops. Figure 18 lists the major mechanisms and institutions available in the United States today for providing economic assistance in retirement. These are divided into two broad groups—private and public. The private mechanisms are either individual preparation or preparation undertaken by the individual as a part of group action. For the public mechanisms it is important to distinguish two major categories: those mechanisms for which there is a **means test** and those for which there is no such test.

In this chapter the focus is primarily on private mechanisms, especially the task that faces an individual who wants to prepare for retirement. In the absence of group mechanisms, both public and private, what must the individual do to have adequate retirement income?

We begin with this focus or emphasis not because this is the most common way that preparation for retirement is currently being carried out, nor because it is the most important way that we would expect it to be carried out in the future. Rather, beginning with individual preparation is a useful way of developing a good understanding of many of the concepts and issues involved in income-maintenance problems of old age. By starting at this level, it is easier to show some of the personal options, the major problems, and the magnitude of the task the individual faces. Thus, we can obtain some needed perspective on the whole problem.

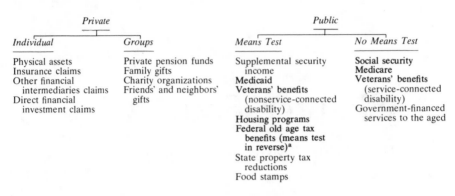

*Figure 18.  Options for Retirement Income*

Source: Adapted from James H. Schulz et al., *Providing Adequate Retirement Income–Pension Reform in the United States and Abroad* (Hanover, N.H.: New England Press for Brandeis University Press, 1974), Figure 1. Used by permission.

[a]Federal tax benefits can be utilized only by people with taxable income high enough to require that they pay taxes and hence take advantage of special tax provisions.

### Retirement Provision by Individuals

First, let us list some of the problems faced by an individual in preparing systematically for retirement:*

1. He doesn't know with certainty when he will die.
2. He doesn't know exactly what his future income flow will be.
3. He doesn't know what his basic retirement needs will be nor what lifestyle he will ultimately prefer for that period.
4. He doesn't know when he will retire.
5. He cannot easily predict the future rate of inflation, which, if it occurs, will depreciate the value of those retirement assets that do not adjust fully and reduce the buying power of income from those assets.
6. He cannot easily predict the rate of economic growth—which is likely to affect his economic position *relative* to the working population.

The number and magnitude of problems listed indicate that individual retirement planning is a very difficult job; the personal decision-making process involved in preparation for retirement is very complex. First, as listed above, not knowing when one is going to die is a major complicating factor in ascertaining the amount of money needed for retirement. To plan for adequate income the individual needs to know the number of years for which income is required. Thus arises a major justification for not providing for retirement entirely by individual mechanisms; one can simplify the

*The pronoun "he" is used generically in this list.

decision-making process and reduce uncertainty by entering into an insurance arrangement, either public or private, that provides collective protection by grouping those who live short, medium, and long lives (discussed further in Chapter 5).

The second problem is the uncertainty of the income flow the individual will receive over his working life. The problem here arises from such possibilities as ill health or disability (either short term or long term). More importantly, problems are created by unemployment in the labor market, job obsolescence, and unequal economic opportunity for various groups. For example, the recurrent periods of recession and inflation are outside the control of the individual and are very difficult to predict, yet these factors have a significant, if not dominating, impact on the flow of income and the total amount of income individuals receive over their lifetimes.

A third problem arises from not knowing what retirement needs will be. A major factor here is the great uncertainty that exists with regard to the state of one's health when one gets old. Will chronic or serious illness develop? Will nursing care be required? Will institutionalization be necessary? Not only does health status directly influence medical costs, it also affects retirement mobility—influencing recreation and transportation expenditures.

Yet another difficulty arises if one is married. There is uncertainty as to whether the family unit will break up (divorce) and about how long each spouse will live. Pension benefits paid out often change if the eligible worker dies. Thus, the amount of money each spouse will need or will have in retirement is essentially unpredictable as far as the individual is concerned.

A fourth problem occurs because of the variability in the age at which people retire. Although the individual has a large measure of control over when he retires, increasingly the decision is becoming institutionalized. This results from mandatory retirement rules, the growth of early retirement options (sometimes accompanied by management and/or union pressures to retire), and, finally, from discriminatory practices in hiring older workers.

Perhaps one of the most difficult retirement preparation problems is that of predicting the rate of **inflation** that will occur *during* retirement. This problem is so very important because to the extent that the individual accumulates assets (or pension rights) for the retirement period that do not automatically adjust in value for inflation, he is faced with the prospect of these assets shrinking in value—being of little worth in the retirement period.

Finally, the individual preparing for retirement might be concerned about changes in his relative economic status in retirement. After he retires the real incomes of the working population will continue to rise over the years. If the retiree wants to keep up with the general rise in living standards, he will have to make some estimate of the growth that will occur while he is in retirement and provide additional retirement funds that can be drawn upon to keep his economic status rising along with that of everybody else. Some people will decide that they do not want to bother dealing with the growth of income problem; they will be content just to keep their standard of living constant. Some may even prefer to allow it to decline. Nevertheless, this is an important point that should not be overlooked. There is a choice to be made, and it should not be made passively because individuals are unaware of the nature of that choice.

### Required Rate of Saving for Retirement

To see the retirement preparation issues clearly, let us assume certain answers to most of the questions listed above in order to answer the following question: Suppose an individual (on his own) wants to save a sufficient amount for his retirement; how much should he save? To put the question another way, suppose you were a preretirement counselor and someone came to you and said, "I'm twenty-five. I don't have much confidence in the present pension mechanisms available to prepare for retirement; I just don't trust them. Instead, I want to sit down and work out a savings plan for myself that will provide me with adequate income in retirement. How much should I save?"

The answer to this question depends on a great many factors. Most important are the following:

1. The standard of adequacy chosen.
2. The number of years one plans to be in retirement.
3. The number of years one plans to work and the earnings over that period.
4. The yield (if any) one can anticipate on one's savings.
5. The expected inflation that will occur over the period.

Let us look first at the standard of adequacy. The two standards described extensively in Chapter 2—the Social Security Administration's poverty index and the Bureau of Labor Statistics' Retired Couple's Budget—are possibilities. But a retirement counselor would probably argue that these are not very good standards for most people to use. Instead, it is becoming increasingly common to propose that individuals with near- or above-average incomes choose a standard of adequacy based upon the concept of "earnings replacement." An earnings replacement standard seeks to provide the individual with income in retirement that is a certain specified percentage of his average earnings prior to retirement. Immediately, two questions arise. What should that replacement goal be; what rate should be chosen—100, 80, or 50 percent? And what period of earnings does one average to get average preretirement earnings?

For those interested, there is a whole book, *Providing Adequate Retirement Income,* devoted to looking at the above two questions (Schulz et al., 1974). The book develops the concept of relative income adequacy in retirement and describes innovative social security systems in Sweden, West Germany, Belgium, and Canada—countries that incorporate variations of the relative adequacy concept into their pensions. Here we briefly summarize some of the most important points connected with providing relative income adequacy.

### What Must I Save for Adequate Retirement Income?

The amount of financial resources needed in retirement depends upon the standard of adequacy used. If the retired person's living standard is to be related in some way to a standard of living experienced before he retired, sources of retirement funds must enable him to replace a certain proportion of the income lost when work stops.

It is generally agreed that expenses in retirement will be somewhat lower than before retirement and, hence, that a 100 percent earnings replacement is not necessary. Various estimates of the differences in pre- and postretirement expenditures have been made by different researchers. For example, the Bureau of Labor Statistics (BLS) has developed an "equivalency income scale" for families of different size and age (on the basis of the relation between food expenditures and income). BLS estimates that an elderly couple generally requires 51 percent as much income for goods and services as a younger four-person husband–wife family living on the same standard. While the BLS equivalence scale shows a difference of 51 percent in expenditures needs when comparing a *middle-aged four-person family* with an *aged couple,* the difference between couples aged 55–64 and couples aged 65 or more is much less. The scales show only a 13.5 percent difference in goods and services needs.

We can use these findings to help establish a retirement living standard. This standard would maintain the same living standard in retirement as existed just prior to retirement. To get our estimate of the preretirement living standard we will (somewhat arbitrarily) average the earnings for the last five years of work before retirement.

The appropriate percentage of replacement needed can then be estimated using the BLS equivalence scale. In addition to the 13.5 percent expenditure difference, one also must take into account the reduced income tax burden in retirement due to special federal and state income tax provisions for persons age 65 and over. Also, presumably the individual upon reaching retirement can discontinue saving for retirement, a requirement that reduces his disposable income in the working years. Taking these three factors into account, the appropriate replacement is about 65–70 percent of *gross* income for a middle income worker.

One can now calculate (using certain assumptions) the saving rate necessary to achieve a specified living standard in retirement. That is, one can determine what amount must be saved every year out of earnings up to the point of retirement. The year one begins saving is arbitrary. One could decide to start saving at, say, age 25, or one could decide to postpone the task till age 45 and then save more over a shorter period.

Let us assume, for example, that one begins to save a certain percent of annual income starting the first year of work and that one saves the same proportion of earnings throughout one's whole lifetime. Assume a life expectancy equal to the current average life expectancy and retirement at age 65. Assume an investment return on savings of 4 percent.

Suppose one's goal is to provide retirement income equal to 60–65 percent replacement of average earnings during the last five years prior to retirement. *To do this, one would have to save about 20 percent of one's earnings each and every year!*

An individual might desire, however, to save at a lower rate in the earlier years when earnings are relatively low compared to anticipated earnings later in his career. In this case, later savings rates would have to be much higher, and disposable income in the years prior to retirement would be lower.

In addition, the question of child-rearing expenses arises. A family with children has a lower standard of living than a family without children but with a similar income. Once a couple's children are self-supporting, the couple's standard of living may rise as a result of the reduced expenditures of this sort. This depends in part on whether the family has incurred previous debts—arising, for example, from educational or unusual medical expenses. Paying off these debts might prevent any significant increase in living standard in the preretirement years.

### The Introduction of Social Security and Private Pensions

Our estimated required saving rate of about 20 percent assumed that one saved for retirement without the help of either public or private **pension** plans. However, such pension plans do exist and are growing; we have some evidence, also, that these plans influence the saving decisions of

---

*A full description of how this estimate was made can be found in Schulz and Carrin (1972). Alternate estimates are found in Morgan (1977) and Diamond (1977).

individuals. Thus, in the case of public pensions, the magnitude of the individual's job in preparing for retirement by saving is partly reduced because of benefits rights acquired through his payments to the social security system. But we should not forget that the substitution of pensions for individual savings also results in the institution of payroll taxes (social security) and lower take-home pay (private pensions). Somebody has to pay for the group benefits.

Different required savings rates can be computed that take into account social security old age pensions. In the past few years social security pensions in the United States have been increased a great deal, the largest single increase occurring in 1972. Table 19 contrasts the required savings rates for three cases: the rates required without social security; those required given social security pensions based on the 1969 formula; and, finally, those required as a result of pensions based on the 1972 social security formula.* The table shows the very large drop in required savings rates as a result of introducing and improving public pensions.

*Table 19.*  Alternative Required Saving Rates, by Percent

| Living Standard | Without Social Security | With Social Security | |
|---|---|---|---|
| | | 1969 Formula | 1972 Formula |
| Replacement of 65 Percent of Preretirement Average Earnings | 20.5 | 11.3 | 5.5 |

Source: James H. Schulz et al., *Providing Adequate Retirement Income—Pension Reform in the United States and Abroad* (Hanover, N.H.: New England Press for Brandeis University Press, 1974). Used by permission.

The required savings rates presented in Table 19 help explain why past generations of older Americans (and many of the current elderly) found themselves in such a relatively poor economic condition. Average personal savings rates in the United States have remained relatively constant over the years and have not at all equaled the rates required to provide adequate funds in retirement. Moreover, *average* rates of saving are an aggregation of the differing rates for many individuals—most of whom save at rates below the average. The introduction of social security in the late thirties provided the aged with benefits that satisfied only a very minimal adequacy standard. At the same time, personal savings have generally been at rates below those required to bring retirement funds to a more acceptable standard of ade-

*The social security amendments passed in 1977 lower future *relative* benefit levels by about 5–8 percent (see Chapter 6).

quacy. Moreover, the introduction of private pension plans, which grew rapidly in the forties and fifties, did not have a significant impact on the economic situation of the many aged who retired without such coverage.

## Future Saving Adequacy

Having looked at required rates of saving, it is appropriate to examine the current saving behavior of individuals and how it might change in the future. In the past, surveys of the aged have shown that the assets of older people are concentrated in the hands of a minority of the aged population. As we saw in Chapter 2 (p. 31), statistics indicate that many people reach old age with little or no savings. In fact, a very large proportion of them reach old age with little or no *liquid* assets. Most of the savings of older people in the lower and middle income groups is in the form of home equity.

One can argue that this situation will change in the future. It is sometimes predicted that future saving behavior will change and that people are now better able to save for their old age as a result of the higher earnings and higher living standard associated with the so-called affluent society. For example, in *Capitalism and Freedom* economist Milton Friedman (1962) argues that the social security system was instituted during the period of the thirties when there were large numbers of people unemployed, when incomes were very low, and when there were large numbers of older people living in poverty. These conditions triggered the demand for social legislation to do something for these people. Friedman argues that present conditions do not justify the continuation of such programs, since they were designed for the conditions of those times, which do not exist at present.

Unfortunately, if we try to assess arguments of this type made by Friedman and others, we find that the data on saving behavior of individuals and asset accumulation are not very good. In Table 10 (Chapter 2), however, we presented data for the 1960s that showed little improvement in the financial status of a group *approaching* retirement as compared to the elderly themselves.

## Inflation and Saving

Some people have argued that saving, particularly personal saving, is discouraged by the uncertainty of not knowing the rate of inflation. Another way of saying this is that people are discouraged from saving by the certainty of knowing that inflation is bound to take place at some rate and that their savings are likely to become devalued over time.

The form in which savings are held determines the impact of inflation on accumulated wealth. Historically, some assets have adjusted very poorly, primarily because of relatively fixed rates of return: bank deposits, insurance contracts, and bonds. Others, which have adjusted better, require considerable financial sophistication or have much higher associated risk: real estate, corporate stock, and gold.

Various proposals have been made for the creation of a different type of financial asset, a constant purchasing power bond. These bonds would be sold by the government to people to protect their savings from inflation. The basic idea of constant purchasing power bonds is that people should be able to buy these bonds from the government to save for retirement or other purposes. They might or might not receive interest from them. Economist James Tobin has argued, for example, that people might even be willing to buy these bonds at a zero rate of interest—as long as there was a firm guarantee that their value would not depreciate from inflation. Having been purchased for a stated amount, the bond would be redeemable at some point in the future for that amount, *adjusted for any inflation that took place over the intervening period.* Thus, the value of the bond would remain constant in real terms and actually increase if there was a rate of interest associated with it.

Henry Wallich (1969), himself an advocate of the bonds, summarizes the *opposition* to them as follows:

> The case against purchasing power bonds every good official can recite in his sleep. If you escalate government obligations, people will say that you are throwing in the towel against inflation. Investors will stop worrying about inflation if they are protected. And the government with its unlimited resources would be competing unfairly with private borrowers who could not take the risk of assuming this kind of open-ended debt.

Milton Friedman (1971) argues against this sort of reasoning:

> The government alone is responsible for inflation. By inflation it has expropriated the capital of persons who bought government securities. Often at the urging of high officials who eloquently proclaimed that patriotism and self-interest went hand-in-hand (the good old government savings bond). The right way to avoid this disgraceful shell game is for the government to borrow in the form of purchasing power securities. Let the Treasury promise to pay not $1,000, but a sum that will have the same purchasing power as $1,000 had when the security was issued. Let it pay as interest each year not a fixed amount of dollars but that number adjusted for any rise in prices. This would be the precise counterpart of the escalator clauses that have become so popular in wage contracts.

The late Senator Pat McNamara from Michigan, when he was chairman of the Special Committee on Aging, introduced legislation in the early sixties to allow the government to sell purchasing power bonds to individuals up to a certain maximum amount, on the condition that the individuals would be willing to hold the bonds until retirement. The proposed legislation specified that if the bonds were cashed in before retirement, there would not be an escalator adjustment; instead, individuals would only get back the original amount plus a stipulated amount of interest. Senator McNamara introduced the bill over a period of many years, but hearings were never held on the proposal.

The principal opposition to purchasing power bonds is centered in the U.S. Treasury Department. In addition to the reasons cited by Wallich (see above), the Treasury worries about possible destabilizing effects on the bond markets of introducing this new type of bond and the possibility of making more difficult the government's debt financing. In this particular area—debt management and federal debt issue—the Treasury is politically very powerful. Thus far, it has been persuasive in preventing Congress from seriously considering legislation of this sort.

We will return to the question of protecting the real value of savings later in the book. One of the proposals for reforming social security we discuss in Chapter 8 is the Buchanan plan for compulsory saving through private and public retirement bonds indexed to adjust, at a minimum, for inflation.

### Suggested Readings

The American Enterprise Institute. *Indexing and Inflation.* Washington, D.C.: The American Enterprise Institute, 1974.

   A round-table discussion by economists Milton Friedman, Robert J. Gordon, William Fellner, and former Deputy Secretary of the Treasury Charles Walker presenting arguments for and against indexing.

Federal Council on the Aging. *The Treatment of Assets and Income from Assets in Income-Conditioned Government Programs.* Technical Papers. Washington, D.C.: Federal Council on the Aging, 1977.

   A collection of papers by members of the Institute for Research on Poverty, University of Wisconsin, on a topic of continuing controversy.

Kreps, Juanita. "The Economy and the Aged." In Robert H. Binstock and Ethel Shanas, eds., *The Handbook of Aging and the Social Sciences.* New York: Van Nostrand Reinhold, 1976.

   This includes a good review of the literature regarding growth and economic fluctuations as they affect the aged's economic position. Also discussed is the interrelation among education, productivity, and lifetime earnings.

Reich, Murray H. "Group Preretirement Education Programs: Whither the Proliferation?" *Industrial Gerontology* 4 (Winter 1977): 29–43.

   A recent survey of the growing preretirement education literature.

Schulz, James H. et al. *Providing Adequate Retirement Income—Pension Reform in the United States and Abroad.* Hanover, N.H.: New England Press for Brandeis University Press, 1974.

   This book presents a more extensive treatment of the topics in this chapter. It emphasizes the replacement of average preretirement earnings by pensions as a measure of adequacy. Innovative pension systems in five countries are analyzed.

# Chapter Five
## The Role of Pensions

The Great Depression of the 1930s went a long way toward exposing the great political lie of American welfare debates: that poverty was generally the result of the laziness or personal unworthiness of particular individuals. In the thirties it became painfully obvious to everyone that this was not the case. Millions of jobless workers and their families suffered severe financial problems because of an economic catastrophe caused by factors unrelated to their own personal activities. Moreover, the cures for their problems lay almost entirely outside the range of their individual reactions.

Up until this depression there had been a great deal of controversy in the United States with regard to the role of (and need for) some sort of public **pension** system. Many other countries had quickly followed the example of Germany, which established the first comprehensive social insurance program in the 1880s. But in the United States there was no widespread public support for public pensions until the economic upheavals of the Great Depression. And although there was a scattered handful of employee pensions provided by government and private firms in existence during the first half of the twentieth century, the significant growth of these pension programs has occurred in the relatively recent years of the 1950s and 1960s.

Thus, the social institution of pensions has had a relatively short history in the United States. And there has been continuing discussion and debate over just what are the appropriate roles to be played by both public and private pensions. In this chapter we look at this question and discuss some of the important goals for a good pension program; in the next chapters we look at social security and private pensions as they currently operate in the United States.

## Why Pensions?

Some of the debate over pensions has revolved around the advantages and disadvantages of public versus private pensions, but there are two even more basic questions that should be discussed: Why is there a need for *any kind* of pension program, and should individuals be compelled (either by the government or an employer) to join a particular pension program?

You will recall that in Chapter 4 we listed and discussed a number of problems confronting an individual making economic preparations for retirement on his own. The first problem is that the individual does not know exactly when he or she will die—that is, how long a period to provide for. This means that any person, or family, preparing for retirement must assume the "worst"—a long life—and put aside enough money to take care of that eventuality; or one must be prepared to rely on private or public charity if one lives "too long" and one's own economic support is exhausted.

A pension program provides an attractive option by utilizing a basic insurance principle. If the number of individuals in a pension program is sufficiently large, mortality tables of life expectancy can be constructed that estimate average **life expectancy** at particular ages. Retirement preparation costs can then be geared to *average* life expectancy, with the "excess" payments of individuals who die before the average age going to those who live beyond it. The result is that no one has to pay more than he or she would need to put aside personally if it was known with certainty that he or she would live for a period of years equal to the average life expectancy.

The second problem discussed in Chapter 4 in connection with individual retirement preparation is the lack of predictability of future income. For example, chronic low earnings, ill health, or periods of unemployment as a result of a variety of factors may make sufficient saving for retirement very difficult or even impossible. Also, health or employment problems may force an individual to leave the labor force unexpectedly and much earlier than was originally planned.

Collective arrangements to deal with this problem are not new. Since earliest times people have attempted to mitigate or eliminate economic insecurity by banding together in groups—families, tribes, associations, guilds. Especially important has been the family. Throughout history individuals have relied heavily on family ties to protect themselves from economic insecurity in old age. Even today in the United States, the family remains an important source of economic and social support for many older persons. And in some other countries—particularly those less industrialized—the family still remains the major source of economic protection and security in old age.

The major problem with the family (and many other group associations) for sharing risk is that the number of people involved is relatively small. As Kenneth Boulding (1958) has observed, "It is when the 'sharing group' becomes too small to ensure that there will always be enough producers in it to support the unproductive that devices for insurance become necessary. When the 'sharing group' is small there is always a danger that sheer accident will bring the proportion of earners to nonearners to a level at which the group cannot function."

The commonly held view that in earlier America most of the aged lived in rural communities together with, or in close proximity to, adult children who provided financial support in the later years is not supported by the facts (Tibbitts, 1977). Nuclear parent-child families have always been the more common family type in the United States, and the three-generation family has been relatively rare.

Thus, the need for better collective arrangements to deal with the economic problems of old age has probably always been with us. The earliest available statistics on the economic status of the elderly prior to the establishment of pensions indicate that most of the aged were poor and that, in fact, many were completely destitute. The reasons why pension programs were not developed sooner are not entirely clear, but various writers have pointed to the *relative* economic prosperity throughout America's history, the country's decentralized governmental structure, and (most importantly) the individualistic ethic of much of the population.

### Why Compulsory Pensions?

Although individual self-reliance and voluntary preparation for retirement—together with family interdependence—dominated the early discussions of old age security provision, it is now generally accepted that this is not the appropriate cornerstone of an income maintenance policy for the aged. Instead, there is widespread support for relying on compulsory pensions. A number of prominent American economists have written about the rationale for compulsory pensions. In a chapter in his book on the *Principles of Economic Policy,* Kenneth Boulding (1958) concisely states the principal argument:

> [If an individual] were rationally motivated, [he] would be aware of the evils that might beset him, and would insure against them. It is argued, however, that many people are not so motivated, and that hardly anyone is completely motivated by these rational considerations, and that therefore under a purely voluntary system some will insure and some will not. This means, however, that those

*who do not insure will have to be supported anyway—perhaps at lower levels
and in humiliating and respect-destroying ways—when they are in the non-
productive phase of life, but that they will escape the burden of paying premiums
when they are in the productive phase. In fairness to those who insure voluntarily, and in order to maintain the self-respect of those who would not otherwise
insure, insurance should be compulsory.*

Richard Musgrave (1968), writing on the role of social insurance,
makes a similar point:

*Insurance could be purchased privately, but becomes a matter of public con-
cern only because [some] will not do so, while [others] will. Given their humani-
tarian premise, Calvin and Homer must bail out Jack should the contingency
arise. They will require therefore that Jack should insure. Social insurance is not
insurance in the technical sense, but its basic function (and especially the
rationale for making it mandatory) is again to avoid burdening the prudent.*

And finally Pechman, Aaron, and Taussig (1968) in their book on
social security, after an extensive discussion of the rationale for pensions,
conclude:

*There is widespread myopia with respect to retirement needs. Empirical evi-
dence shows that most people fail to save enough to prevent catastrophic drops
in postretirement income. . . . Not only do people fail to plan ahead carefully for
retirement; even in the later years of their working life, many remain unaware of
impending retirement needs. . . . In an urban, industrial society, government in-
tervention in the saving-consumption decision is needed to implement personal
preferences over the life cycle.* There is nothing inconsistent in the decision to
undertake through the political process a course of action which would not be
undertaken individually through the marketplace. [*Emphasis added.*]

J. Douglas Brown, who helped draft the original social security program, writes in his book on the history of social security that the drafting
group never seriously considered anything other than a compulsory program. The drafting group did worry, however, about whether a national
compulsory program would be constitutional.

Hoping that it might be possible to avoid a court test of the constitu-
tionality of social security, the drafting group did consider briefly a plan that
would have permitted elective social security coverage by states and various
industrial groups, but rejected it. According to Brown, the plan was "so
cumbersome, ineffective, and actuarially unsound that no further attempt
was made to avoid a head-on constitutional test of a truly workable system"
(Brown, 1972).

As it turned out, during the debates that followed, the principal argument for compulsion was a financial one. It was argued that an optional
coverage program would make it actuarially impossible to project both benefits (costs) and revenue. It was feared that this problem would create
financial instability and make it difficult to guarantee adequate, equitable,
and improved benefits as social security developed.

The original Social Security Act required participation by all workers in commerce and industry except those working for railroads.* A number of groups, however, were specifically excluded from coverage—the major ones being farm workers, the self-employed, and government employees (including military personnel). Over the years, as coverage was extended to these groups, optional coverage was introduced for certain specific groups: employees of nonprofit institutions, state and local governments, and most clergymen. But in each case, coverage was not optional for the individual, depending instead on the collective decision of the organizational unit.

The decision of the United States to have a compulsory pension program is in no way unique. There is no country in the world with a social security old age pension program that has designed a large amount of voluntary coverage into the program. Like the United States, many countries have special public pension programs for certain groups of workers (especially government employees), and many exclude from coverage certain groups (such as farm workers, the self-employed, or employees of very small firms). Currently only a few countries—Ghana, the Federal Republic of Germany, Kuwait, Liberia, Peru, and Zambia—have any voluntary coverage, and these noncompulsory provisions are all limited to certain (usually small) groups.

If we shift our attention from public pensions to private pensions in the United States, we find that the situation is not very different. The vast majority of workers who are covered or not covered by private pension plans have not achieved that status by personal election. Not all firms have established private pension plans for their employees, but almost all private pension schemes that have been set up are compulsory. Typically, once a worker joins a firm he automatically becomes a member of the pension plan—sometimes after a short waiting period. There are a few private plans, however, that provide for an employee contribution out of salary; such plans sometimes make coverage optional.

In summary, we see that the usefulness of pensions in helping to provide for economic security in old age is generally accepted and that compulsory coverage remains a feature of both public and private programs.

### What Makes a "Good" Pension Program?

If one wants to evaluate a pension program or a pension proposal, what characteristics or features of the plan should be examined? With an institutional arrangement as complex as pensions, one can generate a long

---

*Railroad workers were exempted because similar legislation on their behalf had already been enacted in 1934. Although this original legislation was later declared unconstitutional, new (and still separate) railroad pension legislation was enacted in 1935 and 1937.

list of plan features that might be studied. Opinions differ widely as to which of these are most important. Moreover, there is little agreement on the relative weights that should be assigned to each feature when making an overall judgment about a particular pension plan. Some important characteristics of pension plans, however, that would probably appear on almost everyone's list, are discussed in the pages that follow.

*The Adequacy of Pension Benefits*    Any discussion of a particular pension plan's adequacy must explicitly recognize the variety of means available to the individual (or society) in achieving a particular level of income in old age. A pension plan is rarely designed to be the sole source of such income. Thus, in evaluating the adequacy of any particular pension benefit, it is necessary to relate such analysis to a general framework for evaluating individuals' general economic status and the variety of means available to achieve or change that status. Are individuals *expected* to accumulate personal savings for their old age? Are all individuals *able* to save for old age? What noncash programs (such as health insurance) are available to provide economic support? How large are both public and private pension benefits; who is currently covered by each; who should be covered?

There will never be complete agreement about the appropriate roles for the various means of providing income in old age—collective pension schemes are only one major way (see Figure 18, page 74). Rather, it is almost certain that there will be continuing political debate and private discussion among bargaining groups over these matters. Out of such discussions come decisions on legislation, employment contracts, and employer policies in the area of pensions. As these decisions are made, it is possible to evaluate their economic implications for retirement income adequacy, estimating the contribution the resulting pensions will make to a particular individual's or group's goal.

*The Certainty of Benefits*    In addition to estimating or projecting the size of pension benefits, one can examine particular pension plans and estimate the degree of uncertainty associated with the *promised* benefits. Three major contingencies can be evaluated:

1. Plan termination: what provisions are made to ensure that the plan will survive economic or political adversity, such as a change in government (public pensions) or bankruptcy of the firm (private pensions)?
2. Inflation: how well are the workers' future benefits and the pension recipients' actual benefits protected from general increases in the level of prices?
3. Job termination: what happens to pension rights if a worker involuntarily or by choice stops working or changes jobs?

*Flexibility and Discretion for Varying Conditions or Preferences*
The larger the pension program in terms of people covered, the greater the differences in the circumstances and preferences of these participants. It is generally desirable for pension plan provisions and rules not to be too rigid. The introduction of greater flexibility, however, usually results in greater administrative costs (see Low Administrative Costs, below). And by complicating the program, flexibility often makes it more difficult for participants to become knowledgeable and to understand their pension program.

*Adequate and Nondiscriminatory Coverage*    The determination of eligibility for pension coverage is a very complex but important factor in assessing pension plans. Most people would agree that individuals in similar circumstances (e.g., working for the same employer) should not be arbitrarily excluded from coverage under a pension plan or excluded because of age, sex, race, etc. But the actual determination of who should and who should not be included is often difficult because of a variety of administrative, technical, political, and economic considerations.

*Equity*    Whether a pension program is perceived as fair depends in large measure on how the program treats different individuals and how these individuals think they *should* be treated. The major issue around which equity questions usually cluster is financing—how much do the benefits received cost the individual in contrast to other benefit recipients and, possibly, nonrecipients? Chapter 8 of this book is devoted to financing pensions and a discussion of some of the most important equity questions.

*Low Administrative Costs*    Apart from the benefits paid out by a pension program, there are a variety of expenditures connected with keeping records, determining benefit elegibility, collecting and managing the funds used to pay benefits, and informing individuals of their rights under the plan.
Boulding (1958) has argued that one valid criterion for choosing between private and public programs is whether there can be significant economies of scale in their operation. "If there are these economies—that is, if the cost of administering the insurance declines with every increase in the amount of insurance written—then a state monopoly will almost inevitably be cheaper than a number of competing private companies. . . . We may venture a hypothesis that where the operations of insurance are fairly routine, the case for state or national monopoly is stronger than where the operations involve great difficulties of definition of rights."

*Simplicity and Ease of Understanding*    It is important that individuals know whether they are covered by a pension plan, what the conditions of entitlement are, what benefits they (or their family) can or will receive, what the risks of losing benefits are, and various other facts about the plan. Over the years a large amount of evidence has accumulated that indicates a great lack of knowledge and misinformation exists among workers in the United States with regard to their own expected pensions, both public and private. As the number and variety of pension programs grow and many of these programs become more complicated, this problem will also grow. Therefore, in reviewing existing programs or proposals for pension changes, the complexity of the program should be considered. An assessment should be made of the resultant impact on the employees' ability to understand the pension program and to incorporate it realistically into their preretirement planning.

*Integration*   Pensions are almost always only one of a number of collective programs operating to provide economic assistance. It is not sufficient to view a particular pension program in isolation from these other programs. For example, eligibility or benefit determination under one program is sometimes related to benefits received from another program.

This is an especially important issue with regard to public programs. The value of social security pension benefits to the elderly depends, for example, on (a) the tax treatment of these benefits and (b) whether the benefits are counted as income in determining eligibility for Supplemental Security Income, food stamps, Medicare and Medicaid, housing subsidies, etc. (see, for example, Federal Council on Aging, 1975).

### Suggested Readings

Boulding, Kenneth. "Income Maintenance Policy." In *Principles of Economic Policy.* Englewood Cliffs, N.J.: Prentice-Hall, 1958, pp. 233–257.
     One of the best discussions of the rationale for pension insurance and one of the few discussions available on the relative merits of public versus private pensions.
Diamond, P. A. "A Framework for Social Security Analysis." *Journal of Public Economics* 8 (1977): 275–298.
     The rationale for social security is examined relative to conventional economic arguments for public intervention. Empirical estimates of individual saving are made that indicate "a sizable fraction of American workers would not follow sensible savings plans in the absence of social security."
Friedman, Milton, *Capitalism and Freedom.* Chicago: University of Chicago Press, 1962.
     Arguments are presented in Chapter 11 against compulsory pensions.
Heidenheimer, Arnold J., Hugh Heclo, and Carolyn Teich Adams. *Comparative Public Policy—The Politics of Social Choice in Europe and America.* New York: St. Martin's Press, 1975.

Chapter 7 of this book is an excellent comparative discussion of various social welfare programs. Included in the discussion is consideration of issues influencing how and when social insurance was introduced in each country.

Wilensky, Harold L. *The Welfare State and Equality: The Structural and Ideological Roots of Public Expenditures.* Berkeley: University of California Press, 1975.

Wilensky attempts to investigate empirically how ideology, politics, and the economy affect the development of the welfare state. The book presents evidence indicating that the level of economic development is the most important factor influencing the level of welfare programs, including pensions.

# Chapter Six

## Social Security

The first American social security benefit ever paid was $22 a month and was received by Miss Ida Fuller, a retired law firm secretary, in early 1940. Ida Fuller's experience with social security dramatically illustrates one of the major benefits of public pensions discussed in the prior chapter. Miss Fuller (who died in 1975) lived to be over a hundred, paid into the program less than $100, and over the years received more than $20,000 in social security benefits.*

In response to the needs of Ida Fuller and millions of other persons approaching retirement, the United States social security system was created in 1935 and has grown over the years to be one of the major expenditure programs of the federal government.

The Social Security Act of 1935 established a federal old age pension program (OAI) and a federal-state system of unemployment insurance. In 1939 survivors' and dependents' benefits were added (OASI). In 1956 social security was expanded to include disability insurance to protect severely disabled workers (OASDI). In 1965 Medicare was added, establishing a comprehensive health program for the elderly (OASDHI). Over the period of 1950–1967, successive groups of workers were brought into the system: certain farm and domestic workers (1950), most of the self-employed (1954), members of the uniformed services (1956), Americans

---

*As we discuss in Chapter 8, one of the reasons why many people like Ida Fuller receive significantly more benefits than the contributions they paid into the program is because Congress decided to reduce the eligibility requirements (i.e., the work/payment period) for older workers approaching retirement when the program was first established (and later when new groups were brought into the program). Of course, Ida Fuller lived far beyond the average life expectancy, and this also raised her benefits relative to her contributions.

employed by foreign governments or international organizations (1960), physicians (1965), and ministers (1967). Automatic adjustment of benefits for inflation was legislated in 1972 and begun in 1975. The railroad retirement program was integrated with the social security system in 1974.* Finally, **indexing** of earnings was legislated in 1977 (see page 97).

Total annual OASDHI expenditures have grown from less than $1 billion in 1950 to $85 billion in 1977. This chapter focuses primarily on the social security old age pension program (OASI). The pension discussion is mainly on benefits, however, since Chapter 8 is devoted to a discussion of financing issues. At the end of the chapter, we briefly discuss disability programs, public medical insurance, and the Supplemental Security Income program.

### The Changing Social Security System

Paradoxically, the major motivating force behind the passage of the Social Security Act in 1935 was not the provision of adequate retirement income but the creation of jobs. Passed in a period that at one point witnessed more than a quarter of the labor force without jobs, the social security legislation was one of many New Deal laws aimed at job creation and relief for those out of work. The 1935 legislation encouraged the creation of state-administered unemployment programs to help unemployed workers find work and to provide them with financial support while they looked. Old age pensions were provided to help the elderly financially but also *to encourage them to leave or remain out of the work force.* Old age benefits to otherwise eligible persons age 65 or over were made conditional on meeting a "retirement test." In the original 1935 act, benefits were *not* to be paid to persons receiving any "covered wages from regular employment."

Regular employment, however, was not specifically defined in the 1935 act. In the 1939 social security amendments, the retirement test was made less ambiguous; it specified that no benefits would be paid to anyone earning more than $14.99 a month in covered employment.

Over the years the earnings exemption was increased periodically by specific increments. In 1977, the exemption amount, or retirement test, was $3,000. Legislation passed in 1977 schedules further liberalization (see page 104).

Over the past three and a half decades there have been a great many adjustments in the social security system, but except for the introduction of disability insurance in 1956, medical insurance (Medicare) in 1965, and

---

*We do not discuss the railroad retirement system in this book. Those interested in recent developments should read Skolnik (1975).

price indexing in 1972, there have been few, if any, major changes. Two historical developments are of particular interest, however. First, as a result of a series of legislated liberalizations, there was an expansion of persons covered by the system. Currently the only major groups of gainfully employed workers not covered are (a) federal civilian employees and certain state and local government employees with other pension coverage, (b) farm and domestic workers who do not earn or work "enough," and (c) self-employed persons with very low net earnings. Second, legislation over the years has gradually moved the system further away from financing procedures that would result in the creation of a large monetary reserve fund.

Although we discuss pension financing in Chapter 8, some initial remarks are appropriate here. Currently the social security system is almost completely "unfunded" (i.e., few reserves are accumulated and obligations are met essentially on a pay-as-you-go basis). From the very beginning social security was never completely funded. It was recognized from the start that this was not necessary since mandatory participation resulted in the involvement of a large part of the employed population, since the pension system could be assumed to operate indefinitely, and since the taxing power of the government ultimately stood behind the system.

Initially, legislated contribution rates were expected to provide the money for a fairly large trust fund as payments came in over the years. But as this reserve fund began to accumulate and **actuarial** projections predicted that it would grow much bigger, congressional leaders began to argue that there was no reason for the fund to grow so big. Instead, the decision was made to liberalize the system and to use the scheduled increases in contributions to pay for these liberalizations.

Historically, the gradual adoption of an almost completely pay-as-you-go funding policy facilitated the liberalization and improvement of the system. New groups were added to the system with retroactive benefits provided. Cost-of-living increases in benefits were legislated periodically. And, in 1972, a major increase in real benefits was provided for everyone in the system.

### The Principles of Social Security

The social security legislation that was accepted by President Roosevelt and the Congress was based on a number of principles.

First, for the designated groups participation was compulsory. Workers could not opt out of the system. Nor were high income or high earnings members of the covered groups entirely excluded.

Second, it was set up as an earnings related system. When this decision was made in the 1930s, it was not at all obvious that social security should be based upon an earnings related principle. Many countries in Europe had flat-rate pensions. And Dr. Francis E. Townsend, a California physician, had proposed in 1933 a flat pension of $200 per month for all persons aged 60 and over—resulting in the Townsend movement of 4,550 clubs within two years.

The decision against the flat rate is explained by J. Douglas Brown, one of the architects of the system: "It was early recognized that a single flat rate of benefits for a country as diversified as the United States would fail to meet the needs of those living in the high-cost urban areas of the Northeast while being unduly favorable to those in the rural South."

Third, it was decided that social security should be only one of many sources of economic protection and that further supplementation, either through group or individual means, would be needed to maintain an adequate living standard in retirement. Social security was often referred to as providing "a floor of protection."

Fourth, funds for operating the program were to come from ear-marked taxes, called contributions. Social insurance was to be "a cooperative institution taken over by the state, but still a reflection of the responses of workers who are willing to contribute from their earnings today to protect themselves and their families from the hazards of tomorrow" (Brown, 1972).

Social security benefits were to be a matter of right; there was to be no **means test**. Workers were to earn their benefits through participation in and contributions to the program. The system was to be self-supporting through these worker contributions, together with so-called employer contributions.*

Fifth, social adequacy was to be taken into account in the determination of benefits for various recipients. A set of weighted benefits that favored workers with lower earnings was established. Also, a contribution cutoff point (the maximum contribution ceiling) was established; the earnings above the ceiling of very highly paid earners were excluded. The intent was to restrict the focus of the program to those people who would have the greatest problems and the greatest need for a public benefit (while allowing all eligible earners to participate).

Sixth, as indicated above, a retirement test was established; pension benefits were to be withheld, initially, if an age-eligible person worked and eventually if a person earned above a specified amount.

---

*We discuss in Chapter 8 the question of who actually pays the employer contribution—the employee through reduced wages, consumers through higher prices, or the firm itself.

### Retirement Benefit Provisions *

To be eligible for retirement benefits under the old age and survivors' insurance program, a worker must have worked in covered employment for the required number of calendar quarters. Prior to 1978 a quarter of coverage was defined as a calendar quarter in which the worker earned at least $50 in covered employment. In 1978 the reporting of social security wages was changed from a quarterly basis to an annual basis (to reduce administrative costs). Currently, therefore, the number of quarters credited depends on annual earnings, one quarter (up to four) credited for each $250 of wages paid in 1978.**

The number of quarters required for eligibility varies by age—this, to make it easier for older workers to achieve eligibility during the early history of the program (see page 153). A worker age 62 in 1979 needed 28 quarters. The total number of quarters required increases by one quarter in each succeeding year. Ultimately the maximum number of quarters required will be 40, or about 10 years of covered employment.

Benefits paid under the old age and survivors' insurance program to eligible workers and their spouses can be broken down into the following components:

1. The *basic benefit*, paid at age 65, is based on the worker's average indexed monthly earnings below the "earnings ceiling" in covered employment and is derived from a legislated benefit formula that is weighted to provide workers with lower "average earnings" a relatively greater percentage of earnings replacement than workers with higher earnings. Benefits are limited by the ceiling placed on the earnings on which a worker previously paid contributions. Only taxed earnings below this ceiling enter into the calculation of the average monthly earnings used in the benefit formula. Also, total family benefits are limited by a maximum amount.
2. A *minimum benefit* of $1,464 is provided workers (and survivors) who would otherwise be eligible for very low basic benefits. A special minimum benefit (which is larger and increased annually according to the Consumer Price Index) is payable to those with twenty or more years of covered employment, the size of the benefit being dependent on the number of years of covered employment between 20 and 30.
3. A *dependent benefit*, equal to 50 percent of the worker's basic benefit, may be paid to a spouse and children under age 18 (and those age 18 to 21 if full-time students); spouse benefits are reduced by federal, state, or local pensions payable to the spouse based on earnings in noncovered employment. Disabled children and divorced wives may also receive a benefit if certain specified conditions are met.

---

*The disability program is not discussed until later in this chapter. Some students of social security, however, see it as an important part of a *retirement* program, providing transitional protection for many of those unable to continue working up to the OASI eligibility ages. See Chapter 9 (page 191) for a discussion of this issue.

**The $250 amount is adjusted annually to keep pace with average earnings.

4. *Early retirement benefits* may be paid to beneficiaries at age 62–64, but these benefits are actuarially reduced (by 20 percent at age 62) to take into account the longer period over which they will be paid.
5. *Delayed benefit credits* are given to workers whenever they they do not receive benefits after age 65. An additional 3 percent is added to benefits (for those reaching age 62 in 1979 or later) for each year between ages 65 and 72 that they do not get benefits.
6. A *retirement test* reduces benefits paid persons under age 72 (and their dependents) who earn more than a certain amount. Benefits are reduced one dollar for every two dollars earned above the exempt amount. The exemption for beneficiaries age 65 and over ($4,500 in 1979) increases to $6,000 in 1982 and automatically thereafter with increases in average wages.
7. *Survivors' benefits* are payable to a surviving spouse beginning at age 60 or, if disabled, at age 50, or if there is a dependent child (under 18) or disabled), at any age. This benefit equals 100 percent of the basic benefit (see 1 above) for widows age 65 or over and disabled widows age 60 or over. Reduced benefits are paid to widows age 60–64 and to disabled widows age 50–59. Unmarried and disabled children, dependent parents, divorced wives, and remarried widows are also eligible for survivors' benefits when meeting certain specified conditions. Benefits for surviving spouses are reduced by government pension income (see 3 above).

Each of these components of the social security program is discussed in more detail below.

*Benefit Levels*   Benefits are based on a worker's yearly earnings (after 1950 or age 21, whichever is later) on which he or she previously paid payroll tax contributions. These earnings are adjusted upward by a wage index; the five years of lowest indexed earnings (or no earnings) are excluded; and the resulting total earnings are averaged to produce average indexed monthly earnings (AIME).

The law specifies a formula to determine the amount of benefit based on the worker's calculated AIME. The benefit formula for those reaching age 62 in 1979 is 90 percent of the first $180 of AIME, plus 32 percent of AIME over $180 and through $1,085, plus 15 percent of AIME over $1,085. The AIME dollar amounts in this formula change each year as part of a mechanism to stabilize replacement rates over time (see Chapter 8).

One of the best ways of evaluating the resulting level of pension benefits is to look at pension replacement rates. You will remember from Chapter 4 that a *pension replacement rate* specifies the proportion of a worker's prior earnings that is replaced by the pension he receives.

The Social Security Administration's Retirement History Study (Social Security Administration, 1976) provides us with comprehensive information on the amount of earnings replaced (in the recent past) by public and private pensions. Using these data, a Social Security Administration study (Fox, 1979) reports on the pension replacement rates achieved by social

Table 20. Social Security Replacement Rates for Husbands, Couples, and Nonmarried Men, 1973–74[a]

| Social Security Replacement Rate | Husband's Benefit Only | Couple's Benefit Wife Retired Worker | Couple's Benefit Wife Dependent | Nonmarried Men |
|---|---|---|---|---|
| 0.1–19.9 Percent | 11 | 2 | 0 | 6 |
| 20–39.9 | 66 | 38 | 32 | 59 |
| 40–59.9 | 21 | 47 | 47 | 29 |
| 60–79.9 | 1 | 9 | 18 | 2 |
| 80 and Above | 0 | 4 | 3 | 3 |
| Total Percent | 100 | 100 | 100 | 100 |
| Median | 32 | 43 | 49 | 39 |

Source: Alan Fox, "Earnings Replacement Rates of Retired Couples: Findings from the Retirement History Study," *Social Security Bulletin* 42 (January 1979): 17–39.
[a]Restricted to workers first receiving benefits between 1973 and 1974. Preretirement earnings are estimated total earnings in the three highest years of the ten before initial benefit.

security recipients who were married and began receiving benefits during the 1968 to 1974 period. Table 20 presents the replacement rates for 1973–74 "retirees": husbands alone, couples combined, and nonmarried men. The **median** social security pension replacement rates varied between 32 and 49 percent.

*Minimum Benefits* Since its inception, the old age pension program has had a minimum benefit. In the original legislation the guarantee was $10 per month. Over the years the minimum benefit has been periodically increased, and equaled $1,464 in 1979.

Pechman, Aaron, and Taussig (1968) have succinctly summarized the major problem that arises when a minimum is provided:

> *If minimum and low benefits were paid exclusively to aged householders with little or no other money income, the case for sharply increasing the minimum would be overwhelming. In the absence of an income test, however, many beneficiaries receive minimum or low benefits because they have had limited attachment to occupations covered by social security, not because they have had low lifetime earnings. Former employees of federal, state, and local governments can enter covered employment late in life and acquire insured status sufficient to entitle them to low or minimum benefits. . . .*

In response to such criticism, Congress created a special minimum for long-term workers in 1972 and froze in 1977 the regular minimum for future beneficiaries.

The minimum is frozen at an amount equal to the minimum benefit in effect December 1978 ($1,464). Benefits based on the minimum will be kept up to date with increases in the Consumer Price Index beginning with the year the person receives a benefit or reaches age 65.

Under the provisions of the special minimum, persons with 20 or more years in covered employment have a guaranteed level equal (in 1979) to $11.50 per month times the years of coverage in excess of 10 years (but not exceeding $230 per month). In succeeding years the special minimum will be adjusted automatically for increases in the cost of living.

*Dependent Benefits* In 1939 the social security program was amended to provide dependent benefits for wives over age 64 and for children under age 18. Successive legislation liberalized these provisions and extended benefits to children age 18–21, disabled children age 18 and over, divorced wives, and "dependent" husbands meeting various eligibility conditions. In 1977 the Supreme Court further liberalized benefits by ruling unconstitutional the social security provision that men (unlike women) must prove they were financially dependent on their wives in order to get dependent benefits.

As indicated above, an eligible dependent can receive a benefit based on the related worker's earnings and work history. If a spouse also works and becomes qualified for benefits based on his or her own work experience, he or she receives either the dependent benefit based on the spouse's pension or a pension based on his or her own work history, *whichever is greater.* Thus, a wife may pay social security taxes without adding to the family's retirement income.* The problem is further aggravated by the fact that the husband and wife are treated as separate taxable units and consequently may collectively pay more taxes than a family with only a single worker earning the same amount. This occurs as a result of the taxable earnings ceiling that limits the taxed earnings of the single-earner family to the ceiling but taxes each earner of the dual-earner family up to the maximum.

As with the weighted benefit formula, the justification for the spouse benefit is made on social adequacy grounds: on a given earnings history, two people are less able (than one person) to provide *for* retirement and need more income *in* retirement. Pechman, Aaron, and Taussig (1968) argue, however, that the greater amount a couple receives (currently 50 percent more than the single worker) is too large: "The benefits of single workers should be raised substantially, relative to those of married couples. A smaller increment than 50 percent is justified because, at any given earnings level, single persons now receive smaller benefits relative to their previous standard of living than do married couples."

Other arguments against the spouse benefit are (a) that a majority (but not all) of women in the future will be covered by social security on the basis of their own earnings, (b) that since few husband–wife families are poor, the spouse benefit is an extremely inefficient way to channel money to low income families, and (c) that as a result of rising earnings by women, most families are now characterized by the mutual economic dependence of husbands and wives (Munnell, 1977).

The treatment of women under social security provisions is currently receiving considerable attention (see page 112). In the area of spouse benefits three approaches are most frequently proposed as changes:

1. Eliminating the spouse benefit and splitting the earnings of the husband and wife for purposes of calculating benefits (see Consultant Panel on Social Security, 1976, and U.S. Department of Health, Education, and Welfare, 1979).
2. Increasing the worker's benefit rate, at the same time reducing the spouse rate (see Ball, 1978b, p. 322).
3. Extending coverage and benefits directly to nonsalaried household workers, as is currently done in West Germany (for example, see Task Force on Women and Social Security, 1975, p. 35).

*If a husband and wife both work, the working wife has several advantages not available to the nonworking wife. She can retire and draw benefits at 62 or over even if her husband works on. Survivors' benefits—lump-sum, children's benefits, and parents' benefits—may be paid on her earnings record. Also, before age 65 she may draw disability benefits on her own record.

*Early Retirement*    Up until 1956 workers could not receive their old age pension until they reached the age of 65. The selection of age 65 for the receipt of benefits was a somewhat arbitrary decision of those who drafted the legislation. In large part the decision was simply to copy the age provisions of existing public and private pension programs, almost all of which used age 65.

In 1956 the social security law was changed to permit *women* workers to receive reduced benefits between the ages of 62 and 64; and in 1961 this option was extended to men. In both cases the reduction was to be the full actuarial amount. That is, persons receiving benefits before age 65 were to receive over their remaining lifetime amounts that—based on average life expectancy—would not exceed (on average) the total amounts received by those retiring at age 65.

From the very beginning, the early retirement option was exceedingly popular and has been exercised by large numbers of workers. The Social Security Administration reports that over half the men awarded initial retirement benefits each year since 1962 have received reduced benefits. Figure 19 shows the consequent rise in the proportion of social security ben-

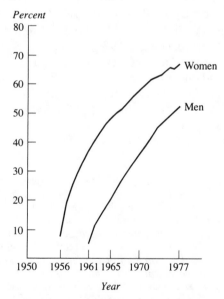

*Figure 19.    Percent of All OASDI*
*Beneficiaries with Reduced Benefits for Early Retirement*

Source: Lenore E. Bixby, "Retirement Patterns in the United States: Research and Policy Interactions," *Social Security Bulletin* 39 (August 1976): 3–19, and *Social Security Bulletin* 41 (June 1978): Table Q4.

eficiaries receiving reduced benefits. Almost 70 percent of women and over 50 percent of men do *not* receive full benefits.

*Delayed Retirement*   In 1939 the calculation of the social security pension was changed to include a percent benefit increment for each year that credited earnings were at least $200. "This provision thus gave an individual who postponed his retirement after 65 a larger benefit when he retired than if he began to draw his benefits at 65. This provision was the subject of much controversy and was repealed in the 1950 law so that higher current benefits could be paid without a cost increase" (Cohen, 1957).

In 1972 a provision was added to social security that raised benefits for those who delayed retirement beyond age 65. Subsequent to the provision canceled in 1950, persons who continued to work beyond age 64 lost their total *potential* pension benefits available each year thereafter that they worked. The new provision reduces the loss somewhat but does not totally eliminate it. For there to be no loss in the actuarial value of a worker's benefit would require that his benefit level be increased by about 9 percent a year, instead of the 3 percent adjustment in the current law.*

*The Retirement Test*   The retirement test reduces or eliminates social security benefit payments if an otherwise eligible recipient has earnings above an exemption ceiling; in 1973 about 1.4 million retired workers age 62 to 71 were affected (Lingg, 1977). Over the years officials of the Social Security Administration have acknowledged that this test generates the most questions and the most criticisms among people covered by the social security program. Further evidence of the controversy is that in every session of Congress since 1940, numerous bills have been introduced to eliminate or liberalize the test.

A recent Advisory Council on Social Security (1975) gives the following rationale for the test:

> The Council has reviewed the provisions of the retirement test and believes that the test is consistent with the basic purpose and principles of social security: to replace, in part, earnings lost because of retirement in old age, disability, or death. Complete elimination of the retirement test is inadvisable.
> The retirement test has been criticized because it does not take into account a beneficiary's income from such nonwork sources as dividends, rent, or pension payments. If the test took account of income other than earnings from work, it would no longer be a retirement test but an income test. If it became an income test, the fundamental idea that social security benefits are intended as partial replacement of earnings from work would be diluted or lost.

While the reasoning advanced by the Advisory Council has also been the official position of the Social Security Administration, it is impor-

---

*The credit was set at 1 percent in the 1972 law but was raised to 3 percent in 1977.

tant to recognize two other arguments that are frequently made in support of the test.*

First, since there are still many workers age 62 or older who do not receive social security benefits and since most of them are working full time, repeal of the retirement test would be relatively expensive and benefit most those who need help the least.

Second, given the fact that relatively high rates of unemployment have been a frequent phenomenon in the American economy, the retirement test encourages older workers to retire and thereby opens up job opportunities for younger workers. Moreover, older workers with pensions are discouraged from competing for jobs with younger workers by offering their services at wages below prevailing levels.

The work-disincentive result of the retirement test arises principally from the fact that, in effect, earnings above the maximum are "taxed" at the relatively high rate of 50 percent. Studies have shown that some older workers have a strong aversion to loss of benefits at this tax rate (Campbell and Campbell, 1976). The effect of the test, therefore, is to discourage some workers from staying in the labor force and also to set a limit on part-time work activity so that earnings do not go beyond the maximum.

Whereas complete elimination of the retirement test would be costly and benefit many high earners, it can be argued alternatively that the test should be liberalized significantly to encourage and allow those people with low or moderate pension incomes to work in retirement. Various proposals have been advanced that would effectively exclude people with high earnings from the receipt of benefits but would not penalize low earners who wanted or needed to supplement their pension income. Complete *elimination* of the test is estimated by the Social Security Actuary to cost $6 or $7 billion, but substantial *liberalization,* while maintaining some earnings ceiling, could cost less than a billion (Schulz, 1978).

The second argument—that older workers should retire to make room for younger workers—raises a number of very complex issues. Ideally, an appropriate mix of monetary and fiscal policy by the government could promote an expansionary economy with jobs for almost everyone—thereby avoiding the dilemma of the older versus younger worker trade-off. The problem that arises, however, is that as the economy approaches full employment, inflationary factors tend to push up the general level of prices. Economic policymakers are thus faced with the unpleasant trade-off of less employment to prevent more **inflation.** In addition to having to choose between inflation and unemployment (sometimes referred to as the problem of "fine tuning" the economy) there is the problem of the **recessions** and **depres-**

---

*For a more detailed listing and discussion of arguments for and against the test, see Schulz (1977) or Colberg (1978).

**sions** that have occurred throughout the century. The result of these has been millions of unemployed workers.

The causes of downturns in the economy are varied. While it is generally agreed that increased economic sophistication now provides nations with the necessary tools to prevent or moderate economic instability, the application of this knowledge has been far from perfect. Given, then, the recurring instability and joblessness that have characterized the American economy, it is not surprising to find workers and unions supporting policies that promise to moderate the situation. The retirement test appears to be one policy that falls into this category.

In contrast, the recent aging of the population is a factor that may undermine future worker support for the retirement test. As the costs to the working population of providing pensions to a growing segment of the total population significantly increase, there is apt to be better recognition that there is a relatively high price tag associated with our present policies, which encourage or force people to retire. As indicated above, significantly liberalizing the test would probably encourage work without incurring the high costs of completely eliminating the test.

Responding to intense political pressure to abolish the test, Congress significantly liberalized the test as a part of the social security amendments of 1977. As shown in Table 21, the new law provides for annual increases in the exempt amount *for beneficiaries age 65 or over*—reaching an annual level of $6,000 by 1982. Adjustments equal to the average increase in workers' earnings (i.e., by a **wage index**) will occur automatically in succeeding years. Also, effective in 1982, the age at which the retirement test no longer applies is lowered from 72 to 70.

No change in the law was made for workers under age 65. Under the provisions of social security amendments passed in 1972, the exempt amount for those under 65 will continue to be periodically adjusted by a wage index.

*Table 21.*   Retirement Test Earnings Exemption Amounts

| Year | Under Age 65[a] | Age 65 or Older |
|------|------|------|
| 1977 | $3,000 | $3,000 |
| 1978 | 3,240 | 4,000 |
| 1979 | 3,480 | 4,500 |
| 1980 | 3,720 | 5,000 |
| 1981 | 3,960 | 5,500 |
| 1982 | 4,320[b] | 6,000 |

Source: John Snee and Mary Ross, "Social Security Amendments of 1977: Legislative History and Summary of Provisions," *Social Security Bulletin* 41 (March 1978): 14.
[a]Amounts for the years after 1978 are estimated under the automatic adjustment provisions.
[b]Corrected amount different from amount published in cited source.

Finally, the 1977 amendments eliminated the monthly exemption test except for the first year of retirement. Under this monthly measure, a beneficiary who did not earn over the specified monthly exemption, or render substantial services in self-employment in a month, received a benefit for that month *regardless of the level of his annual earnings.* Now only an annual test applies.

*Survivors' Benefits*    We are apt to forget that social security provides more than worker retirement pensions. Currently about 40 percent of the social security pensions being paid are to survivors and to disabled workers and their dependents—totaling about 12.5 million pensions in 1977.

When a worker protected by social security dies, a modest $255 lump sum payment is made to the widow, widower, or (if neither) a person responsible for burial expenses. Qualifying widows, surviving divorced wives, children, and dependent parents are also paid monthly pensions. Conditions for receipt of a survivor's benefit vary considerably depending on the relation of the relative to the deceased.

Probably the two most important categories are widows and children. A widow who was married to a fully insured worker for at least nine months and who has reached age 60 is entitled to a benefit of 100 percent of the worker's pension if payments begin at age 65 and a reduced benefit at an earlier age (71.5 percent at age 60). Benefits are subject to reduction if any earnings exceed the retirement test. Widows with eligible children, unmarried dependent children under age 18, disabled, and full-time students under 22 are entitled to a pension equal to 75 percent of the deceased's pension. Supreme Court decisions in 1975 and 1977 struck down provisions of the Social Security Act that prohibited widowers from receiving survivor benefits based on their wives' earnings.

The monetary value of survivors' benefits is often very large. Ball (1978b) reports, for example, that a male worker with median earnings in 1977 who dies at age 35—leaving a wife age 32 and two children age 3 and 5—"would have left his family the social security equivalent of an estate worth $129,265." And a study by Lucy Mallan (1975) found that if social security were omitted from the total 1971 income of widows under age 60 with children, the proportion with poverty incomes would double, rising from one-third to almost 60 percent.

## Social Security Pension Reform

Over the years there has been continuous complaining about the inadequacy of social security, given the economic situation of the elderly. In the early years the Congress did not respond to these complaints and to the generally acknowledged inadequate income situation of most elderly. Some people point to the legislated benefit increases occurring over the early years; but the fact is that except for the very early and the most recent years, these periodic increases did little more than keep benefit levels in line with the changing price level—which was also rising over time.

In recent years mounting criticism of the old age pension program has centered on three major issues: the adequacy of benefits (always a major complaint), alleged inequities existing among various recipient groups (a more recent development), and recent and projected increases in the payroll taxes financing social security (the focus of most current discussions). These mounting criticisms have stimulated a renewed interest in both reform of social security and alternatives to it. In this section we examine the views of a number of groups and individuals who have studied the social security program and proposed various reforms.

*The Social Security Advisory Councils* The 1937–38 Advisory Council, authorized by the Senate Committee on Finance, was the first group of eminent persons asked to review the social security laws. Under current law, a new council is to be appointed every four years. Its function is to review all aspects of the social security program and to recommend improvements.

Over the years the various advisory councils have not called for any fundamental changes in the system. In general, they have concentrated on ways of *improving* the program through incremental changes. This does not mean that the advisory councils have not made important suggestions. The 1938–39 council recommended survivors' benefits, for example; the one in 1948–49 recommended expanded coverage; and the council that met in 1970–71 recommended raising the widow's benefit to 100 percent of the worker's benefit (as opposed to the 82.5 percent under the then current law). Such recommendations result in important improvements in the social security program but do not satisfy many critics of the system, who charge that it is fundamentally inadequate and inequitable.

The large benefit increase passed by Congress in 1972, which greatly exceeded rising cost-of-living needs, and legislation to adjust benefits automatically for inflation were major efforts to alleviate the inadequacy and erosion of social security benefits. It is interesting that the legislation was not stimulated by (or the result of) any recommendations of the Social Security Advisory Council or, for that matter, by recommendations of the various governmental task forces that had been appointed in earlier years to review the problems of the elderly. Instead, early in his first term (1969) President Nixon sent a message to Congress proposing changes in social security. The key recommendations were, first, a 10 percent increase in benefits; second, and more important, a proposal that the Consumer Price Index be used to adjust future benefits automatically and that a wage index be used to adjust the contribution and benefit base.

At the same time that the President proposed changes in social security, he proposed a welfare reform bill—the Family Assistance Act. The House Ways and Means Committee and the Senate Finance Committee held hearings that simultaneously considered both the social security and welfare reforms. The major focus of these hearings, however, was on welfare reform and not on social security. Therefore, most of the testimony did not even mention the social security proposals.

At about the same time a new Social Security Advisory Council met and reported. This council had been appointed in the early part of the first Nixon administration, which had taken the position that aside from the changes recommended in its social security message, it would make no other legislative suggestions until the advisory council made its report. It argued that it would be premature for the administration to propose legislation while this very illustrious group, which was given the job of surveying the whole situation, was still deliberating.

This position, of course, set up expectations that something significant would come out of the council's report. Nothing did. The council looked at a number of incremental changes, mostly equity changes, and rejected most of the proposals people had made. Instead, the 20 percent increase was first proposed by Senator Frank Church on the floor of the Senate and then supported by the then powerful chairman of the House Ways and Means Committee, Wilbur Mills (at the time a presidential hopeful).

The council's only important recommendations were in the area of financing. The report argued strongly in favor of moving toward a pay-as-you-go system (changing from a "three-year reserve" to a "one-year reserve") and strongly recommended that the actuarial assumptions for projecting benefit outlays and contributions into the system be nonstatic—that is, assume that earnings levels will rise over time, that the contribution and benefit base will increase as earnings rise, and that benefits will be increased as prices rise. Both recommendations facilitated the benefit increases that occurred, but the council itself never recommended the increases.

An advisory council was appointed in 1974 and issued its report in 1975. The main focus of that report was again financing issues (discussed in Chapter 8). Another advisory council was appointed in 1978 and reports at the end of 1979.

*Separating "Public Assistance" from Social Security*    Let us now look at some recommendations that have been made by a group of economists at The Brookings Institution. Pechman, Aaron, and Taussig argue in their book *Social Security—Perspectives for Reform* that the aged should be eligible for either an earnings-related pension or a negative income tax payment—whichever is the greater. They argue further that the earnings-related pension should have a replacement rate that is roughly the same at all earnings levels between subsistence and the level of median earnings. They also recommend that there be no spouse benefits but that pensions be based on total family earnings instead.

Their major point is that the social security system *should not operate both as a welfare system and a pension system*. If a person receives income in old age (including a social security pension) that places him in a taxable bracket, they feel that such a person should pay taxes (regardless of age). On the other hand, if the elderly person's income is too low, they argue, he should be eligible for a negative tax program:

> *The advantage of the dual system is its efficiency and flexibility. Either part of the system could be altered independently of the other. At present any effort to improve social security with respect to the income support function typically requires substantial improvements with respect to the earnings replacement function. For example, a program to raise minimum benefits to help the aged poor must in practice be joined with a general benefit increase, thereby making the cost of aiding the poor seem greater than it is. This is aggravated, of course, by the fact that the present system supplements income regardless of the income status of the beneficiaries. In many instances higher minimum benefits would be paid to individuals with adequate income. Under the proposed system the earnings related benefit could be set at any desired percentage of past earnings. Negative income tax allowances to those with low earnings histories would be sufficient to keep income above poverty level. Thus, policy makers and the public could identify immediately the cost of performing the two distinct functions of the system. [Pechman, Aaron, and Taussig, 1968]*

The advantage Pechman, Aaron, and Taussig (and various other economists) see in separating the two issues is considered a drawback by others (see, for example, Brown, 1972, Chapter 4). Some writers in the field of income maintenance policy argue that when you separate the two groups (and hence make it very clear whom you're helping), it is very difficult to get sufficient political support for improving the situation of the poor. They argue that the only way one can get help for the poor is to piggyback it onto help for middle (and even upper) income groups. For example, one authority on social security, Wilbur Cohen, has argued that "in the United States, a program that deals only with the poor will end up being a poor program. There is every evidence that this is true. Ever since the Elizabethan Poor Law of 1601, programs only for the poor have been lousy, no good, *poor* programs. And a program that is only for the poor—one that has nothing in it for the middle income and the upper income—is, in the long run, a program the American public won't support. This is why I think we must try to find a way to link the interests of all classes in these programs" (Cohen and Friedman, 1972).

Another Brookings book by Alicia Munnell (1977) has updated the discussion of this issue and was the basis for a two-day social security conference in 1976. The conference gave major attention to whether the social adequacy function of social security should be reduced or transferred to the new supplemental security income (SSI) program (described at the end of this chapter). In addition to repeating the opposing arguments summarized above, there was general agreement that several serious problems had to be dealt with before SSI could assume a larger role.

Most conference participants felt that the SSI asset test was unreasonably stringent and needed a complete overhaul. Some participants pointed out that it would be difficult to reduce the current dollar-for-dollar SSI reduction for social security benefits (after a $20 **disregard**) to, say, 50 cents for each dollar so that low-wage workers would be insulated from a decline in retirement income as a result of a (more) proportional OASI formula. Supplementary state SSI programs in many, but not all, states would make it difficult to ensure uniformity of welfare programs in the face of large-scale changes in the relationship between OASI and SSI. And simply changing the federal SSI tax rate (i.e., the income offset rules) would not in itself be sufficient; state tax rates would also have to be changed. But that raises issues of state autonomy and whether states would be willing to bear the increased costs of the new program. Finally, a shift to an expanded SSI program would mean that more people would be subject to the much more stringent SSI earnings test. Munnell reports the conference viewpoint that "any attempt to encourage labor force participation of the elderly must take into account that with an expanded SSI program over 50 percent of the aged would be subject to the more stringent SSI test."

The Brookings conference discussion reminds us of an important fact. The implementation of any policy objective (in this case, a proposed reduction in the social adequacy function of social security) is often very difficult, especially given existing programs and the complex distribution of political authority. Alvin Schorr observes: "A political difficulty of many welfare reform proposals is that they are presented as if they were in a closed system. They ignore both other income-tested programs (notably Medicaid) and social security, or assume that these programs will adjust rationally. In particular, they raise daunting problems of reducing the benefits of large numbers of people at the moment of introduction."

*Changing the Pension Adequacy Standard*    In recent years there has been less talk about eliminating poverty among the elderly and more attention given to providing them with "adequate income." Many people have begun to argue that benefits should be related to some kind of retirement budget based on observed needs and lifestyles of the elderly. The 1971

White House Conference on Aging, for example, recommended that adequate income be defined by the Bureau of Labor Statistics' budget for an elderly couple (see p. 40).

The Bureau of Labor Statistics' budgets are for retired couples who are "self-supporting, living independently in their own home, in reasonably good health, and able to take care of themselves." The generalized conception of the living standard is translated into a list of commodities and services that can be priced. The "intermediate level" budget is currently around $8,000 per year for an elderly couple.

The establishment of such a budget standard (or even a variety of budgets) for various groups or categories of the aged can never (and is not intended to) adequately reflect the even greater variety of economic circumstances of these aged families prior to retirement. The budgets do "not show how an 'average' retired couple actually spends its money, nor do they show how a couple should spend its money. . . . In general, however, the representative list of goods and services comprising the standard reflects the collective judgment of families as to what is necessary and desirable . . ." (U.S. Bureau of Labor Statistics, 1966). Thus, the Nixon Administration responded to the adequacy-of-income recommendations of the 1971 White House Conference delegates as follows: "The Administration does not concur in the recommendations of the delegates to the Conference that the 'intermediate' budget developed by the Bureau of Labor Statistics become the national goal in this area. . . . While these [budget] studies are interesting and useful in their own right, they provide no basis for knowing whether any particular level of income is 'adequate' under varying sets of circumstances."

Also, while it is easy to adjust these budgets for price changes, it is much more difficult to adjust them to reflect the changing levels of living in the economy; such adjustments are largely arbitrary.

Besides poverty indexes or budget levels, there is another way to define the operational income maintenance goals of various pension programs. This is to specify the proportion of prior earnings to be guaranteed to the worker upon retirement through a pension program. In recent years the pension systems of many countries have sought to express pension benefits as a proportion of earnings.

But in the United States, aside from general recommendations calling for help to the aged by improving social security (often in the form of requesting 5, 10, 20, or 50 percent benefit increases), there has been very little discussion of just what the level of old age benefits should be.

Over the years the principal architect of United States social security reform has been the House Committee on Ways and Means. In 1967 that committee issued a report discussing the earnings replacement objective governing the benefit levels specified in the social security amendments of 1967. The report said, in part:

*The bill embodies the principle that the retirement benefit of a man age 65 and his wife should represent at least 50 percent of his average wages under the social security system. . . . In establishing the benefit levels, it was necessary for your committee to consider not only benefit levels but also earnings levels and other factors. It was the committee's judgment that when all factors were taken in conjunction, the benefit for a couple which is based on the maximum credited earnings ought to be approximately 50 percent of the average earnings of the worker, with an appropriate increase in the percentage as the earnings fell below the maximum, until benefits reached what in the light of existing conditions seemed to be an appropriate minimum benefit. [U.S. House Committee on Ways and Means, 1967b]*

A pension formula that seeks to replace 50 percent of *lifetime* average earnings, however, usually replaces a much lower percentage of earnings *just prior to retirement*. The actual social security pension replacement rates for American couples retiring, for example, between 1960 and 1980 (estimated by a simulation model) tend to be much lower than the committee's goal. If pensions are compared with the average of earnings five years prior to retirement, one finds that a majority of the couples will receive at least 50 percent replacement only in the earnings groups below $4,000. In general, couples will receive much lower than 50 percent replacement (Schulz et al., 1974).

In *Providing Adequate Income in Retirement* Schulz et al. argue that a pension program that replaces such a low proportion of prior earnings is not an adequate floor of protection and that the House Ways and Means Committee's 50 percent standard is inadequate *as long as it is based upon unadjusted lifetime earnings*. Pensions based on a lifetime earnings average, by the very nature of the averaging process, are reflective of a living standard experienced decades before retirement. One would expect families to have become accustomed to the higher living standard typical of the later years before retirement and would not expect the act of retirement to change dramatically their living expectations.

Another major defect of the lifetime earnings measure is that it does not take inflation into account. Over the lifetime of any individual it is certain that some significant amount of inflation will occur. Failure to adjust past earnings for subsequent inflation gives a distorted and unmeaningful measure.

Thus, it is certainly not unreasonable to base individual and collective retirement pension plans on a goal of preventing any major decline in lifestyle as a result of retirement. In fact, the "golden years" of retirement are often glamorized as those years when an individual is finally free of work constraints and able to enjoy life more.

In their book, Schulz et al. (1974) report on innovative pension reform that has taken place in four countries. In three of these countries— Germany, Sweden, and Belgium—the objective of maintaining living standards during retirement was an important consideration in designing the current pension program. In the United States the social security amendments of 1977 have changed the measure of "average earnings" for purposes of benefit calculation. The earnings credited over a participant's working life will now be indexed to allow for historical changes in wage levels resulting from inflation and higher levels of productivity.

In adopting this **indexing** procedure Congress rejected several alternative indexing proposals that emphasized the maintenance of real *absolute* levels of income. They chose instead an indexing mechanism related to a *relative* standard of adequacy. This relative adequacy standard represents a substantial movement away from a view of social security as a minimal floor or protection.

*Women and Social Security*     There is widespread agreement that social security provisions related to women need to be reformed. As observed by Flowers (1977), "The social security benefit structure reflects a pattern of marital life and family obligations which is no longer typical in the United States." Benefits (and payments) are designed to provide family protection under an assumption that there are just two major family types: single workers and married couples consisting of lifelong paid workers and lifelong unpaid homemakers.

A number of important social trends have made that assumption increasingly unrealistic. First, female participation in the paid labor force has changed dramatically. Over half of the married women under age 60 are now in the labor force (Hayghe, 1978), and labor force participation for women age 25 to 54 is projected to rise even further—to about 70 percent in 1990. Moreover, increasing numbers of married women spend part of their lives solely as homemakers and another part in the paid labor force.

Second, there is a changing perception of roles within families. A recent report (HEW Task Force on the Treatment of Women Under Social Security, 1978) describes these changes as follows:

> As more married women work and have broader employment opportunities, the homemaker role is more frequently viewed as a career choice in itself; the decision to have a spouse at home full-time is viewed as a conscious decision rather than a foregone conclusion. The idea that the homemaker role has economic value—though difficult to measure—is gaining acceptance.... Both the rising labor-force participation of married women and the changing perceptions of the homemaker role tend to lead toward a view of marriage as an interdependent relationship between spouses.

Third, there is a rapidly rising number of women who are divorced, separated, or widowed. Table 22 indicates that the United States has one of the highest divorce rates in the world. And there are currently about five widowed women for every widowed man in the United States (Lopata,

*Table 22.*   Divorce Rates per 1,000 Population for Selected Countries, 1957–1975

| Country | 1957 | 1967 | 1975 |
|---|---|---|---|
| United States | 2.23 | 2.63 | 4.82 |
| Sweden | 1.20 | 1.36 | 3.14 |
| U.S.S.R. | — | 2.74 | 3.08 |
| German Democratic Republic | 1.33 | 1.66 | 2.47 |
| Czechoslovakia | 1.07 | 1.39 | 2.18 |
| Finland | 0.81 | 1.13 | 1.99 |
| Canada | 0.40 | 0.55 | 2.22 |
| Federal Republic of Germany | 0.77 | 1.05 | 1.73 |
| Netherlands | 0.48 | 0.59 | 1.47 |
| Australia | 0.65 | 0.82 | 1.76 |
| Japan | 0.79 | 0.84 | 1.08 |

Source: Extracted from United Nations, *Demographic Yearbook* (New York: United Nations, 1976 and 1977).

1977). Reporting on the economic consequences of families breaking up, the University of Michigan Survey Research Center's five-year study of American families found that "the economic status of former husbands improves while that of the former wives deteriorates" (Morgan et al., 1974). And almost half of women becoming widows find their income falling below the poverty line (Lopata, 1977).

In reaction to the many new issues that emerged, increasing attention has been given to changing the way social security programs treat women. A number of countries in Europe have already instituted major reforms, and many other countries have legislative proposals actively under consideration (Weise, 1976). In the United States, discussion has centered on three issues: the equity and adequacy of spouse and survivor benefits (see pp. 100 and 105, fairness of coverage for one-earner versus two-earner couples (see p. 162), and coverage of homemakers and divorced persons.

The first two issues are discussed in other parts of the book. With regard to homemakers, persons who stay out of the paid labor force to raise children or maintain a household currently accumulate no earnings credits for that period of their lives. If they later take a job outside the household, they find their average lifetime earnings depressed and hence receive lower social security benefits. Furthermore, those homemakers who do not work outside the home must depend entirely on the earnings records of their spouses for any social security benefits. Consequently, a divorce, disablement, or death *of a spouse* (especially in the early years) could result in the homemaker receiving very meager benefits or no benefits at all. Alternatively, the death or disability *of the homemaker* deprives the household of valuable services, but lack of homemaker coverage precludes any social security compensation.

Several proposals before Congress would provide social security credits for people performing homemaker services, providing social security protection independent of marital status. A number of problems arise in connection with these proposals, however. How would the provision be financed—by general revenue, by a special earmarked tax, or by the covered person? How would the value of household services be determined for both tax and benefit purposes? Who should be eligible? And how would proper reporting of homemaker services be assured?

An alternative approach would divide social security earnings credits of married couples equally between spouses. Retirement credits could be split and credit given on three alternative occasions: (a) as the credits are earned, (b) only in case of a marriage dissolution, or (c) at the time of retirement. As pointed out by Weise (1976), the use of "credit splitting could have disadvantages and present certain administrative problems, especially if there have been several marriages or common-law partners." And the HEW Task Force (1978) concludes that such proposals raise "issues of fairness and adequacy of protection when only one spouse is retired, becomes disabled, or dies."

Changes in the social security laws in this area can be expected. For example, the 1977 amendments reduced the duration-of-marriage requirement for "retiring" or surviving divorced wives from 20 years to 10 years, thereby expanding eligibility and increasing the social adequacy of benefits for such women. In addition, it called for a government study and report on proposals (a) to eliminate dependency as a factor in social security entitlement and (b) to bring about equal treatment of men and women under the program.

### Other Social Security Programs

In previous chapters we have referred to a number of programs other than retirement pensions that have an important impact on the economic welfare of the aged. It is appropriate at this point to discuss some of them, since they are all important complements to pension programs.*

*Disability* About 16 million noninstitutionalized Americans between the ages of 20 and 64 have limited ability to work because of chronic health conditions and impairments. And more than three times that number suffer from one or more chronic health conditions. Approximately half the disabled (8 million) are unable either to work altogether or to work regularly (Krute and Burdette, 1978).

*Not discussed are the food stamp program and veterans' benefits.

In general, whatever the degree of impairment, the chance of disability increases with age, as shown in Figure 20. The figure also shows how the prevalence of *total* disability rises sharply. Among persons age 20 to 34, total disability occurs at a rate of 22 per 1,000 population. The rate approximately doubles for each succeeding 10-year age group—reaching 190 per 1,000 for those 55 to 64.

There are currently more than 85 public and private programs dealing with disability (Berkowitz, Johnson, and Murphy, 1976). Disability protection under social security is currently provided to: (a) disabled insured workers and their dependents , (b) disabled widows and widowers of insured workers, and (c) the adult (18 or older) sons and daughters of insured disabled, retired, or deceased workers who become disabled before age 22. Disability protection was not legislated until 1956. Although it had been proposed repeatedly, major groups opposed it, and early social security advisory groups disagreed about the predictability of disability program costs and about whether one could administratively determine eligibility for this type of benefit (i.e., distinguish legitimate disability from malingering).

When the first major legislative proposals for disability protection were debated in 1949 and 1950, strong criticism and opposition were voiced by the American Medical Association, the United States Chamber of Com-

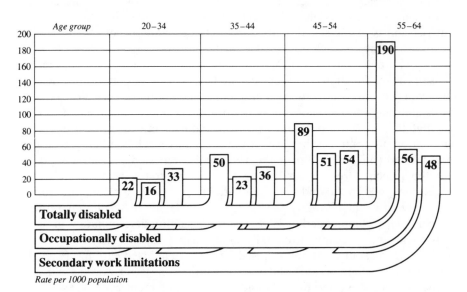

*Figure 20.   Disability by Age, 1972*

Source: *Work Disability in the United States—A Chartbook* (Washington, D.C.: U.S. Government Printing Office, 1977).

merce, the National Manufacturers Association, and representatives of private insurance organizations. After the defeat of the 1949–50 bill, strong opposition continued in succeeding years to the various new proposals that were introduced—including the disability freeze amendment of 1954* and the social security disability benefits finally legislated in 1956. All the disability proposals were attacked as potentially costly, difficult to administer, and the beginning of "socialized medicine." Given this strong opposition over the years, the ultimate passage of disability legislation in 1956 is viewed by many as a major development in the legislative history of social security in the United States.

To be eligible for social security disability payments a worker must be screened on three levels: (a) determination of insured status, (b) assessment of physical condition and level of functional impairment, and (c) determination of ability to work. To achieve insured status, the worker must have 1 quarter of work coverage credit for each year since 1950 (or since age 21, if later) and 20 quarters of coverage during the 40-quarter period prior to disability. Disability, for purposes of benefit entitlement, is defined as "inability to engage in any substantial gainful activity by reason of any medically determinable physical or mental impairment which can be expected to result in death or which has lasted or can be expected to last for a continuous period of not less than 12 months." This strict disability definition excludes many people with relatively severe incapacities. Surveys find that two-thirds of the self-described severely disabled do not receive social security disability payments (Van De Water, 1979).

The determination of an applicant's disability is by a state agency whose primary function is to develop medical, vocational, and other necessary evidence and then evaluate it and make a decision. The principal reason for establishing the federal–state relationship was that it was deemed essential that the disability program be linked with an effective vocational rehabilitation program. But because of the extremely small number of workers rehabilitated (only 20,000 over the 1967 to 1976 period), some now argue that the principal reason for having the federal–state arrangement is no longer completely valid and that the relationship should be modified. After a recent review of the disability program, the U.S. General Accounting Office, for example, recommended in 1978 that the disability determination process be brought under complete federal management (Ahart, 1978).

The disability pension is based on average indexed earnings (excluding the disablement period) and is calculated in the same way as old age pensions, using the same formula and the same minimum benefit level. Ini-

---

*A provision that prevented periods of disability from reducing or wiping out retirement and survivors' benefits by "freezing" the individual's rights at the time of disablement. For a good discussion of the legislative history of this and other disability provisions, see Cohen (1957, Chapter 4).

tially the social security disability benefit was reduced dollar-for-dollar by any workmen's compensation benefits received by the same worker. Then in 1958 this deduction was removed, and considerable controversy followed. Turnbull, Williams, and Cheit (1967) report that with the deduction removed, "it became possible in some states for a seriously injured worker to receive combined benefits that would exceed his wages prior to his disability." Faced with the criticisms of those who feared the encroachment and possible supplantation of federal disability insurance for state and private programs, Congress reintroduced an offset provision in 1965. Under the new provision, social security disability and workmen's compensation payments together could not exceed 80 percent of a high-five-year average of earnings in covered employment (adjusted periodically for rises in wage levels). Then in 1972 the definition of average earnings was changed to permit benefits to be based (if a higher benefit resulted) on average monthly earnings in the calendar year of *highest* earnings during the five years preceding the year in which disability began.

Thus, as the disability benefit has evolved, the disabled worker is guaranteed the social security minimum pension and up to 80 percent earnings replacement (in cases of dual eligibility for social security and workmen's compensation). In 1978 the average family benefit was about $4,400, and the average replacement rate of "recent gross earnings" was about 50 percent (Van De Water, 1979).

In fact, there are not two but three major public disability programs: the federal social security disability program; the federal Supplemental Security Income program, which provides benefits to low income disabled, aged, and blind persons; and the workmen's compensation programs (administered by state governments), which provide insurance against industrial accident and occupational disease. In addition, about two-thirds of private wage and salary workers have some kind of protection against loss of earnings caused by *short-term, nonoccupational* disability. Most of this protection comes from private group disability insurance or formal paid sick-leave plans. Five states (and Puerto Rico), however, have established state plans, which currently cover about 15 million workers.

The existence of multiple and overlapping public and private disability programs has resulted in a continuing debate over the adequacy and equity of the resulting nonsystem. Merton Bernstein (1973), for example, has charged that the ensuing "web of protection provided by separate public and private programs is full of holes, with those most in need receiving less protection than those with lesser need." As we indicate in Chapter 9, the problems of workers unable to continue working until the normal retirement age because of disability and other causes represents one of the policy areas requiring major attention in the years to come.

Another issue receiving increasing attention in recent years is the rapid and unexpected growth of payments under the social security disability program. Begun in 1956, disability program expenditures had begun to grow faster than revenue by the mid-1960s. In response, Congress tightened the definition of disabilities in 1968. Even under the revised definition, however, claims mushroomed, with the number of disability beneficiaries tripling between 1965 and 1978 to a total of about 5 million disabled workers and their eligible dependents.

During the same period, the costs of the program grew from $1.5 billion in 1965 to $11 billion in 1977. If not for a legislative reallocation in 1977 of OASDHI payroll tax revenues—less to the retirement (OASI) and health (HI) programs and more to disability (DI)—the disability program would have exhausted its reserves and been faced with a financial crisis. While some part of the increased costs result from program maturation (i.e., more workers meeting the years-of-coverage requirements), much of the increase has come from unanticipated increases in claims and the approval of claims (Cardwell, 1976).

Analysts do not fully understand why the disability rolls have expanded so rapidly, especially "since surveys of the disabled show no increase in the number of disabled" (Berkowitz, 1979)*, but the following are some commonly cited reasons:

1. Improved benefit levels, which reduce the need and desire to work. Six percent of awards in 1977 actually increased the disabled person's after-tax income. Almost one-fifth of the awards produced earnings replacement rates of more than 80 percent (Subcommittee on Social Security, U.S. House Committee on Ways and Means, 1978).
2. High unemployment in recent years that makes it harder for disabled persons to keep old jobs and find new ones.
3. Problems with state rehabilitation programs and laxity in disability reassessment procedures. A recent Social Security Administration study of 1,000 beneficiary reassessment cases revealed substantial state errors and deficiencies in procedures (Wortman, 1978).
4. Increased public awareness of the program, spurred in part by the government itself.
5. A liberal, elaborate, multileveled appeals process with a high reversal rate (about 30 percent at the state level and 50 percent by administrative law judges). Moreover, appeal is increasingly encouraged by the rising number of legal services lawyers (and private lawyers) who assist people with their claims.
6. More liberal, or looser, administrative action by officials confronted by many applicants who are disadvantaged and who have little chance of getting a job.

*Berkowitz, however, thinks we need much better information. He points out that past survey results are not entirely reliable since they asked people "for a result or outcome, i.e., the fact that they are limited or prevented from working, and then we confine them to one reason for that outcome—their health."

Considerable attention is now focused on these and related issues. Legislative and administrative action attempting to improve the disability program's operations and to keep costs down can be expected in the near future.

*Medicaid and Medicare*    Major legislation to help individuals meet health costs was passed in 1965: hospital insurance and supplementary medical insurance (collectively known as Medicare) and a medical assistance program (Medicaid).

An amendment of the Social Security Act in 1950 had provided for federal financial participation in providing medical care to public assistance recipients, and in 1960 another amendment authorized additional federal matching for medical care payments for Old Age Assistance recipients. The Medicaid program, enacted as Title XIX of the Social Security Act, greatly expanded the access of low income people to health care.

Medicaid provides federal funds appropriated from general revenue to states establishing qualifying medical assistance programs. All states except Arizona participate. The federal cost-sharing ranges from 50 percent to 80 percent, based on a formula that varies the percentage in accordance with a state's per capita income.

Medicaid is not a program limited to aged persons. All states cover recipients of Aid to Families with Dependent Children (AFDC); about 30 percent cover all aged, blind, and disabled recipients of Supplemental Security Income (SSI); the other states limit coverage of SSI eligibles to persons who meet restrictive medical assistance standards. In addition, about two-thirds of the states cover medically needy persons who are aged, blind, disabled, or members of AFDC families and ineligible for cash assistance but not able to afford medical services.

A wide measure of discretion is allowed states under the Medicaid legislation with regard to what income and asset "means tests" will be applied to various individuals. Consequently, actual practice among the states varies greatly. In 1970, only 39 percent of Medicaid dollars were spent to provide medical care for persons age 65 or older (U.S. Joint Economic Committee, 1972).

Participating states are required to provide both inpatient and outpatient hospital services, skilled nursing home or home health care services, and physicians' services. Other services, such as drugs, dental services, and physical therapy, are provided at the option of the state.

The 1965 social security amendments also established the Medicare programs. The "hospital insurance" program provides benefits financed by *compulsory* payroll taxes and covers all persons age 65 or over entitled under either OASDI or the railroad retirement system and most disability beneficiaries under age 65. Hospital insurance benefits are also available to *noninsured* persons who were over age 65 in July 1966, and to other persons age 65 and over who voluntarily enroll and pay a premium rate that meets the entire cost of their protection. "Supplementary medical insurance" is a *voluntary* program financed by participant premiums ($8.20 per month in early 1979) and a matching contribution by the federal government out of general revenue; with certain minor exceptions, any person age 65 or over in the United States can participate.

The hospital insurance program provides a variety of hospital and posthospital benefits (subject to certain deductible and cost-sharing charges). Reimbursement for services provided are made on a "reasonable cost basis" directly to hospitals, skilled nursing facilities, and home health service agencies. With regard to the major type of expenditure, hospitalization, an individual is entitled to inpatient hospital benefits for the first 90 days in a spell of illness and for an additional "lifetime reserve" of 60 days that can be used on an elective basis. In addition, 20 days of skilled nursing care are provided without cost to eligible persons for each spell of illness, and 80 days following are provided on a cost-sharing basis. Finally, a maximum of 100 home health services are provided within a spell of illness, with no provision for cost-sharing after the maximum is exceeded.

The supplementary medical insurance program covers certain nonhospital medical costs, primarily the cost of physician services. In general the program reimburses 80 percent of "reasonable charges" after an initial deductible of $60 per calendar year (with certain carry-over provisions). There are, however, two very different administrative procedures available for reimbursing covered services. If a doctor accepts "assignment" and therefore agrees to bill for no more than "reasonable charges," he is paid directly by the government (after taking into account any deductible and coinsurance). If the doctor does not accept assignment, the beneficiary must pay the doctor's actual charges, present an itemized bill from the doctor to the government, and be reimbursed on the basis of "reasonable charges" (which may be lower than the actual charges). In actuality, a great many doctors will not accept assignment—some because of strong personal views against dealing with government agencies and having fees "dictated" by them, others because it is the American Medical Association's recommended action, and still others because of the alleged red tape involved.

In recent years public funds have financed about 70 percent of health expenses for the aged, and Medicare and Medicaid together accounted for almost 60 percent of those expenses (Gibson, Mueller, and Fisher, 1977).

*The Supplemental Security Income Program*   A new cash-assistance program for the needy aged, blind, and disabled went into operation at the beginning of 1974. This Supplemental Security Income program

(SSI) replaced federal grants to three programs: the state-administered programs of old age assistance (OAA), aid to the blind (AB), and aid to the permanently and totally disabled (APTD). The SSI program is financed from general revenues of the federal government and establishes uniform eligibility requirements and benefits levels for the whole nation. In addition, states are encouraged (and some are required) to supplement the federal benefits with their own payments.

Eligibility for this program requires meeting an assets test, and benefits are phased out as income increases. Nonexcluded assets may not exceed $1,500 for an individual and $2,250 for a couple. Excluded assets are (a) the value of a home up to $25,000 (fair market value), (b) nonliquid-income-producing property, (c) assets of a blind or disabled person needed to establish a "self-support plan," (d) the value of household goods and personal effects up to $1,500, an automobile (up to $1,200), and life insurance (cash surrender value up to $1,500), (e) self-support business property, and (f) cash reimbursement from qualifying indemnity insurance.

Benefits are reduced by 100 percent of all *unearned* income and by 50 percent of *earned* income amounts above the "disregard." The two major income disregards are $60 per quarter of irregular unearned income and the first $85 per month of earned income.

The benefit paid to eligible individuals is $2,273 per year (1978) and $3,409 for couples. This benefit is about 75 percent of the nonfarm poverty level for aged individuals and about 90 percent for a couple. The federal benefit is automatically increased for changes in the cost of living.

There are now about 5 million people receiving SSI payments. Surprisingly, about half of these recipients are disabled persons—not aged. Expenditures totaled about $7 billion in 1978.

When SSI was legislated, its supporters argued that it would reduce many of the traditional problems associated with other programs to help the poor—that it would produce more efficient program administration, less stigma to recipients, and more adequate benefits using a national standard. During the first years of the program the Social Security Administration had difficulty coping with the new responsibilities and workload suddenly thrust upon it as the chief administrator of the new program. In 1977, three years after its operations began, the SSI program was described by the U.S. Senate Committee on Finance staff as follows: "The early months of the program were characterized by near total administrative breakdown, primarily as a result of insufficient and inaccurate planning and inadequate resources. The crisis stage has passed, and steady improvements in administrative capabilities are taking place; however, the program continues to operate with apparently insufficient resources and at a clearly unacceptable level of accuracy" (U.S. Senate Committee on Finance, 1977).

An analysis (Schieber, 1978) of the first year of program operations indicated that comparatively few people were moved out of poverty by SSI; but most of the individuals transferred into SSI from abolished programs did experience an increase in income levels (after adjusting for general price increases). As intended, the greatest income increases accrued to persons who had been the poorest before SSI was implemented.

In 1973 and 1974 nearly 16,000 persons who had first received old age assistance and then the new SSI benefit were asked their attitudes about the two programs. Tissue (1978) reports that most aged and disabled welfare recipients did not feel embarrassed or troubled about receiving old age assistance. SSI, however, achieved an even higher degree of approval. Only 14 percent of respondents indicated that they were "ever bothered by the fact that . . . [they] had to accept aid from SSI." In addition, when asked to compare old age assistance with SSI, only 6 percent felt SSI was worse than the program it replaced. In other words, SSI was the clear choice when recipients were asked to pick the system they preferred. Tissue concludes that "from the perspective of needy persons who had experienced both programs, SSI represented a definite step forward."

### Suggested Readings

Ball, Robert M. *Social Security Today and Tomorrow*. New York: Columbia University Press, 1978.

    An outstanding (and very readable) discussion of all major issues connected with social security.

Cockburn, Christine, and Dalmer Hoskins. "Social Security and Divorced Persons." *International Social Security Review* 29 (1976): 111–151.

    A comprehensive survey of practices in twenty-six countries related to this growing problem.

Cohen, Wilbur, J., and Milton Friedman. *Social Security: Universal or Selective?* Rational Debate Seminars. Washington, D.C.: The American Enterprise Institute, 1972.

    A debate between former HEW Secretary Cohen, who defends social security, and economist Friedman, who argues for its abolition.

International Labour Office. *An Introduction to Social Security*. Geneva: ILO, 1970.

    Developed for use throughout the world, this comprehensive discussion stresses the basic principles and alternatives for social security systems. Conceptual issues and practical problems are given extensive examination.

Lubove, Roy. *The Struggle for Social Security, 1900–1935.* Cambridge, Mass.: Harvard University Press, 1968.

    An interpretive, historical analysis of the passage of the 1935 Social Security Act.

Munnell, Alicia H. *The Future of Social Security*. Washington, D.C.: The Brookings Institution, 1977.

    A good overview from an economist's viewpoint.

Myers, Robert J. *Social Security*. Homewood, Ill.: Irwin for the McCahan Foundation, 1975.

    A comprehensive discussion of all aspects of OASDHI by a former Chief Actuary of the Social Security Administration.

Pechman, Joseph A.; Henry J. Aaron; and Michael K. Taussig. *Social Security—Perspectives for Reform*. Washington, D.C.: The Brookings Institution, 1968.

Despite its age (which means that program descriptions are not up to date), this book remains one of the best discussions of the issues associated with old age pensions under social security.

Rimlinger, Gaston. *Welfare Policy and Industrialization in Europe, America, and Russia*. New York: Wiley, 1971.

A comparative analysis of the historical development of the social security systems in Germany, Russia, Great Britain, and the United States.

Schorr, Alvin L. "Welfare Reform and Social Insurance." *Challenge* 20 (November-December 1977: 14–22.

A leading spokesman against removal of the social adequacy function from OASDI presents his views on social security reform.

U.S. Social Security Administration. *Social Security Programs in the United States*. Washington, D.C.: U.S. Government Printing Office, various years.

Describes the provisions of the OASDHI, unemployment insurance, workmen's compensation, temporary disability, and public assistance programs in the United States. It is revised periodically so readers should make sure they have the most recent issue.

# Chapter Seven
## What Role for Private Pensions?

Pension plans set up by private industry or employee groups did not appear in the United States until the end of the nineteenth century. The first company pension plan was established by the American Express Company in 1875 but provided benefits only to permanently incapacitated workers over age 60 who had at least twenty years' service. Thereafter plans were established in the railroad industry and by a few firms in other industries. However, a congressional study reports that such pension schemes "were by and large slow in developing and [that] there were probably fewer than ten plans in operation by the end of the 19th century" (U.S. House Committee on Education and Labor, 1972).

The Civil Service Retirement Act was enacted in 1920, providing pension coverage for the first time to federal civilian employees. A year later the implementation of private plans was encouraged by the Revenue Act of 1921; this legislation exempted from income taxation both the *income* of pension and profit sharing trusts and the *employer contributions* to these plans.

Although between 3 and 4 million workers were covered by private pensions prior to the establishment of social security, coverage was concentrated in only a few industries; benefits were very limited; less than 15 percent of the work force was covered; and payments were made only if certain very stringent age and service requirements were met. It was not until the 1940s and 1950s that the growth of private pensions mushroomed. Coverage rose from about 4 million employees in the late thirties to roughly 10 million in 1950 and 20 million in 1960.

Various factors have been cited as responsible for this rather dramatic increase in private pension coverage:

1.  Continued industrialization of the American economy, together with a movement of workers out of agriculture, which stimulated increasing interest in alternatives other than the family for providing retirement security.
2.  The introduction of private pensions by some employers as a way of creating employee loyalty and discouraging job shifting, since most early plans called for the worker to lose his rights to the pension if he left the firm.
3.  Wage freezes during World War II and the Korean War that encouraged fringe benefit growth in lieu of wages.
4.  A series of favorable tax inducements offered by the federal government beginning with the Revenue Acts of 1921 and 1926. Probably the most important inducement was offered in the Revenue Act of 1942. Coming at a time of sharp personal and corporate federal income tax increases, the 1942 act (a) treated employer contributions to qualified pension plans as tax deductible, (b) excluded plan investment income from taxation, and (c) deferred taxes on participant beneficiaries until actually received in retirement.
5.  A favorable decision by the Supreme Court in 1949 supporting the National Labor Relations Board's decision that pensions were a proper issue for collective bargaining.
6.  The report of the Steel Industry Fact-Finding Committee in 1949, which included a recommendation that the industry had a social obligation to provide workers with pensions.
7.  Growing recognition by unions of the inadequacy of social security benefits and the need for supplementation.
8.  The development of multiemployer pension plans—particularly in the construction, transportation, trade, and service industries.

In years past there have been numerous serious problems related to worker protection under private pensions. Workers lost benefit rights as a result of unemployment, company mergers, plant closures, or firm bankruptcies—often after long years of service. Many workers did not know about, or understand, the sometimes very stringent age and service requirements that had to be met to actually receive benefits. Pension reserve funds, supposedly put aside to guarantee benefits to workers, were sometimes mismanaged or misused. Benefits, when actually paid, were often inadequate.

A great deal of attention was given these problems by investigating groups and legislative committees in the 1950s. Congressional concern for the protection of employees' private pensions eventually caused the enactment of the Welfare and Pension Plan Disclosure Act. This act, however, placed primary responsibility for policing the plans on the participants themselves. Dissatisfaction and problems continued. Finally in 1974 Congress passed much stronger, more comprehensive legislation: the Employee Retirement Income Security Act (**ERISA**). This legislation, which is summarized later in the chapter, was a major step in providing protection to covered workers against benefit loss.

This chapter, then, focuses on the progress made in developing private pensions into a viable institution for providing income in old age. The role that private pensions will ultimately play in the economics of aging depends on the resolution of a number of remaining issues: extending coverage, protecting benefits, and dealing with the problem of inflation. To these issues we now turn.

### Who Is Covered?

Estimates of the total number of workers covered under private pension plans vary and are subject to large error. The Social Security Administration's published estimates, however, are the most frequently cited. These indicate for various years the percentage of private wage and salary employees covered by either a private pension or a **deferred profit sharing plan.**

The nature of the retirement income promise from private pensions is very different from that of profit sharing benefits; it is not desirable to lump the two together statistically. Contributions into profit sharing plans vary with the amount of a particular company's profits and are more directly tied to the vicissitudes of the economy. Hence, profit sharing plans—less certain with regard to ultimate payout—are a more debatable way of providing retirement benefits for the approximately 2 million workers with *only* this type of coverage. In contrast, most pension plans make a pension promise that is generally independent of fluctuations in the economy or the prosperity of a particular business enterprise. Given this distinction, then, we have made an estimate of the percentage of workers covered only by profit sharing plans and have deducted this type of coverage from the Social Security Administration's estimates. Both sets of coverage data are shown in Table 23.

The total number of workers covered under private pension plans has increased from about 4 million workers in 1940 (12 percent of the private wage and salary labor force) to 27 million workers (42 percent) in 1975, and currently is probably over 30 million. The major increases occurred in the 1940s and the 1950s, averaging about 12 percent and 7 percent a year respectively. More recently the growth rate has slowed in the 1960s and 1970s to a little over 3 percent a year.

It has been especially difficult to extend private pension coverage among small employee groups. Among the factors that have been cited for this difficulty are:

1. The high costs per employee of establishing and maintaining a private plan
2. The lack of pressure in some companies from employees or unions
3. The fact that small business firms are often relatively young and, on average, short-lived
4. The fact that small employers tend to view pensions as personal costs
5. The personality of small business owners who tend to emphasize individual self-reliance in financial matters
6. The often unstable and insecure financial status of many small businesses and the competitive pressures for cost-cutting

As a result of these and other factors, a sizable proportion of the work force in the United States is not likely to be covered by such pensions.

*Table 23.*   Private Pension Coverage Estimates, 1940–1975

| Year | Private Pension and Profit Sharing (in thousands) | Percent of Wage and Salary Labor Force | Private Pensions Only[a] (in thousands) | Percent of Wage and Salary Labor Force |
|---|---|---|---|---|
| 1940 | 4,100 | 12.2 | 3,936 | 11.7 |
| 1952 | 11,300 | 24.2 | 10,215 | 21.9 |
| 1958 | 17,200 | 35.8 | 15,549 | 32.4 |
| 1962 | 19,700 | 38.3 | 17,357 | 34.7 |
| 1969 | 26,000 | 41.7 | 23,504 | 37.7 |
| 1974 | 29,800 | 44.0 | 26,939 | 39.8 |
| 1975 | 30,300 | 46.2 | 27,391 | 42.0 |

Sources: Coverage data for combined private pension and profit sharing plans are from Alfred E. Skolnik, "Private Pension Plans, 1950–74," *Social Security Bulletin* 39 (June 1976): 3–17; and Martha R. Yohalem, "Employee-Benefit Plans, 1975," *Social Security Bulletin* 40 (November 1977): 19–38.

[a]The profit sharing factor was estimated as 9.6 percent of the private pension and profit sharing data. The estimate is based on tabulations of information reported to the government on Form EBS-1 and data from Gunnar Engen, "A New Direction and Growth in Profit-Sharing," *Monthly Labor Review* 90 (July 1967): 1–8.

Table 24 shows how pension coverage in the United States varies by work status, sex, race, industry, and earnings. Part-time workers, women, nonwhites, and low earners have the lowest coverage. The industries with the lowest coverage are service, wholesale and retail trade, and construction.

Table 24 shows coverage among current workers *of all ages.* Similar findings were found for *recently retired workers*—based on examination of data from the Social Security Administration's Retirement History Survey. Of all retirees who had ever worked, 45 percent were covered by a pension on their longest or most recent job. But many who had been covered at one time by private pensions never received a benefit—28 percent of covered men and 45 percent (!) of covered women (Thompson, 1978).

*Table 24.*  Private Pension Coverage[a], April 1972

| Wage and Salary Workers in Private Industry | Percent |
|---|---|
| All Full-time and Part-time Employees | 43.7 |
| Full-time Employees Only | 47.0 |
| Men | 52.0 |
| Women | 36.0 |
| Whites | 48.0 |
| Nonwhites | 39.0 |
| Full-time Employees, by Industry | |
| Communications and Public Utilities | 82.0 |
| Mining | 72.0 |
| Manufacturing | |
| Durable Goods | 63.0 |
| Nondurable Goods | 57.0 |
| Finance, Insurance, and Real Estate | 52.0 |
| Transportation | 45.0 |
| Trade | |
| Wholesale | 48.0 |
| Retail | 31.0 |
| Construction | 34.0 |
| Services | 29.0 |
| Full-time Employees, by Earnings | |
| Men Earning Less than $5,000 | 26.0 |
| Women Earning Less than $5,000 | 31.0 |
| Men Earning $5,000–9,999 | 58.0 |
| Women Earning $5,000–9,999 | 58.0 |

Sources: Walter W. Kolodrubetz, "Employee-Benefit Plans, 1972," *Social Security Bulletin* 37 (May 1974): 15–21; and Walter W. Kolodrubetz and Donald M. Landay, "Coverage and Vesting of Full-Time Employees Under Private Retirement Plans," *Social Security Bulletin* 36 (November 1973): 20–36.
[a]Includes profit-sharing coverage.

## Alternative Types of Coverage

As we mentioned above, profit sharing plans are usually counted statistically as part of private pension coverage, but workers with only profit sharing coverage may face problems in retirement. The case of Sears and Roebuck employees is a good example.

Over 20 percent of Sears' common stock is owned by Sears employees through the company's profit sharing plan. In the good profit years of the sixties and early seventies, employees realized huge investment gains through the profit sharing plan. But when business conditions became poor, the price of Sears' stock fell dramatically, and workers became very angry. Sears responded by creating a regular pension fund to complement the profit sharing plan, thereby giving more security to workers approaching retirement.

Today millions of workers covered only by profit sharing plans still face the issue raised by the Sears example: How secure is their retirement income promise? A recent study (Profit Sharing Research Foundation, 1978) of the largest profit sharing plans reports, for example, that only 58 percent of the companies surveyed also had a regular private pension for their employees' retirement security.

Another mechanism that helps workers prepare for retirement is thrift or savings plans set up by employers. Sixty-one of the top 100 industrial corporations have one of these plans (Bankers Trust, 1977). Company contributions are a deductible business expense. Also, the employee pays no income tax until pay-out on both the company's contributions and the *earnings* on his own (and the company's) contributions.

Again, thrift plans are not necessarily alternatives to a pension plan; most companies with such plans also provide a pension plan for employees. Some companies, however, just have thrift plans.*

Perhaps the most important mechanism created to deal with the private pension coverage issue is the **Individual Retirement Account** (IRA). In a message to Congress on December 8, 1971, President Nixon first proposed that pension legislation be enacted that would contain saving incentives. The legislation was ultimately enacted as part of the private pension reform legislation (ERISA) that became law in September 1974.

President Nixon's proposal, and the subsequent law, permits wage and salary earners to set up their own individual retirement plans (IRAs) if they are not covered by any qualified pension plan. Employees not covered by private pension plans can deduct up to 15 percent of earned income (up to $1,500 a year) to be set aside free of taxation until subsequently paid out.** In addition, the 1974 pension-reform legislation liberalized existing limitations on contributions to retirement plans for the self-employed (generally called Keogh or HR 10 plans). The self-employed are now allowed to deduct 15 percent of earned income up to $7,500 (instead of 10 percent up to $2,500 under previous law).

In proposing the legislation, President Nixon argued that it would encourage people to save and that public policy should reward and reinforce this type of activity. In transmitting the legislation, he said: "Self-reliance, prudence, and independence are qualities which our government should work to encourage among our people. These are also the qualities which are involved when a person chooses to invest in a retirement savings plan, set-

---

*Not discussed are Tax Reduction Act Stock Ownership Plans (TRASOP) that allow companies to make contributions for employees, primarily in the company's common stock.
**Also, the 1976 Tax Reform Act permits a nonworking spouse of an eligible worker to establish an IRA in a separate account. The maximum for both accounts is $1,750, with up to $875 in each.

ting aside money today so that he will have greater security tomorrow. In this respect pension plans are a direct expression of some of the finest elements in the American character. Public policy should be designed to reward and reinforce these qualities."

The President also argued that this legislation would be responsive to the inequity that existed between those people who were covered by private pensions and those who were not. People covered by private pensions receive favorable tax treatment because contributions made by the employer on their behalf are not taxable. These private pension contributions are only taxable at the time they are paid out, usually at much lower tax rates because retirement income levels are lower than those of work periods.

These were the President's two principal arguments in favor of such legislation. Other people have argued that by encouraging people to save for retirement individually, one allows them to control their own investments and decide what they want to invest in and the amount of risk they want to take. If you are a member of a private pension plan you have nothing to say about the investment policy of the plan. Often the gains of good investment accrue only to the employer. If you are sophisticated about financial matters and economics, you might be able to do better with the same amount of funds, especially if you are willing to take some risks.

And, finally, it has been argued that this approach is an alternative to increasing and expanding the social welfare programs that currently exist to help older people. Such tax incentives, it is argued, give people the option to build upon their social security base and give them the freedom to choose how to do it.

A major objection to the "incentive for saving" tax plan is that it provides greater benefits to workers with higher earnings. These workers will be able to set aside a larger absolute amount of income; 15 percent of $6,000, for example, is not as much as 15 percent of $10,000 ($900 versus $1,500). Moreover, if you are a higher income person you are in a better financial position to save up to the maximum and get the maximum tax deduction.

But, more importantly, the proportion of lower paid workers who will take advantage of this opportunity for tax-sheltered saving is likely to be smaller than that of more highly paid persons. The fear that such tax-exemption proposals would turn into tax loopholes for higher income people was the principal argument voiced in Congress against the legislation when it was proposed.

Table 25 shows that this is in fact what has happened. The only income group that has a high IRA utilization rate is the one for people with incomes over $50,000. Less than 1 percent of eligible wage earners with incomes under $15,000 took advantage of the IRA opportunity in 1976.

Table 25.  The Proportion of Eligible Workers in 1976 Utilizing IRAs, by Income Class

| Income Class[a] | Number of IRA Eligible Taxpayers[b] (millions) | Percent of Eligible Workers Utilizing IRAs |
|---|---|---|
| Up to $5,000 | 17.1 | 0.2 |
| $5,000–9,999 | 13.5 | 1.4 |
| 10,000–14,999 | 11.8 | 2.5 |
| 15,000–19,999 | 6.5 | 5.2 |
| 20,000–49,999 | 6.1 | 14.8 |
| 50,000 and Over | 0.4 | 45.0 |
| Total | 55.4 | 3.5 |

Source: U.S. Treasury Department data reported in *BNA Pension Reporter* (February 20, 1978): R–9.
[a] Adjusted gross income class.
[b] Excludes persons covered by public or private retirement systems.

## Private Plan Characteristics

It is difficult to generalize about the provisions of private pension plans because of the large number of different plans with widely varying characteristics. There are about a half-million corporate pension plans in the United States. These can be generally divided into *single employer* and *multi-employer* plans. Multiemployer plans usually require employers to make contributions into a central fund (typically a specified percent of payroll or cents-per-hours-worked), and employees can qualify for benefits from the fund by meeting eligibility requirements through employment in the various firms participating in the program. Reciprocity agreements among some of these multiemployer plans (and a few single employer plans) allow workers to move between plans. Another important difference between the two types of plans is in their administration. Single employer plans are generally managed by the employer alone; multiemployer plans are almost invariably administered by a group of trustees, with equal representation from labor and management (in accordance with terms of the Taft-Hartley Act).

Another common way of classifying private plans is to distinguish between *contributory* and *noncontributory* plans. Contributory plans require that the employee pay part of the cost, whereas noncontributory plans are financed solely by the employer. In the United States, most covered workers (80 percent) participate in noncontributory plans—in part because employer contributions are tax free but under current federal laws employee contributions (unless sheltered by special arrangements) are not. Also, noncontributory plans do not require the employer to put aside money for *each* worker at the time benefit rights accrue. And employers can use actuarial assumptions that permit them (a) to take account of employee turnover (reducing current pension expenses) and (b) to raise the level of funding of the plan over an extended period of time (see Chapter 8).

Multiemployer plans cover about one-third of all covered workers. These multiemployer plans tend to be concentrated, however, in particular industries (mining, construction, trade, transportation, and service) and, in these industries, affect more than 50 percent of all covered workers.

In surveying the specific provisions of various pension plans, there are four key characteristics that are generally considered most important: the benefit formulas, vesting and portability requirements, the availability of survivors' benefits, and early retirement options.

*Benefit Determination*  While there is a great deal of variation among private plans in the way benefits are calculated, three major types can be identified:

Defined Benefit Plans:

1. *Dollar amount times service*—benefits are determined by multiplying a specified dollar amount by the number of years of employed service credited under the plan.
2. *Combined service/earnings formulas*—benefits are based upon (a) the employee's earnings over a specified period of employment (e.g., career, high five of the last ten, or last ten years of earnings) and (b) years of service.

Defined Contribution Plan:*

3. *Money-purchase arrangements*—periodic contributions are set aside according to a predetermined, or agreed upon, formula (usually a percent of earnings). Pensions are paid out based on the accumulated funds (contributions plus investment income) in individual employee accounts.

The overwhelming proportion of workers covered by *single employer plans* belong to plans that use the defined benefit formula basing benefits on earnings. In contrast, only a small proportion of workers under *multiemployer plans* participate in plans using earnings-based formulas. Instead, most multiemployer plans use the "dollar amount times service" formula. Money-purchase plans are most common in public employee retirement systems and nonprofit organizations.

---

*Deferred profit sharing plans are often listed as defined contribution plans. For the reasons given previously, we exclude them.

The most important recent trend has been a shift to basing benefits on earnings just prior to retirement. The major advantage of this type of formula is a built-in adjustment for inflation *prior to retirement*—since earnings over time are usually adjusted upward for cost-of-living increases.

Another important feature of many benefit calculations is the attempt of some private plans to integrate private pensions with social security. Some plans deduct (typically) 50 to 75 percent of the social security benefit from the amount computed according to the private plan formula. Other plans use a formula that provides higher benefits on earnings above a certain specified amount—often the social security maximum earnings ceiling.

In a study of 977 defined benefit plans in 1974, Schulz, Leavitt, and Kelly (1979) estimated that men retiring with thirty years' pension service would receive average benefits of about $2,700 annually; women would receive about $2,000. The average pension replacement rate for men and women working thirty years in the same plan was about 25 percent. The replacement rate, however, varied widely by industry, type of plan, and size of plan (see Table 26).

*Table 26.*    Estimated Replacement Rates for the Median Male Worker with Thirty Years of Work, by Industry, Size of Plan, and Type of Plan

| *Industry* | *Replacement Rate*[a] |
|---|---|
| Mining | 17 |
| Construction | 17 |
| Manufacturing | 22 |
| Transportation | 27 |
| Communication/Utilities | 34 |
| Wholesale and Retail Trade | 21 |
| Finance/Insurance/Real Estate | 34 |
| Service | 15 |
| *Type and Size of Plan* | |
| Single Employer Plans | 24 |
|    100 to 1,000 employees | 20 |
|    1,001 to 10,000 employees | 24 |
|    10,001 to 50,000 employees | 27 |
|    More than 50,000 employees | 26 |
| | |
| Multiemployer Plans | 16 |
|    100 to 1,000 employees | 19 |
|    1,001 to 10,000 employees | 19 |
|    10,001 to 50,000 employees | 18 |
|    More than 50,000 employees | 10 |

Source: James H. Schulz, Thomas Leavitt, and Leslie Kelly, "Private Pensions Fall Far Short of Preretirement Income Levels," *Monthly Labor Review* 102 (February 1979): 28–32.
[a]Replacement rate equals the ratio between pension income and before-tax gross earnings in the year before benefits begin.

*Vesting and Portability Requirements*    **Vesting** and **portability** are related pension concepts but are not identical. Vesting refers to the provision in pension plans that guarantees that those covered by the plan will receive all or part of the benefit that they have earned (i.e., accrued), whether or not they are working under the plan at the time of their retirement. Through vesting, the pension rights of otherwise qualified workers are protected whether they are discharged, are furloughed, or quit voluntarily. Prior to ERISA (which established a variety of controls over private pensions), vesting provisions were often nonexistent. Where vesting was available, eligibility conditions varied greatly, and many workers lost their pension rights—sometimes after long years of service and sometimes just prior to retirement. The 1974 law now requires all plans covered by the law to provide minimum vested benefits meeting one of three alternative standards:

1. Vesting of 100 percent of accrued benefits after 10 years of service.
2. Vesting of 25 percent of accrued benefits after 5 years of service, going up by 5 percent each year for the next 5 years and by 10 percent thereafter (until 100 percent vesting is reached after 15 years).
3. Vesting of 50 percent of accrued benefits when age and service add up to 45 years, with 100 percent vesting 5 years thereafter—subject to a minimum 5 years service and the constraint that employees must be 50 percent vested after 10 years of service and 100 percent vested after 15 years.

Almost all companies have adopted the 10 year–100 percent option. Hence, those workers who change jobs before accumulating 10 years of service receive no pension credits.

Another problem is that vested benefits left in a pension plan after a worker voluntarily or involuntarily leaves the firm are not adjusted upward if the pension plan's formula for *continuing* workers is changed either to compensate for inflation or to provide a higher level of real benefits.* "Portability" of pension rights permits employees to transfer the money value of these rights into another plan and, hopefully, by this process to reduce the inflationary losses that arise when benefits are left behind. Unfortunately, although portability has received a lot of public attention (and is often confused with vesting), the administrative, financial, and actuarial complexities of setting up such arrangements have discouraged any significant action in this area. The multiemployer plan, however, reduces the problems associated with job change by introducing limited portability (i.e., within the boundaries of the plan) through a centralized pension fund.

The 1974 pension reform law permits a separated employee to transfer *tax free* the value of a vested benefit into an "individual retirement

---

*Also, vested benefits left in plans with earnings related formulas do not reflect the rise in earnings that would occur if the worker remained employed by the firm.

account" *if permitted by the plan* or to another plan *if permitted by both plans.* In fact, an employer with a noncontributory plan has a positive financial incentive not to agree to this transfer, since he can earn interest or dividends on any "funded" money he keeps and need not pass on any of these earnings to the former employee.

*Survivors' Benefits* Half of the aged who are poor are widowed women. Provisions for survivors in pension plans, both public and private, play an important role in determining this outcome. For example, in a study of members of the United Auto Workers (UAW) and their survivors, Eugene Loren and Thomas Barker (1968) found that total resources available to survivors were inadequate for long-term needs. More importantly, they found *that without group survivors' benefits, vast numbers of survivors would be virtually destitute.* About 65 percent of the surveyed UAW families had financial resources at the worker's death of less than $3,000; approximately half of the dependent surviving units had little or no net assets to supplement survivors' benefits or work income.

Responsibility for protecting the family against economic insecurity arising from the death of family members (especially wage earners) has been evolving over time. In 1939, individual responsibility through savings and life insurance was supplemented in a major way by the addition of survivor benefits in the social security retirement program.

There is great variation in the provisions various private companies have made for dealing with problems arising from the death of an employee. Employers provide benefits to employees' survivors through group life insurance, a profit sharing plan, and/or a pension plan. Death protection through private pensions, however, was not a high priority item in most early pension planning. Consequently, until recently some plans made little or no provision for the survivors of workers. In 1974, before ERISA became effective, for example, about 20 percent of the workers covered by defined benefit plans were in plans with no survivor provisions of any kind. The most common type of survivor benefit in those private plans that did have provisions was a **joint and survivor option.** This option provides a lifetime income for a spouse in the event of the worker's death. The survivor benefit is paid regularly and equals a specified percentage (typically 50 to 75 percent) of the worker's accrued or actual benefit. The cost of this option is paid for either by lowering the worker's retirement benefit by about 15 percent or by the employer absorbing the charge as part of company fringe benefit costs.

ERISA now mandates that all pension plans subject to its provisions at a minimum give certain workers an opportunity to elect a 50 percent joint and survivor option covering *some* of the preretirement years. This preretirement option must be offered at the initial age the worker becomes eligible for early retirement benefits, or ten years before normal retirement, whichever comes later. In both cases, the cost of these options may be imposed on the worker through a lower amount of pension paid out. In addition, plans must provide all workers with this type of survivor protection *at the time of retirement* (unless it is specifically rejected by the worker).

Some companies provide employee survivor benefits that go beyond the ERISA mandated provisions. For example, some automatically provide benefits at no cost to the worker. The most recent information on survivor benefits is found in the Bureau of Labor Statistics' *Digest of Selected Pension Plans 1976–78 Edition.* The *Digest* gives information on plans which "cover a large number of employees in major industries or illustrate different approaches to pension planning."

How many plans do better than the ERISA mandated survivor provisions? There still exists a significant percentage of plans that require workers to pay for their survivor protection; 26 percent of plans in the sample have no preretirement automatic death benefits and 52 percent have no retirement automatic death benefits. Typically, those plans with no preretirement death benefits also have no retirement death benefits.

Even in plans with death benefits, not all workers are eligible. Most of the automatic preretirement death benefits shown in Table 27 require that the worker be eligible for early retirement benefits. Thus, if the worker dies before reaching early retirement eligibility the spouse does not receive these benefits.

Table 27 also shows that in many cases the automatically provided benefits are not generous. Nearly 70 percent of the plans *with* employer-paid preretirement death benefits provide a specified percentage of the worker's accumulated benefit. In most cases the percentage is the ERISA minimum. Eleven plans pay a monthly benefit to survivors for a six-month to a five-year period. After this stipulated period, benefits cease entirely—ignoring the fact that the survivor's living expenses continue and no doubt increase over time. Alternatively, a few plans give a lump sum to the survivor; usually the amount is sufficient to cover little more than burial expenses.

Finally, *contributory* plans return the employees' contributions with interest. Since there is no employer expense in such cases, it is difficult to construe this return of contributions as a benefit. Thus, excluding this contributory survivor provision, Table 27 shows that nearly 38 percent of the surveyed plans have no employer-paid preretirement death benefits, and over 65 percent have no employer-paid retirement death benefits.

Automatic death benefits during retirement, Table 27 shows, are generally less generous than benefits before retirement. The most generous retirement benefits are those that provide some percentage (usually 50 percent) of the worker's benefit. In effect, these plans provide joint and survivor benefits

*Table 27.* Type of Survivor Benefit Provided to Worker at No Direct Cost

| | Percent of Plans | |
|---|---|---|
| *Type of Benefit* | *Before Retirement* | *After Retirement* |
| Percent of Worker's Benefit:[a] | | |
| Less than 50 percent | 3 | ⎫ |
| 50 percent | 28 | ⎬ 6 |
| More than 50 percent | 13 | ⎭ |
| Fixed Period of Monthly Payments: | | |
| 5 years | 1 | 10 |
| 3 years | 5 | 4 |
| Other | 1 | 1 |
| Lump Sum Payment: | | |
| $1,200–1,500 | 1 | ⎫ |
| 3,000 | 1 | ⎬ 6 |
| 5,000 | 1 | ⎭ |
| Worker's Contribution Returned (plus interest) | 12 | 13 |
| Other Types | 8 | 6 |
| None | 26 | 52 |
| Total[b] | 100 | 100 |

Source: Tabulation of data in U.S. Bureau of Labor Statistics, *Digest of Selected Pension Plans, 1976–78 Edition* (Washington, D.C.: U.S. Government Printing Office, 1977).
[a]A joint and survivor reduction is often applied to the worker's benefit before the percentage is applied.
[b]May not add up to 100% due to rounding.

without the worker having to make an election and without any reduction of the pension.

The most common type of retirement death benefit, however, makes a monthly payment to the survivor—but only for a six-month to a five-year period. Most plans of this type reduce the length of the postdeath payment period by the length of time that regular pension payments were made prior to the death of the retired worker. Thus, given a five-year certain plan, if the worker died two years after retirement, the spouse would receive a benefit for three years.

In summary, the existing data indicate that the most important means of providing survivor protection through private pensions continues to be the joint and survivor option, typically at the cost of a lower benefit paid to the retiring worker. Survivor benefits provided over and above the joint and survivor option are not widespread, are of generally limited duration, and are often of small magnitude.

Some firms do have life insurance and/or supplemental plans which add to the level of benefits provided, but it seems obvious, nevertheless, that current benefits often do not reflect the needs of employees and their survivors. For a large number of long-term employees, there remains the very real possibility that many years of employer contributions in his or her name provide little or no survivor protection. In Chapter 9 we discuss the implications of this situation for the economic condition of older women.

*Early Retirement Options*    Early retirement options in private pension plans permit workers to leave employment and receive benefits before the normal retirement age specified in the plan. Receipt of pension benefits at an earlier age almost always requires that the worker meet a minimum age requirement, a years-of-service requirement, or both. Many plans permit early retirement only with the employer's consent, and a few plans permit the employer to involuntarily retire the worker at an early age. The most common service requirement for early retirement is 10–15 years.

More than 90 percent of all workers covered by private pension plans are in plans having early retirement options. In almost every plan up until the 1970s a worker exercising the early retirement option had his or her benefit reduced, usually by (or close to) the appropriate actuarial reduction. In recent years, however, a number of plans have begun providing a benefit that is greater than the actuarial equivalent.

One special type of early retirement option gives the worker a bigger benefit before social security benefits begin and then reduces the private pension benefit when social security begins. The benefit plan is usually constructed so that the worker receives a uniform benefit throughout his retirement—initially from the private pension alone and then from his combined pensions.

A study of major pension plans by the Bureau of Labor Statistics (Frumpkin and Schmitt, 1979) found that many changes had been made between 1974 and 1978. Of the 131 plans studied, 94 had liberalized retirement benefit formulas, 58 had lowered age and service requirements, 37 had raised benefits given to early retirees, and almost all provided vesting as mandated by ERISA.

## Private Pension Legislation

Benefit formulas, vesting, survivors' provisions, and early retirement options are four of the most important aspects of private pensions, but there are still others that have great significance for evaluating private pensions and determining public policy toward them. One of these areas concerns the danger of lost pension rights as a result of inadequate pension funding, misuse of pension funds, or the termination of plans because of plant closures, bankruptcy, or other reasons.

A great deal of attention has been given to this area by investigating groups and legislative committees. Congressional concern for the protection of employee benefit funds caused the enactment of the Welfare and Pension Plan Disclosure Act in 1959 but placed primary responsibility for policing the plans on the participants themselves. The Employee Retirement Income Security Act of 1974 set up a more comprehensive set of safeguards— establishing participation, vesting, funding standards, plan-termination insurance, and extensive reporting and disclosure requirements. The following are the major provisions of the act:

1. Plans must minimally vest benefits using one of three alternatives (see page 134).
2. Plan-termination insurance is established, up to $750 monthly, for employees whose plans terminate with insufficient funds.*
3. Funding standards are established and fiduciary standards are strengthened.
4. Individual retirement accounts (exempt from federal income taxation) may be established by workers (and their spouses) without private or public employee pension coverage, up to $1,750 annually or 15 percent of annual compensation (whichever is less) may be invested (see pages 129–131).
5. New disclosure regulations permit participants to request once each year a statement from the plan administrator of total benefits, both vested and nonvested, that have accrued and the earliest date on which unvested benefits will become nonforfeitable.
6. The Social Security Administration receives reports from employers (through the Treasury Department) of vested benefits due separated workers; Social Security notifies employees of all vested pension rights at the time they apply for social security benefits.
7. With the consent and cooperation of their employers, employees may transfer upon separation vested pension rights on a tax-free basis from one employer to another; or the employee may transfer the funds to an individual retirement account.

Passed by both houses of Congress by wide vote margins, the new law (as its name implies) is an attempt to provide greater certainty that private pension promises will be fulfilled. But the legislation does not deal with all the problems that have been discussed in connection with private pensions. Critics have been quick to cite the problems they think still remain:

1. A large segment (over half) of the private work force still remains uncovered.
2. Very few private pensions adjust pension benefits *during* retirement for inflation.
3. State and local government pension plans are excluded from the 1974 law.
4. The lack of "portability" in pensions may result in a reduction in

*At the time of writing, this insurance covered only single employer plans; problems developed in covering multiemployer plans (see page 172).

mobility and, for those who move, a reduction in the value of pension rights relative to what the value would be if they did not change jobs (see discussion above).

5. The availability of survivors' benefits remains relatively low, and those benefits paid are often small.

6. Private pension provisions may discourage the hiring of older workers because it typically costs more to provide such workers with a specified pension benefit.

While the drafters of the 1974 private pension legislation admitted in debate that the legislation did not deal with all the problems, they argued that it was a major step forward. And they pointed out that the legislation itself calls for further study of many of the unresolved issues.

### What Mix of Public and Private Pensions?

Despite the fact that the first pension plans were established about a century ago, there is still little agreement about the relative virtues of public versus private pensions and what the ideal combination of the two types should be. There is great diversity in the mix of pensions existing in various countries—but there are fewer countries where private programs assume a major role than there are countries that rely primarily on public pensions.

Relatively little has been written that attempts objectively to approach the question of the most desirable pension mix and present data for evaluation purposes. In the United States, the well-known economist Milton Friedman has been a consistent critic of social security and one of the few academics actually to advocate complete abolition of public pensions: "Social Security combines a highly regressive tax with largely indiscriminate benefits and, in overall effect, probably redistributes income from lower to higher income persons. I believe that it serves no essential social function. Existing commitments make it impossible to eliminate it overnight, but it should be unwound and terminated as soon as possible" (Cohen and Friedman, 1972).

There has been very little support for Friedman's rather extreme position. Instead, the more common negative view toward social security advocates a relatively minor role for it and, consequently, seeks to limit severely any future growth of the program—either by expansion of real benefits or by adding additional functions.

Robert J. Myers, chief actuary for the social security program between 1947 and 1971, labels advocates of a greater role for social security in aged income maintenance as "expansionists" and designates as "moderates" those persons who believe the program should not be expanded. Myers summarizes the moderate viewpoint as one that seeks a governmental program that would provide benefits "sufficient so that, with assets and real estate normally accumulated, the vast majority of beneficiaries will be able to have at least a reasonable subsistence."

Myers (1970) sees social security in the United States at a crossroad:

> It is impossible to predict with any exactitude whether there will be any changes in the relative role of the social security program in our society—and if so, specifically what the changes will be. If the philosophy of moderation largely prevails, the relative role of the social security program will not change significantly. Its provisions will be modified from time to time to keep it up to date and to solve such problems and anomalies as arise, especially those which are not being handled in a reasonably satisfactory manner by the private sector. On the other hand, if the expansionist philosophy prevails, the role of the social security program would be greatly enlarged.

Over the years concern about an expanded role for social security and rising social security benefits has not been the major issue raised by critics. Rather, most of the concern and criticism has centered on the way benefits have been financed. In Chapter 8, which is devoted exclusively to public and private pension financing, we discuss many of the issues connected with social security financing. In general, the program is criticized because of the heavy tax burden it places on the poor and near-poor and because of the very great differences in contributions paid in versus benefits received among different socioeconomic groups and between the current and future generations.

Criticism of social security, however, has been relatively limited in comparison to support voiced for it. On the positive side, three major arguments have been advanced in its favor:

1. That the nonbenefit costs of social insurance are much lower than the costs for *private pension* administration, fund investment, mobility, disclosure to recipients, supervision and regulation, and reinsurance.
2. That it is easier to make social security pensions both inflation proof—adjusting for inflation at and during retirement—and adjustable for economic growth.
3. That it is relatively easy to cover all workers and provide complete portability of credits under social security, whereas private pensions present formidable problems in this regard (unless mandated by the government).

*Costs* Although the structure of social security in the United States is far from being uncomplicated, there are many aspects of its operation that are relatively simple. Consequently, the collection and benefit payout process permits the extensive use of computers. This in turn permits the handling of large numbers of claims in a way that allows significant economies of large-scale operation to be realized. In fiscal year 1977, for example, administrative expenses were only 1.4 percent of OASI payroll contributions.

Comparing costs between social security and private pensions is complicated by the fact that social security financing in the United States is essentially on a pay-as-you-go basis, whereas private pensions are funded (see Chapter 8). Private pension funding costs generated as a result of financial investment on behalf of employers (and, in part, indirectly benefiting the economy) have no analogous counterpart in the United States social security program. Also, another difference between the two types of pensions is the fact that employers and the Internal Revenue Service give lots of "free" administrative services to the social security system.

Insurance companies, unions, corporations, and banks administer private pension plans. Although there has been no study of the costs of private pension plans compared to social security, it is hard to imagine that the current conglomeration of thousands of private plans, many covering less than a hundred workers, can have lower administrative costs. A study by Jerry Caswell (1974), for example, of a representative sample of multi-employer plans in the construction industry found that total administrative expenses averaged slightly less than 4 percent of current contributions and that significant economies of scale were associated with larger plans.

*Pension Adjustments for Inflation*    Another important argument made in favor of public pensions is their ability, in contrast to private plans, to deal with the need to respond to inflation and economic growth. The problem of inflation has plagued pension programs since their inception. All countries have had to struggle with this problem, continually adjusting pension programs and benefits to offset increases in price levels. Inflation has varied, for example, from the catastrophic rate in post–World War I Germany (which completely wiped out the monetary value of that country's social security reserves and benefits) to the relatively mild price increases averaging less than 2 percent in the United States during the 1958–68 period, to the more than 6 percent per year rate in the United States since 1968.

Gradually most industrialized countries (including the United States in 1972) have introduced some sort of automatic benefit adjustment mechanisms into the social security program to deal more effectively with the inflation problem. In contrast, private pension plans, with few exceptions, virtually ignore the need for regularized adjustment mechanisms. This results, in large part, because of employers' unwillingness to make financial commitments based on guesses about future price levels and the fear that the cost of these adjustments may be too high. In addition, most private pension analysts feel that it is virtually impossible to devise an acceptable inflation-proofing mechanism (see Munnell, 1979).

It is much easier for governments to deal with the inflation problem, given their inherent taxing powers and their ability to minimize the size of the monetary fund necessary to guarantee the financial soundness of the pension program. A pay-as-you-go system, for example, makes it easier to increase revenues to pay for inflation-adjusted wages because the earnings base is also rising with inflation. In contrast, many securities in a reserve fund will not adjust upward in value with the inflation.

The actual history of social security programs in various countries dealing with inflation supports that conclusion; even after runaway inflations, countries have been able to adjust pensions to the new price level. In addition, public pension programs have shown an ability to devise equitable ways of permitting retired persons to share systematically in the real economic growth of the country. Social security programs in some countries—such as Belgium, Canada, Norway, and West Germany—provide for automatic or semiautomatic adjustments in *real* benefit levels. Still others adjust benefits systematically by various ad hoc processes.

*Coverage*   It has proven to be a relatively easy matter in all countries to extend social security coverage to large segments of the labor force. Coverage of agricultural workers and the self-employed has presented problems—especially in developing countries—but, in general, extension of coverage all over the world has been quite comprehensive. In the United States, for example, coverage of the gainfully employed is now complete.

In contrast, as we discussed in the first part of the chapter, extension of private pension coverage presents serious problems. It has been especially difficult to extend coverage to workers in small firms. As a result, a sizable proportion of the work force in countries with private pensions may not be covered by such pensions.

One possible solution to the coverage problem is for the government to require that all employers provide private pension benefits. Some countries have done this. Great Britain, for example, is in the process of implementing such a requirement as a supplement to social security. British employers must privately provide pension protection equal to government minimums or contribute to a quasi-public funded pension scheme.

### Arguments in Support of Private Pensions

There are two major arguments supporting the existence and expansion of private pensions:

1. That social security—because of its broad coverage—must remain very uniform in its benefit provisions, while private pensions are flexible and can be tailored to meet differing situations and conditions (e.g., hazardous conditions) of various industries, particular firms, or different occupational groups.
2. That private pensions are vital to assure the saving necessary to provide sufficient investment in a growing economy.

*Flexibility*    On the one hand, a private pension can be a flexible management tool. As Charles A. Siegfried (1970) of the Metropolitan Life Insurance Company has observed, "a pension plan can be devised to attract and hold employees or it can be devised to facilitate the separation of employees from employment." On the other hand, pension objectives may vary to accommodate different employee wishes and aspirations, these being determined by decisions of the employers (unilaterally or in consultation with workers) or by collective bargaining.

The late Edwin S. Hewitt, a well-known pension consultant, arguing the case for private pensions before the U.S. Senate Special Committee on Aging, emphasized the flexibility factor:

> *It is extraordinary how flexible an instrument for providing adequate security the private plan has proved to be. There are two kinds of flexibility and perhaps this fact is underrated when we oppose what private plans are doing.*
>
> *First is their flexibility in terms of adapting to different needs. Very real differences in security problems exist among different companies, different industries, different age groups. . . .*
>
> *The second dimension is the flexibility between periods of time. Private plans have exhibited amazing flexibility to make their provisions meet the different needs that a group may have at different times.*
>
> *The initial job of most pension plans when first established is to concentrate on retirement income for the older worker, hence the importance of past service benefits.\* As plans become better funded, they tend to branch into other areas. Variety increases as plans are able to spend more money and give attention to tailormade benefits to meet specific needs. [Hewitt, 1970]*

*Pension Saving and Capital Formation*    A much more controversial argument made in favor of private pensions is their role in the mobilization of national saving for economic **investment.** Charles Moeller, an economist for the Metropolitan Life Insurance Company, has argued the positive aspects this way:

> *The key to any nation's economic growth is its ability to direct substantial portions of its output into real investment, i.e., to defer current consumption of output through saving and to permit investment in productive facilities for use in future production processes. . . . In effect, what pension funding operations and other forms of contractual saving do is to improve the efficiency and stability of the capital markets. . . .*
>
> *The importance of the saving function for private pension plans cannot be too strongly emphasized. The need for encouraging the accumulation of individual saving flows and for recirculating these funds back into the economy through the investment process has been spotlighted by the dramatic events of recent years including the "crunch" of 1966 and the "liquidity crisis" of 1970. [Moeller, 1972]*

---

\*Past service benefits are credits for years of work in the firm prior to the establishment of the pension plan. Most benefit formulas pay benefits that rise with years of service with the company.

While there is wide agreement that there is a need for saving in an economy, there are a variety of ways such saving can be accumulated and, hence, no agreement on the need or importance of any one accumulation process—such as through private pensions. In the key growth sector of *corporate* production, the overwhelming majority of funds needed to finance new investment comes from the *internal* funds saved by the corporations themselves. "If you subtract housing investment from total capital investment funds, more than 99 percent of real capital investment funds took the form of corporate **retained earnings** or **depreciation allowance** in 1973" (Thurow, 1976). Other possible sources of savings are unincorporated business, individuals, and government budget surpluses.

Moreover, there is disagreement over the extent to which there is any insufficiency of saving in the United States relative to investment opportunities and the willingness of business to undertake investment. Bosworth, Duesenberry, and Carron (1975), for example, predict no short-run shortages in their study *Capital Needs in the Seventies* (see also Bernstein, 1975). And economist Arthur Okun (1975) has observed that "the specter of depressed saving is not only empirically implausible but logically fake. . . . The nation can have the level of saving and investment it wants with more or less [income] redistribution, so long as it is willing to twist some other dials."

Currently there is also disagreement among economists about the impact of social security on personal savings. Feldstein (1975) and Munnell (1974) present statistical evidence that growing social security benefits have reduced total personal savings in the United States; Feldstein and Munnell disagree, however, on the magnitude of this effect. In contrast, Barro (1978) argues that evolving social security has changed the pattern of voluntary intergenerational transfers (from parents to children and vice versa). Barro presents statistical evidence (disputed by Feldstein) indicating that this changing pattern of family transfers offsets the savings impact of social security.

Finally, it should be noted that the generation of savings through pensions is not limited to private pensions. Public social security reserve funds can also be generated. For example, the financing rates for the social security program in Sweden have been deliberately set high enough to help the chronic shortage of savings in the Swedish economy. In fact, public pension reserves may be a particularly attractive means of mobilizing savings in developing countries where private pensions are virtually nonexistent.

## The Pension Mix in Various Countries

If we look at the pension programs currently existing in various industrialized countries, we find that there is a tendency to rely heavily either on public pensions or on some sort of private/public combination *with extensive regulation of the private sector.* In countries that rely heavily on private pensions, the tendency is for the private and public pension programs to be closely coordinated by a large number of complex legislative and administrative mechanisms and regulations. In France, for example, it is difficult to make a distinction between social security and the widespread private pension programs—given the elaborate coordinating mechanisms that have been established.

In the United States, both public and private pension plans have assumed a growing share of responsibility for providing retirement income needs. The indications are that this collective share will continue to grow. But it is not yet clear how that responsibility ultimately will be divided.

### Government Employee Pension Plans

Our discussion of pension plans would not be complete without mentioning one other category: federal, state, and local plans for government employees. These plans have many characteristics similar to the public and private plans discussed above but are unique in some respects.

Most civilians working for the federal government are covered by the civil service retirement pension program. In 1976 there were 4.5 million beneficiaries receiving about $2 billion in pension, survivor, and disability benefits under this program (Social Security Administration, 1978). Benefits are computed on the basis of length of service and the average of the highest three consecutive years of earnings. An automatic cost-of-living adjustment is made to this benefit.

Federal employee fringe benefits now comprise a third of the government's compensation payments (Marcou, 1978). The major item in this outlay is the payments for pensions. "Of all pension plans, probably none is better than the military's" (Aspin, 1976). This pension is based on the final year of service and is automatically adjusted for general price increases. About 10 percent of the defense budget currently goes to meet these pension obligations.

While federal civilian employees are not covered by social security, the relatively low number of quarters needed to qualify for social security in the past has encouraged them to seek dual coverage. Many federal employees work part time while employed by the government and/or retire (perhaps early) from government employment, take a new job to obtain social security eligibility, and eventually obtain a minimum (or better) social security benefit. In fact, the U.S. Joint Economic Committee estimated in 1973 that 40 percent of all civil service pensioners also received social security pensions (Storey, 1973).

The cost and inequity of providing social security benefits to federal pensioners has been condemned by many, and the Social Security Advisory Council has recommended mandatory social security coverage for all government employees.

State and local pension plans are similar in many ways to private employer plans. James A. Maxwell (1975) has summarized some of the differences: "Overall, the state and local government pension systems provide more generous benefits than do private systems. The normal retirement age and service requirements are more generous. . . . And they are more likely to have generous disability and survivor coverage. Most state and local government pensions are based on final average pay. . . . [Most] require employee contributions, whereas most private plans do not."

Tilove's recent study (1976) of state and local plans finds two other important differences between private and public employee plans. In a sharp reversal from previous studies, Tilove finds that vesting provisions in public plans have improved greatly and compare favorably with private plans. And while automatic postretirement benefit adjustments are almost nonexistent in private plans, they "are the most recent and most rapidly expanding changes among public systems." Currently a little over half of all state and local employees are covered by some sort of automatic adjustment mechanism when they retire.

Various amendments to the Social Security Act have permitted state and local governments to cover their employees by social security. Consequently, close to two-thirds of state and local employees are currently covered by both social security and a state or local pension plan. Again, for workers not covered by social security, dual coverage is often achieved by early retirement from state or local service followed by work for a nongovernment employer.

Benefits are typically very good under state and local plans; Tilove (1976) reports that in the future "many public employees will be retiring with more net income than while they were working." These high benefits have resulted in considerable concern about the rising costs of these benefits and the way state and local governments are planning (or, some would say, not planning) to finance them. It is to this question of pension financing that we now turn.

## Suggested Readings

American Council of Life Insurance. *Pension Facts*. Washington, D.C.: yearly.
    A good source of up-to-date statistics on both private and public plans. Also provided is a succinct summary of pension history and legislation and an excellent selected bibliography.
Ball, Robert M. "Social Security and Private Pension Plans." *National Tax Journal* (September 1974): 467–471.
    A former commissioner of Social Security argues that the role of social security should be increased but explains why he also feels that the role of private pensions will not diminish significantly in the near future.
Bernstein, Merton. *The Future of Private Pensions*. New York: The Free Press, 1964.
    Despite its date, this book is a useful introduction to the various aspects

of private pensions. Bernstein emphasizes the lack of portability and the inflation problems associated with private pensions and argues for the development of a workable portability mechanism.

Clark, Robert. *The Role of Private Pensions in Maintaining Living Standards in Retirement.* Washington, D.C.: National Planning Association, 1977.

Retirement income goals are discussed, and a brief review of private pension data is presented.

Esposito, Louis. "Effect of Social Security on Saving." *Social Security Bulletin* 41 (May 1978): 9–17.

An explanation for noneconomists of the relationship of social security to saving and capital formation. A variety of relevant data and recent research findings are summarized.

McGill, Dan M. *Fundamentals of Private Pensions.* 3rd ed. Homewood, Ill.: Irwin, 1975.

A comprehensive and authoritative book that traces the historical development and regulation of private pensions, explains plan design, reviews funding procedures, and discusses actuarial practices.

Schulz, James H. "Private Pensions and Women." In *Women in Midlife—Security and Fulfillment Part I*, a compendium of papers submitted to the U.S. House Select Committee on Aging, U.S. House of Representatives, 95th Congress, 2nd session. Washington, D.C.: U.S. Government Printing Office, 1979, pp. 205–221.

A discussion of coverage issues, vesting, and survivors' benefits.

Tilove, Robert. *Public Employee Pension Funds.* Twentieth Century Fund. New York: Columbia University Press, 1976.

A study of 129 of the largest state and local retirement systems, covering (in 1972) about 70 percent of all employees in such plans. In addition to simply surveying plan characteristics, Tilove presents a comprehensive and careful analysis of many important pension issues, including the relationship between social security and public employee plans.

U.S. Subcommittee on Retirement Income and Employment, House Select Committee on Aging. *National Pension Policies: Private Pension Plans.* Hearings. Washington, D.C.: U.S. Government Printing Office, 1978.

Testimony by government, academic, and business experts on the role and problems of private pensions.

# Chapter Eight

*Pension Financing: Who Pays?*
*Who Should Pay?*

In the article "The Young Pay for the Old," journalist Edwin L. Dale, Jr. (1973) wrote:

> *A funny thing happened to your taxes on the way to 1973. Congress passed the biggest federal increase since the Korean war (and that one was temporary), and hardly anybody peeped except a few intellectuals. This was happening at the time of the "taxpayers' revolt" at federal, state, and local levels. It was at the time when even George Wallace was appealing to a sense of frustration in the middle and lower middle classes, telling them the tax system was unfair. It was an election year. . . .*
>
> *Before anyone wonders whether he missed some important news development, or has been somehow bamboozled, it is best to explain the mystery. The paradox is resolved in two words: social security . . . a $7 billion tax increase enacted in 1972 with scarcely a voice of protest.* [*]

In 1977 Congress again found it necessary to schedule further increases in social security payroll taxes, and it is not yet clear what the long-term political reaction will be: "President Carter and Congress have a bear by the tail. Having decided . . . [in 1977] that the only way to rescue the social security system from bankruptcy was to raise an additional $227 billion in payroll taxes over the next ten years, they now have discovered—big surprise!—that this isn't very popular with the voters" (Rowan, 1978).

For the public, one of the most important aspects of pension policy is the way these programs are financed; yet until recently there has been little controversy over these matters. Few people realize the magnitude of

---

[*] © 1973 by the New York Times Company. Reprinted by permission.

the expenditures involved in pension programs and hence the huge amount of funds that must be raised through taxes, worker "contributions," and employer allocations for pension purposes. In 1976, $119.3 billion in pension benefits were paid to Americans (see Table 28). This amount, by way of comparison, was $30 billion *more* than national defense expenditures in the same year; about ten times the amount spent on "public assistance"; and almost equal to the consumer population's expenditures that year on automobiles, gasoline, and oil. And in order to meet *future* expenditure obligations, private pension funds currently have amassed over $213 billion in financial assets.

*Table 28.*   Pension Expenditures, 1976

| Type of Pension | Billions |
|---|---|
| OASI Benefits | $ 65.7 |
| Private Pension and Deferred Profit-Sharing Plan Benefits | $ 17.0[a] |
| Contributions Paid into Pension Reserves | $ 30.0[b] |
| Pension Reserves, Book Value | $212.6[b] |
| Federal Employee Pension Benefits | $ 16.5 |
| Veterans' Pensions and Compensation | $ 8.4 |
| State and Local Government Pension Plan Benefits | $ 8.1 |
| Railroad Retirement Benefits | $ 3.6 |
| Benefit Total | $119.3 |

Sources: *1978 Annual Report of the Board of Trustees of the Federal OASDI Trust Funds;* M. R. Yohalem, "Employee-Benefit Plans, 1975," *Social Security Bulletin* 40 (November 1977): Tables 5 and 6; "Benefits and Beneficiaries Under Public Employee Retirement Systems, Calendar Year 1976," *Research and Statistics Note* No. 8 (Washington, D.C.: Office of Research and Statistics, Social Security Administration).
[a]Estimated for 1976 by using data for 1974 and 1975.
[b]For year 1975.

In recent years, there has been a sharp increase in criticisms of pension financing techniques—especially those used for social security. Pension financing involves many complex issues, and, no doubt, part of the recent controversy arises because of the confusion and misunderstanding that generally prevail. Is the social security system bankrupt, as is frequently charged? Will younger workers get back less than they contribute to social security? Who pays for private pensions—the employer by tax-subsidized expense write-offs or the worker as a result of reduced take-home pay? Do public and private pension financing burdens fall disproportionately on the poor and treat racial minorities and women unfairly?

We will divide the discussion of pension financing into four broad aspects: (a) current social security financing practices and the role of pension plan reserves, (b) the equity of present practices, (c) a review of various proposed changes in social security financing, and (d) the financing of private and state/local government pensions.

### Financing Social Security

The OASDHI program is financed by a payroll tax that requires workers in covered employment (regardless of age) to pay a percentage of their earnings into the program and employers to pay an equivalent percentage based on their employees' earnings. In both cases the percentage paid is limited to the earnings of each employee up to a specified maximum. In the original legislation (and up to 1950) this maximum, called the *earnings base,* was $3,000. Between 1951 and 1972 the earnings base was increased periodically on an ad hoc basis. Then in 1972, legislation was passed that set the earnings base at $12,000 in 1974 and specified that the base was henceforth to rise *automatically* as average earnings rose. By 1976 the earnings base had reached $15,300.

The 1977 social security amendments scheduled increases in both payroll tax rates and the earnings base (see Table 29). Under the old law, taxes were scheduled to rise in steps from 5.85 to 7.45 percent by the year 2011. The new law does not raise tax rates above those already scheduled until 1979; but by 1990 the tax rates under the new law reach 7.65 percent—totaling 15.3 percent when both worker and employer payments are combined.*

*Table 29.* OASDHI Scheduled Changes in Payroll Tax Rates and Maximum Taxable Earnings

| Calendar Year | Tax Rate Worker and Employer, Each | Earnings Base |
|---|---|---|
| 1977 | 5.85 | $16,500 |
| 1978 | 6.05 | 17,700 |
| 1979 | 6.13 | 22,900 |
| 1980 | 6.13 | 25,900 |
| 1981 | 6.65 | 29,700 |
| 1982–1984 | 6.70 | —[a] |
| 1985 | 7.05 | —[a] |
| 1986–1989 | 7.15 | —[a] |
| 1990 and after | 7.65 | —[a] |

[a]Beginning in 1982 the amounts will be determined automatically under the law on the basis of the annual increase in average earnings in covered employment.

*Tax rates for the self-employed increase from 7.9 percent in 1977 to 10.75 percent in 1990. This lower tax rate was adopted for political reasons, to placate this group when it was initially covered (Myers, 1975a).

A more significant change specifies the level of the maximum taxable earnings base—reaching $29,700 in 1981. If the law had not been changed, it is estimated that the base in 1981 would have reached only $21,900 under the automatic adjustment provisions (Myers, 1978). Robert Myers, former Chief Actuary of the Social Security Administration, points out one important implication of the earnings base increase: "The higher earnings bases will generate higher benefits, albeit not proportionately so (because of the heavily weighted nature of the benefit formula).* Thus, from a benefit standpoint, less need will occur for protection from the private sector" (Myers, 1978).

Concerning reserves, J. Douglas Brown (1972) writes that "as originally enacted the old age insurance system would have accumulated in time a reserve of $47 billion, more than the outstanding debt of the government in 1935." But before any benefits were actually paid by the new pension program, Congress quickly revised the contribution rates, postponing scheduled increases in the payroll tax. This action set the pattern for future financing action, with tax rates being set below the rates that would be appropriate for a private pension or insurance plan.

Over the years there has been considerable controversy over whether adequate financing of social insurance programs requires the accumulation of large financial reserves. Much of the discussion has centered on the extent to which public insurance programs require financing practices conforming to the traditional tenets of actuarial soundness associated with private insurance.

The term *actuarial soundness* refers to the ability of insurance programs to provide sufficient (i.e., legally obligated) payments to eligible recipients at the time they come due. A private insurance company, for example, must necessarily operate on the basis that it will not sell any new policies in the future. Therefore, it should always have sufficient funds on hand to meet its obligations for existing policyholders, even if they all surrender their policies at once. Similarly, private pension plans generally try to maintain reserve funds sufficient to meet current contracted obligations but, at the same time, often amortize (i.e., pay over a period of years, usually ten or more) the cost of benefits provided for employee services rendered *before the pension plan began operation.*

There is now widely accepted agreement among pension specialists that social security programs do *not* require the accumulation of large amounts of reserves to be actuarially sound (see, for example, Myers, 1975a, Chapter 4). It is recognized that the taxing power of the government helps

*The benefit formula factor applicable to the *highest* amounts of covered earnings (15 percent) is only about half as large as the *average* factor applicable to persons at the higher earnings level (say, at about 150 percent of average earnings).

to guarantee the long-run financial integrity of such programs and that, unlike private insurance, it is appropriate to assume that the programs will operate indefinitely—with a consequent continuous flow of revenue. And perhaps more fundamentally, the fact that public insurance is usually compulsory and covers most of the population avoids the financing problems arising from a fluctuating number of participants.

This way of financing social security is known as the pay-as-you-go method. Benefits are paid to the current aged out of the payroll tax contributions of the current working population. In return, members of the working population know that they are promised benefits when they become eligible, financed out of the taxes of the future working population.

Thus, while OASDI reserves have increased in 32 out of 40 years (1937–1977), total reserves at the end of 1976 were equal to less than one year's disbursement (43 percent of 1977 benefits). Given this small reserve, some people have argued erroneously that social security is a bankrupt program that does not have the money to pay its obligations. Without necessarily characterizing the situation as bankruptcy, others have seriously questioned the financial soundness of the program. For example, an August 23, 1974, editorial in the *Wall Street Journal* argued in part:

> *And unless we are mistaken, the system is not financially sound in its present form.*
> *The one number that jars us, more than any other, is that as of June 30, 1973, the net unfunded liability of the system was $2.1 trillion. What this means is that current members of the system, working and retired, have been promised $2.1 trillion more—in constant dollars—than they will henceforth pay into the system.*

As we indicated above, the unfunded liability results in part from a decision by Congress not to operate a funded system (see Robertson, 1977). Part of the unfunded liability arises, however, from a related decision to grant significant pension benefits to persons reaching retirement age during the initial years of the program ("blanketing in"). To become eligible for social security benefits an individual must work a certain number of calendar quarters. Congress set the required quarters low for the older worker group, which resulted in their receiving benefits that far exceeded their few years of contributions.

*Thus, ever since the social security system began, most retirees have received more benefits than they have paid in.* New groups that were covered in the fifties and sixties also were granted these "windfall gains." And with liberalizations in the benefit structure, most retirees will also experience these gains—and for many years to come.

This policy—*not* to exclude persons with relatively few years of participation in the program and *not* to make them "pay their way"—has been financed on a pay-as-you-go basis out of the rising earnings of the working population with only modest increases in taxes. But it has also added to the "unfunded" liabilities of the social security program.

In answer to critics of these nonfunding practices, five former secretaries of the Department of Health, Education, and Welfare and three former Social Security commissioners issued on February 10, 1975, a statement emphasizing why the government need not amass vast reserves to keep social security financially sound. In part, they argued:

> By earmarking the proceeds of social security taxes for the payment of benefits and depositing them in a trust fund for this purpose, by entitling the system insurance, by continuing actions to assure its financial soundness, and by innumerable pronouncements of congressional committees and individual spokesmen, Congress has made clear beyond question its pledge to the American people that the social security commitment will be honored. [Ad Hoc Advisory Committee, 1975]

Thus, we see that the main argument for nonfunding rests on the quality of the promise made by the government. To fulfill this promise requires that social security planning ensure that over the long run the flow of funds remains in a "satisfactory actuarial status." But what constitutes satisfactory actuarial status? A recent Panel on Social Security Financing—composed of economists and actuaries—argued that this means being able to predict with reasonable confidence (a) that future scheduled income and future scheduled outgo will be in harmony and (b) that future scheduled taxes required to support the program be within the limits of practical acceptability to the population paying the social security tax (U.S. Senate Committee on Finance, 1975).

Actuarial projections of future benefits and taxes are made annually by the Social Security Administration's Office of the Actuary. The projections and a general assessment of financial status are submitted in a report by the Social Security Board of Trustees to Congress each year. Up until recently there had been little concern expressed in these reports about any long-term financing problem. In the 1974 report, however, the actuarial projection forecast a significant actuarial deficit over the 75-year period 1974–2048. This projected deficit, higher than any previously forecasted, *was almost doubled one year later* when the trustees issued their 1975 report!

This long-term financing problem was caused by four major factors: (a) the post–World War II "baby boom," (b) the dramatic decline in recent years of the birthrate, (c) expanding pension expenditures arising from the automatic cost-of-living adjustment mechanism legislated in 1972, and (d) high disability rates.

Figure 21 shows the number of births, deaths, and immigrations during the 1930 to 1976 period. The steady rise in births after World War II (reaching a peak in 1957 at 4.3 million) will cause a rise in the retirement age population relative to the working age population. This will occur around the year 2010, when this baby boom population begins reaching old age. The drop in births in recent years causes the rise in the ratio to be even sharper, since the falling number of births reduces the number of persons who will be in the working population.

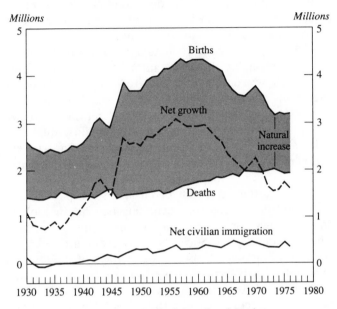

*Figure 21.    Annual Levels of Births,*
*Deaths, Net Immigration, Net Growth, 1930–1976*

Source: U.S. Bureau of the Census, "Estimates of the Population of the United States and Components of Change: 1940 to 1976," *Current Population Reports,* Series P–25, No. 706 (Washington, D.C.: U.S. Government Printing Office, 1977), Figure 1.

Another reason why actuarial deficits were projected to increase relates to the particular way the 1972 legislation specified that pension benefits were to be automatically adjusted for inflation. Soon after this change, various pension analysts demonstrated that the particular inflation adjustment mechanism used had the unintended effect of increasing the replacement rates of benefits for workers retiring in future years. The greater the rate of inflation, the greater the increase in real benefits, and hence the greater the future financial burden on social security.*

---

*We do not present the relatively technical explanation for this result. Interested readers should see the monograph by Lawrence Thompson listed in the Suggested Readings at the end of this chapter.

When the 1972 legislation was passed, much lower inflation rates were anticipated than those of subsequent years, and it is clear that Congress did not fully understand the extreme sensitivity of the mechanism they adopted to general economic conditions. By the time the Advisory Council on Social Security met in 1974, this adjustment problem was recognized, and it became the central issue of the discussion. The council recommended that the adjustment mechanism be changed so that automatic increases in replacement rates would not occur in the future.

The 1977 social security amendments revised the method of calculating benefits—changing the 1972 automatic adjustment methods. The new benefit formula was designed by Congress so that replacement rates for further generations of retiring workers will be stabilized at various relative earnings levels. Thus, single "average workers" retiring currently (but also in the future years) will receive social security benefits equal to about one-third of their earnings just prior to retirement.* The financial effect of this new calculation method is to reduce the long-run projected deficits of OASDI by half.

One can see the net result of changing the payroll tax rates, the earnings base, and the method of calculating benefits by looking at future OASDI dollar inflows and outgoes. To facilitate the presentation of projected financial estimates, the Social Security Administration expresses social security expenditures in terms of a percentage of the total income subject to the social security tax—that is, as a percentage of taxable payroll. "This procedure avoids the difficulties created by the changing value of the dollar and allows a direct comparison to be made between projected expenditures and the tax rates scheduled in the law" (Robertson, 1978).

Figure 22 shows projected OASDI expenditures through the year 2052. The tax rates rise in steps in accordance with the scheduled increases shown in Table 29. Expenditures rise in dollar amounts but decline as a percentage of taxable payroll during the 1979–1981 period (reflecting the rise in the taxable earnings base). Expenditures then rise slowly until the early part of the next century. As the post–World War II baby boom population reaches retirement age, costs as a percent of payroll rise sharply. Shortly after 2010, expenditures are projected to exceed payroll taxes, indicating a need for additional revenues (Robertson, 1978).

Estimating costs so far into the future is difficult, however. Future costs and revenues depend on a large number of uncertain factors (fertility and mortality rates, labor force participation trends, migration, economic growth rates, and retirement patterns). We cannot know with certainty how

---

*We discuss the appropriate way to measure social security replacement rates in Chapter 9. Under the 1977 amendments, replacement rates were actually reduced by about 5–7 percent (restoring them to the levels in effect when indexing was first legislated in 1972).

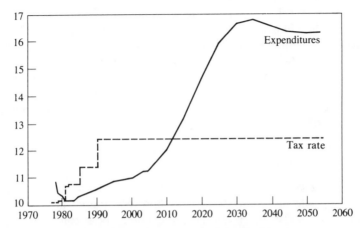

*Figure 22.    Comparison of the Projected
Expenditures and Scheduled Tax Rates of the
Old-Age, Survivors, and Disability Insurance System,
1978–2052 (as Percent of Taxable Payroll)*

Source: Actuarial Study No. 78, *Long-Range Cost Estimates for Old-Age, Survivors, and Disability Insurance System, 1978,* Social Security Administration, June 1978, HEW Publication No. (SSA) 78–11524.

these factors will change over the next fifty years. At present, however, most trends point to no major social security financing problems in the near future but to sharply rising costs early in the next century.

Thus, there is no doubt that the costs of social security will continue to rise over time and that the government is faced with the problem of finding the best means of raising the additional funds. Of course, one way of dealing with the problem would be to reduce benefit levels and/or to raise the eligibility age for beginning to receive benefits.* It is not very likely that future advisory groups will propose a general reduction in social security benefits, but the 1974 Advisory Council on Social Security did recommend that future consideration be given to increasing the social security eligibility age.

Neither of these actions appears likely—not only because of past promises made and the political and moral issues they raise, but also because of the general low level of current benefits; for large numbers of older persons benefit levels fail to meet their rising expectations about "adequate" income in retirement.

A related change *is* likely to take place, however. The current discrimination against older workers and the various encouragements for their

---

*It is also technically possible to *raise* (rather than *reduce*) benefit levels but at a rate that would result in a decline in the pension/earnings ratio (i.e., the replacement rate).

early retirement will probably be moderated. This change in manpower attitudes has already occurred in Europe. Many European countries have experienced a "demographic bulge" problem similar to the one facing the United States. Their bulge is primarily a result of the high loss of young males during World War II. Consequently, these countries have had to impose much higher tax rates but also have had generally more liberal policies to encourage workers to remain in the labor force. The United States is likely eventually to develop similar policies.

### Financing Equity

Rising costs of social security now and in the future increase the importance of developing financing methods considered fair by the population. Our first question in assessing the equity of social security is: Who pays? In the United States, the size of the payroll tax exceeds all other federal, state, and local types of taxes except the federal income tax. Thus, it is important to look at who pays the tax and the relationship between those taxes paid and the benefits ultimately received.

*Who Pays?* Determining "tax incidence" or who ultimately bears the burden of any tax is one of the most complex issues in economics. Although the general population thinks it knows who pays taxes, economists disagree—especially about who actually bears the corporate income tax, sales taxes, and the property tax. Until recently, the payroll tax had received little attention from economists. Most people have assumed the worker bears the burden of *his* payroll contribution, but there has been great disagreement over the employer payments. A variety of recent economic studies indicate that most of the employer tax is ultimately paid by the worker in the form of wages that are lower than what they otherwise would have been (or, to a smaller extent, by consumers in the form of higher prices). In the most thorough study of the question to date, economist John A. Brittain's findings indicate that the worker generally bears all the tax. He found that given the level of productivity, the higher the employer payroll tax rate the lower the basic real wage—the wage rate being lower by the same amount as the payroll tax increase (Brittain, 1972). Not all economists, however, agree with the Brittain findings (see Feldstein, 1972, and Leuthold, 1975).

The payroll tax has been criticized as unfair by numerous people. There have been three major criticisms: (a) that the tax is regressive and a heavy burden on the poor, (b) that the tax is unfair to certain groups of beneficiaries, given the benefits they are likely to receive, and (c) that younger workers who are now paying taxes (and those who will pay in the future) are likely to get an unfair deal. We will examine each of these criticisms in turn.

First is the issue of a regressive tax structure and its impact on the poor. In general a regressive tax is one where the amount of tax paid is a *declining* proportion of income as incomes *increase*. Since the payroll tax is levied only on the "earnings base" and not on earnings above the maximum earnings ceiling, the tax is partly regressive. The proportion that contributions represent of total earnings falls *for earnings levels above the ceiling*.

During the fifties and sixties the maximum ceiling was low relative to average earnings. The proportion of total earnings in covered employment subject to the payroll tax fell from more than 90 percent during the early years of the program to a low of 71 percent in 1965. Thus, for example, in 1972, when the earnings base was $9,000, about one-quarter of the workers paying social security taxes had earnings that exceeded the maximum. With the significant increase and indexing of the earnings ceiling that began in 1973, the proportion of total earnings in covered employment had risen to 85 percent in 1977. Under the 1977 amendments, about 91 percent of total earnings will be subject to the tax after 1980.

What concerns many critics, however, is not the burden on workers with earnings near or above the maximum, but, rather, the taxes paid by low wage earners. On October 4, 1972, a group of economists at the prestigious Brookings Institution wrote to the *Washington Post* to protest the payroll tax:

> The rise of the payroll tax has been a quiet drain on low- and middle-income Americans. For the middle-income workers, payroll tax increases have more than offset the much vaunted reductions of personal income taxes of 1964, 1969, and 1971. . . .
>
> For low-income workers earning $3,000, payroll tax increases have exceeded personal tax cuts. A worker with two or more dependents who is employed year round at the minimum wage is spared personal income tax because of his poverty, but he will pay $176 in payroll taxes himself in 1973 under present law; his employer also pays $176. . . . [Aaron et al., 1972]

Why should people with poverty-level incomes have to pay any taxes—including social security? The principal answer given by supporters of the current payroll tax is that the benefit structure of the program is heavily weighted in favor of low earners and that tampering with the tax structure threatens to turn the program into a welfare program—thereby undermining its general political acceptability. J. Douglas Brown (1973) in a memorandum sent to the U.S. Senate Special Committee on Aging gives some additional arguments:

> Overall, the advantages of uniform proportionate contributions toward one's social insurance protection are of great psychological, social and political importance. They clearly differentiate benefits as a matter of right from those available only on individual proof of need. They reflect a natural desire for self-reliance. They refute a criticism of dependency. They also are a factor in avoiding a class-conscious society in which some classes give and some classes get. Propor-

*tionate contributions are a force for political restraint in the evolution of a total system, both in respect to excessive demands for liberality in the benefit structure and the condoning of abuses in unwarranted payments.*

As the costs of social security rise and the burdens on low earners also rise, however, the pressures for reform will no doubt increase, despite the strong historical resistance to changing the taxing structure. We will discuss a number of reform proposals in a section to follow, but first let us examine the other two major equity issues raised at the beginning of this section.

*Intergenerational Equity*   From time to time people argue, and sometimes present calculations to show, that payments to social security by new entrants into the labor force will be much greater than the retirement benefits they can expect to receive subsequently. Such calculations almost always assume that currently legislated contribution rates and benefit levels will remain unchanged in the future, which is an unrealistic assumption.

A better way to investigate this question is to calculate **lifetime rates of return.** This method mathematically determines the rate of interest or rate of return implicitly earned on payroll tax contributions paid over a worker's lifetime. It is done by comparing the taxes paid (plus an imputed interest rate on them) to the benefits received during the entire retirement period. John Brittain, using 1966 tax and benefit levels, estimated projected yields for hypothetical *average* earners that ranged from about 3 to 6 percent, depending on assumptions with regard to economic growth, birth/mortality rates, the interest rate, and the age when entering the work force. Brittain (1972) concluded that "if the model and the official demographic projections are fairly realistic, new contributors will in the aggregate get neither a very good 'buy' nor a very bad one, but they will fare moderately well." Another study by Chen and Chu of 1974 retirees and entrants calculates similar lifetime rates of return. The rates for 1974 hypothetical retirees ranged from 6 to almost 17 percent. Entrants into the labor force in 1974 were estimated to have much lower rates of return, between 1 and 8 percent (Chen and Chu, 1974).

Both the Brittain and Chen/Chu studies calculate measures of individual equity for *hypothetical* case histories that are thought to be representative of the lifetime experience of various individuals. In contrast, Freiden, Leimer, and Hoffman (1976) calculate measures of individual equity for a sample of *actual* case histories. Using data from Social Security Administration records, they calculate rates of return for a sample of workers retiring between the years 1967 and 1970. Again, relatively large positive rates of return were found, with higher rates for those with histories of lower earnings.

The data Freiden et al. used, however, did not permit them to analyze the differences in mortality that exist between people with different ethnic backgrounds, educational attainment, and/or marital status. In another study, therefore, Leimer (1979) has investigated differences in rates of return for groups of workers with different characteristics. Specifically, Leimer examines the validity of the arguments made by some critics of social security that the disadvantaged (nonwhites, low earners, and women) get a poorer deal from social security (see, for example, Friedman, 1972, and Aaron, 1977). Leimer uses the hypothetical worker approach; projected earnings streams for representative workers are based on cross-sectional age–earnings profiles derived from the 1973 Current Population Survey. Leimer's investigation suggests that in the future nonwhites, low earners, and women will generally fare better than their counterparts.

Prior hypothetical worker studies in this area have all found that entrants to the labor force at early ages have lower rates of return from social security because they contribute payroll taxes over a longer work life. Since going to college may delay entry into the labor force and result in higher lifetime earnings, most researchers have concluded that the actual impact of delayed entry into the labor force is very important. Leimer, however, analyzes data showing that workers with high ultimate education attainment have substantial earnings *during* the education period. This offsetting factor tends to reduce the importance of the delayed entry factor in actual case histories.

Thus we see that, just as in the case of who pays the payroll tax, determining the relative cost–benefit equity of social security is extremely difficult. The wide range of rates of return estimated by various researchers demonstrates the difficulty of giving an unequivocal answer to the question of whether social security is a "good buy"; results are highly sensitive to the assumptions made in the analysis. Also, these studies fail to include in the analysis the federal and state income tax treatment of social security contributions and benefits.

Finally, Brittain (1972) has raised the question: "Why should one ask whether a person ultimately recoups in benefits the equivalent of his taxes when the same question is rarely asked about other taxes? ... Since the taxes and later benefits assigned to a person are not at all closely related, as they are under private insurance, a strong case can be made for a completely separate analysis and evaluation of the tax and benefit structures on their own merits." While many would agree with this point of view, others see social security taxes differently—as special earmarked taxes associated with a *compulsory* pension program, which necessitates analysis of who pays and who should pay.

Examination of the various findings, however, does help focus attention on possible differences between various population groups. Brittain, for example, notes that the wide spread in the rates of return indicates substantial income redistribution among categories of participants. For example, the college graduate who starts work at 22 fares much better than the high school graduate who starts work at 18 if both earn the same average earnings over their respective work lives. Their social security benefits will be very similar, but the college graduate, entering the work force later, will pay less total payroll taxes over his career. Leimer, however, cautions against giving too much weight to such hypothetical findings when evidence indicates that there are more offsetting factors in real life experiences.

*Women and Social Security Financing*     Certain specific groups have been singled out for attention by some critics of social security. The treatment of women has recently come under careful scrutiny.\* In the financing area the most controversial issue has been the differential treatment of working and nonworking women. Currently, a spouse is entitled to a benefit equal to 50 percent of the working partner's pension—regardless of whether or not the spouse participates in the social security program. A spouse who works, however, may become eligible for a regular benefit on the basis of that work. In effect, the law stipulates that such a person can get only one benefit—50 percent of the spouse's pension or his or her own pension, whichever is larger.

An issue arising from this treatment of working spouses is the low rate of return on contributions of the spouse. A working wife may pay social security taxes toward retirement protection, but the resulting benefits of the family may be *no higher* if the spouse doesn't work a sufficient number of quarters to achieve eligibility. Moreover, because of anomalies in the benefit structure, a couple composed of two retired workers can receive lower total benefits than a couple with the same average lifetime earnings credits all earned by one spouse. For example, the annual 1979 benefit for a couple composed of two retired workers who each had average indexed earnings of $6,000 would be $3,173 each. In contrast, the benefit of a couple with one $12,000 earner would be $7,640—nearly $1,300 more annually than the two-earner couple (HEW Task Force, 1978).

Although a working woman's retirement benefits may be little more or no more than a nonworking spouse's, she does receive certain protection under social security not available to a nonworking wife:

1. Disability protection.
2. Benefits payable at or after age 62, even if her husband continues to work.
3. Monthly benefits to her children if she becomes disabled or dies.

As we discussed in Chapter 6, the economic role of women has been shifting over time (see also Kahne, 1975). As a result, a number of social

\*See, for example, the report of the Task Force on Women and Social Security listed in the Suggested Readings at the end of this chapter.

security reform bills have been introduced in Congress over the years to deal with the working woman issue. Thus far, no legislation has been seriously considered. This and other matters, such as whether to have social security benefits for housewives, are likely to be hotly debated in the years to come. When the Advisory Council on Social Security (1975) recommended no major action in this area, Rita Campbell gave a dissenting opinion:

> It is my belief that because of the continuing trends in the increasing labor force participation rate of women, the declining labor force participation rate of men, the increase in divorce and decrease in marriages, and the decline in the birth rate, it is advisable to begin now to restructure the social security system to adapt to these socioeconomic changes rather than wait for dissatisfaction with the system to so increase as to force hurried changes which may be undesirable.

### Differential Life Expectancies

Another issue that has been raised in relation to women, and also by various ethnic minority groups, is the extent to which differences in average **life expectancy** should be taken into account. Women, *on average,* tend to live longer than men; nonwhites, *on average,* have shorter life expectancies than whites. For benefit purposes, social security policy has largely ignored these or any other differences in life expectancies. Some private pensions, however, *have* paid differential pension benefits based on sex, causing certain women's organizations to challenge in the courts such differentials in benefits.

In contrast, some nonwhites argue that they *should* receive preferential social security benefits because of adverse life expectancy rates. For example, the 1971 White House Conference on Aging "special concerns session" on aged blacks recommended: "The minimum age-eligibility requirement for primary beneficiaries of Old Age, Survivors, Disability, and Health Insurance (OASDHI under social security) should be reduced by 8 years for black males so as to erase existing racial inequities."

The average life expectancy *at birth* is different for whites versus nonwhites, in large part because of higher infant mortality rates for nonwhites, but differences in life expectancies at other ages are not nearly as great. At age 65, for example, there are almost no differences for men.

Ubadigbo Okonkwo has investigated "Intragenerational Equity Under Social Security" for subgroups of the United States population differentiated by race, marital status, education, and region of residence. Calculating "internal rates of return" by race, Okonkwo finds that returns are higher for all groups of nonwhite workers except nonwhite couples with 16 or more years of schooling. The highly favorable mortality experience of white female college graduates results in a more favorable internal rate of return for these couples.

Okonkwo (1975) concludes: "In general, the progressivity of the social security benefit structure tended to redistribute lifetime earnings in favor of subgroups with low earnings, exemplified by nonwhites and workers with relatively few years of schooling. However, this redistributive effect was weakened, but not reversed, by the relatively smaller probabilities of survival experienced by these subgroups." These findings are similar to those of Leimer, discussed earlier.

Viscusi and Zeckhauser (1976) in their book *Welfare of the Elderly* argue against public pension differentials based on life expectancy. They cite the widespread resentment that would probably be generated by an explicit set of different eligibility criteria or benefit levels. And they point out the administrative and practical difficulties in taking account of all differentials— smokers versus nonsmokers, drivers of safer cars, persons in occupations or industries with environmental settings that may affect health. Finally, they argue that these differentials are not as important as equalizing benefits per unit of need. "Once we accept the notion that the principal focus of Social Security should be on equalizing income for the periods one is alive, the need to adjust for differing lengths of lifetimes is not only unnecessary, but is also detrimental to this more fundamental objective."

### Reform Proposals

Numerous proposals for changing the financing of social security have been put forth. This section will look at only three approaches: (a) the Buchanan proposal to change social security radically, (b) general revenue financing, and (c) changing the payroll tax structure.

*The Buchanan Proposal*  Economists James Buchanan and Colin Campbell have written about the inequities they see arising from the social security system. In an article published in the *Wall Street Journal* they proposed that a new system of financing be devised that would, in effect, finance the "windfall gains benefits" of current and future social security recipients out of general revenue.*  Once this is done, they recommend that the payroll tax be set at a rate that would make it actuarially certain that the amount people paid into the program would equal, on average, the amount that is paid out to them.

In a later article Buchanan amplified the original proposal, calling for a radical change in the social security structure. The purpose of the pro-

---

*We discuss in the next section of this chapter the matter of windfall gains and the issue of general revenue financing.

posed new program is "to embody the advantages of an intergenerational tax transfer program while at the same time incorporating most of the desirable features of a genuine insurance program" (Buchanan, 1968).

Buchanan refers to the advantages of an intergenerational tax transfer program. As originally described by economist Paul Samuelson (1958), there can be a "subsidy" in public social security programs that moves from one generation to the next as a result of population growth and economic growth. Buchanan seeks to establish a social security program that would embody that subsidy advantage but, at the same time, be more consistent with private insurance principles in terms of a *guaranteed* pension payoff based on law.

Buchanan proposes that the present payroll tax be repealed. In its place, individuals would be required to purchase "social insurance bonds." The pension benefits paid out at any particular time would be financed from revenues (purchases) of bonds sold during the same period.

Thus, when someone bought a bond for retirement, the purchase money would be immediately transferred to people who were currently retired. This would resemble the current practice of taking social security contributions and immediately paying them out to current social security pension recipients. If these bond revenues were insufficient to meet current benefit obligations, Buchanan proposes that general revenue financing be used to pay for the balance of benefits due. In this way, he argues, current bond purchasers would not be paying for the results of blanketing in certain groups (see page 153) or for higher individual benefits that are not based on prior contributions.

If they wanted to, individuals would be allowed to buy more bonds than the compulsory amount. *In either case, however, individuals would be able to buy bonds from either private companies or government.* When the individual turns 65, the bonds mature, and he can then convert them into an annuity.

As far as the government bonds are concerned, Buchanan proposes that the return on them be the higher of either of the following: the interest rate on long-term U.S. Treasury bonds or the rate of growth of the nation's total economic output (gross national product). Thus, the private bonds—in order to compete—would have to promise (with a fair degree of certainty) a rate of return either better than the interest rate on long-term government bonds (if one didn't expect any growth in the economy) or equal to the rate of general economic growth.

Thus, Buchanan accepts the need for compulsory pension programs. He also agrees that there need not be reserve funding—accepting the validity of a nonfunded, pay-as-you-go government program. But he seeks to prevent inequities that occur as a result of combining benefits based on limited contributions ("blanketing-in" coverage and retroactive benefits) with benefits based strictly on contributions paid over a lifetime.

Buchanan tries to incorporate into the system an adjustment procedure that guarantees that the individual in the social security system will benefit from the general growth of the economy. Adjusting the bonds at the same rate as the changing gross national product also takes care of the problem of inflation, for this procedure will automatically adjust for general price increases in the economy. Thus, one would have both a price adjustment and a real growth adjustment factor built into the social security system.

Buchanan argues that such a program would have much wider acceptability than the current system because of its "individualization." The current system, he argues, is politically acceptable because people think of themselves as paying contributions to it and getting back benefits when they retire based upon *their* contributions. It is not a welfare system; it is a system of forced savings in the minds of most people. But Buchanan is worried that increasingly people will find this rationale unacceptable—given the current divergence between individuals' contributions and the amount paid back. He argues that future generations will be less and less certain that they're going to get their money's worth; they may lose faith in the system. The advantage of Buchanan's plan is that the individual gets his own piece of paper with a guaranteed rate of return. He argues that this is a much stronger guarantee than the *implicit* promise of benefits to be paid inherent in the current system.

Buchanan argues that his proposed program also insulates social security from political interference and from *excessive and inequitable* spending on the part of Congress. Congress would not be able to manipulate the system so easily, taking some from one population group and giving more to other groups. Instead, a straight one-to-one relationship would exist on an individual basis—just as in private insurance.

Some critics of the Buchanan proposal argue, however, that it is very important for a government pension program to be able to redistribute income. Indeed, many people think that it is quite justifiable to redistribute income through a social security program.

A more fundamental concern is that the proposal calls for a radical change. The current program has strong support both from a broad segment of the population and within Congress. It is questionable whether the Buchanan proposal would have any chance of acceptance because it is so completely different and does not build on what we have at present. The tendency is for legislation to develop incrementally, and major changes that are proposed still have to embody in some way prior legislation.

Apart from the political feasibility of such a major change, it is questionable whether the resulting gains obtained in equity are worth the great cost. There are major developmental, administrative, and information costs associated with a radical shift to a completely new program that has no established consumer acceptability or understanding.*

*General Revenue Financing*    Other people concerned about the financing of social security have also recommended the introduction of general government revenues to help support the costs. Like Buchanan, many of them see the blanketing in of large groups of persons during the initial years as a burden that need not be financed by the payroll tax. Unlike Buchanan, however, most people call for general revenue financing without abandoning the basic structure of the current social security system.

General revenue financing was first suggested by the Committee on Economic Security, a presidential committee whose recommendations formed the basis of the original Social Security Act. The idea was also supported by the first Advisory Council on Social Security in 1937–38 and the one in 1947. Later advisory councils, however, did not see an immediate need for this additional source of financing or opposed general revenue financing as destructive of the insurance principles embodied in the program.

In 1944 Congress (over presidential veto) froze the payroll tax and authorized an appropriation from general revenue to the trust fund for "such additional sums as may be required to finance the benefits and payment under this title." Rather than representing an enthusiastic endorsement by Congress of the concept of general revenue financing, this action was really a by-product of the division in Congress over when and how large social security reserves should grow. Ignoring the 1947 Advisory Council on Social Security's recommendation for a "government contribution," both the House Committee on Ways and Means and the Senate Finance Committee in 1950 stated that the system "should be on a completely self-supporting basis," and Congress in that year repealed the general revenue provision.

Many who agree with the idea of general revenue financing favor restricting these payments to help meet the costs of "windfall benefits" (i.e., those given without contributions equal to the actuarial value of these benefits). In a working paper prepared for the U.S. Senate Special Committee on Aging, Nelson H. Cruikshank, as president of the National Council of Senior Citizens, presented such a proposal:

> *Workers already close to retirement age when the [social security] system was first started, or when coverage was extended to their employment, received full benefits even though the contributions they and their employers paid would finance only a small part of the benefit. While this was sound public policy and kept many old people off relief, it did mean that these benefits had to be financed from future contributions. There is no justification for expecting presently covered workers to pay for this "accrued liability"—estimated in the long run to*

---

*See Browning (1973) for a discussion of income distribution problems associated with the Buchanan plan and a proposed alternative.

*amount to one-third of the total cost of the program—through a regressive payroll tax. A far fairer method would be to finance this share from general revenue sources to which all taxpayers contribute and through a more progressive tax structure. [U.S. Senate Special Committee on Aging, 1970]*

During the debates leading up to the 1977 social security amendments, President Carter proposed an alternative mechanism: to limit general revenue contributions to the amount of social security revenues lost as a result of an unemployment rate in excess of 6 percent. When workers lose their jobs they (and their employers) do not pay payroll taxes on their behalf, causing a shortfall in projected revenues. Through this proposed mechanism, general revenue financing would not be open-ended but would be used only when economic activity falls significantly short of full employment levels. The proposal was not accepted by the Congress, however, when they considered the 1977 amendments.

A variety of arguments have been raised against general revenue financing. The major ones are:

1. That it would encourage excessive increases in benefits.
2. That it tends to integrate social security into the annual budget review process and to make social security more "political."
3. That it is contrary to the insurance and contributory principles of the program, which promote the political acceptability of social security.
4. That it would turn social security into a welfare program, with an associated congressional and public decline in support.

*Changing the Payroll Tax Structure*   A variety of proposals have been made to change the payroll tax. The principal approach is to make the payroll tax rate progressive. One method is to provide individual lump-sum exemptions to the tax in the same way as exists in the current income tax law. The late union leader Walter Reuther, for example, proposed in 1967 a $600 exemption per earner. Other proposals would allow exemptions for dependents, and some propose a "standard deduction" amount equal to that in the federal income tax law.

Alternatively, it has been proposed that the payroll tax be integrated with the income tax. The present tax withholdings for both social security and income taxes would continue, but at the end of the year the total amounts collected would be added together and applied to satisfy the individual or couple's income tax liability. An excess of taxes over liability would be the basis for a tax refund. To accomplish this would require higher taxes.

Arguments against the above two proposals are similar to those against general revenue financing, but another type of reform proposal actually became law in 1975.

The 1975 Tax Act contained a one-year provision known as the "earned income credit" or "work bonus" for low income workers *with children*. Under this provision, an eligible individual was allowed a tax credit equal to 10 percent of earned income up to $4,000 a year (a rough approximation of his or her combined payroll tax). The tax credit was reduced (till it reached zero at income levels of $8,000) by 10 percent of "adjusted gross income" (or, if greater, the earned income) that exceeded $4,000 per year.

The major justification for the amendment was to remove the work-disincentive effect of social security taxes on low income workers. In 1975 this credit offset most of the total payroll taxes paid on earnings of $4,000 or less.

Again, some of the opposition to the work bonus amendment was based on its welfare character. Senator Sam J. Ervin, for example, charged in one floor debate over the credit that "it is robbery to take social security money and use it for welfare purposes." In addition, the Nixon Administration came out against an early version of the work bonus, arguing that the provision would create serious administrative problems and that it would complicate the development of sound income maintenance policy by "adding yet another program to the many present assistance programs." The Ford Administration, using similar arguments, also argued against the provision.

Despite this initial opposition, the earned income credit has been continuously renewed in all subsequent tax legislation. In fact, the 1978 tax "reform" law extended its application to the first $10,000 of earnings. However, the provision has still not been extended to workers without children, a liberalization recommended by many.

*A Value-Added Tax?*  In 1979, both the chairman of the House Committee on Ways and Means (Al Ullman) and of the Senate Finance Committee (Russell Long) endorsed a value-added tax to supplement social security financing. A value-added tax is similar to an excise or sales tax but levied on manufactured goods *at various stages* of the manufacturing process. While arguing that payroll taxes should remain the principal source of social security revenue, Ullman stated that a value-added tax could facilitate movement to a more simplified system of business taxation and, at the same time, ease the burden of the payroll tax.

Barber Conable, ranking Republican on Ways and Means, immediately countered that a value-added tax is "every bit as bad as putting general Treasury money into social security, because it destroys the insurance character of the system" (BNA, 1979b). And Senate Banking Committee Chairman William Proxmire argued that such a tax would be regressive, inflationary, and hidden.

### Financing State and Local and Private Pensions

No less important are the financing issues associated with other types of pension plans. Whereas social security in the United States operates without accumulating any significant reserves, we find that the reserves of other pension plans have increased dramatically in the past few decades (see Table 30). The federal civil service retirement system is the major exception—being financed, like social security, primarily on the pay-as-you-go principle. Let us first look at private pensions and then the state and local government plans.

*Table 30.* Pension Plan Assets, 1960–1976 (in Billions of Dollars)

| Type | 1960 | 1965 | 1970 | 1973 | 1976 |
|------|------|------|------|------|------|
| Private | 51.9 | 86.5 | 138.2 | 179.0 | 248.8 |
| Insured | 18.8 | 27.3 | 41.2 | 54.6 | 88.4 |
| Noninsured | 33.1 | 59.2 | 97.0 | 124.4 | 160.4 |
| State and Local | 19.6 | 33.1 | 58.0 | 80.2 | 117.2 |

Source: American Council of Life Insurance, *Pension Facts 1977* (Washington, D.C.: n.d.), p. 23.

*Private Pension Financing*   In 1963 the Studebaker Corporation, a small producer of automobiles, went out of business. The company had established fourteen years before a pension plan that ultimately covered about 11,000 employees. When the company closed its South Bend, Indiana, plant, there were assets worth $24 million in the pension fund. But these assets were insufficient to meet all the pension rights that had been accumulated. The result: about 4,500 workers received an average of only $600 apiece, or 15 percent of the value of their rights. And those workers who had accumulated years of service but had not achieved pension vesting status got nothing.

Because of the number of workers affected and the prominence of the industry, the Studebaker case immediately became a favorite example cited by those persons calling for private pension reform. Studebaker (and dozens of others) illustrates the major goal *and also the major hazard* of private pension financing—to ensure that there are adequate funds so that promised benefits are, in fact, paid.

Prior to the 1974 pension reform legislation, most private plans financed pensions on a reserve basis, with a few operating on a partial or full pay-as-you-go basis. Now all plans covered by the 1974 act are required to meet its minimum funding standards.

In reviewing financing practices it is useful to group plans into three categories: (a) noninsured or trusteed plans, (b) insured plans, and (c) multiemployer plans. The majority of plans are noninsured or trusteed plans whose reserves are either self-administered by the individual company or administered by a trustee, in most cases commercial banks. Significantly, the great bulk of these reserves are administered by only about twenty-five banks. Insured plans are administered by various insurance companies. Multiemployer funds, usually the result of union collective bargaining, are often run by the unions themselves.

Less than a quarter of private plans require employee contributions to the plan; the rest are financed entirely by the employer. A major reason for the prevalence of noncontributory plans is that employee contributions from earnings are subject, with certain exceptions, to federal income taxes. In contrast, the money employers put into a pension fund is not subject to any taxes. In addition, employee contributions greatly complicate the administration of a plan—requiring the establishment of a pension account for each worker and policies regulating these accounts. And, as we indicated in Chapter 7, noncontributory plans usually reduce employer pension costs during the earning years.

Although most firms have established reserve funds to be built up over the years as their pension liabilities grow, many of the pension rights granted under the plans remain in jeopardy as a result of "past service credits." When new plans are established or old plans liberalized, the usual practice is to give workers full pension credits for their years of work prior to the plan's establishment or liberalization. While the pension liabilities for these past service credits accrue immediately, employers usually adopt a payment schedule for funding these liabilities that in the past extended over a ten- to forty-year period (and sometimes longer). As long as this unfunded liability remains, a plan that terminates will be unable to pay all of its promised future pension benefits. This is what happened in the Studebaker case. And, in fact, many plans have terminated over the years—with a resultant loss of pension rights to thousands of workers.

A study by Frank Griffin and Charles L. Trowbridge (1969) of funding status indicated that "the level of funding achieved by 1966 within the private pension movement as a whole [was] higher than we might expect" (Trowbridge, 1970). As might be expected, they found that the longer a plan had been in existence, the higher the level of funding. Plans in existence for 15 or more years had assets, on average, sufficient to cover about 95 percent of all accrued benefits. And more than half of all plans studied were fully funded.

Many plans, however, still have sizable unfunded liabilities. Griffin and Trowbridge found in their study that about one-third of the plans ten years old or younger had unfunded liabilities of 40 percent or more. More recently, articles in *Fortune* and *Business Week* gave startling statistics on the magnitude of current liabilities. *Business Week*'s study of 1,500 companies in

1976 found $48 billion in unfunded vested benefits (*Business Week*, 1977). The Big Three car manufacturers (General Motors, Ford, and Chrysler), for example, reported unfunded pension liabilities of about $13 billion.

What may be even more significant is that, historically, unfunded liabilities have been rising dramatically, not falling. *Business Week* reports that between 1975 and 1976, unfunded past service credits increased almost 62 percent and unfunded vested benefits increased 48 percent. Furthermore, A. F. Ehrbar (1977) argues that reported figures "are ridiculously understated" and that unfunded liabilities "might actually come to several hundred billion dollars."

The 1974 pension reform legislation (ERISA) requires that all new plans fund past service liabilities in no more than thirty years; plans in existence prior to the 1975 law have forty years. A study by Randall Weiss (1976), however, concludes that these ERISA provisions are not likely to have much impact: ERISA funding provisions "are likely to have very little, if any, effect on the flow of funds into pension funds. Plans covering at least half of the workers covered by pensions will not be affected, either because they are not defined benefit plans or because they had already been following the rules ERISA dictates." Weiss argues that the quicker funding requirements for the other plans will be minimized by liberalized actuarial assumptions and the relatively long (thirty to forty years) period involved.

It seems reasonable to assume, therefore, that many pension plans in the years to come will not be sufficiently funded to meet all obligations in the event of plan termination. In addition to the funding requirements discussed above, ERISA attempts to deal with this problem by establishing a benefit insurance program. This program seeks to protect employees against the loss of vested benefits (up to specified maximum levels) in the event a plan is terminated for any reason (firm bankruptcy, plant shut down, merger, etc.).

A new Pension Benefit Guaranty Corporation (PBGC) is in charge of this program. All covered plans must pay into the insurance fund. In addition, the corporation has authority to borrow up to $100 million from the federal treasury. The resulting insurance program is a major step forward in providing workers covered by private pensions significant protection from the potential financing problems connected with plan termination. By April 1979, PBGC had assumed trustee status for over 300 plans covering 33,000 vested workers (BNA, 1979b).

One major problem, however, is yet to be resolved. When termination insurance was established under the supervision of PBGC, single employer plan coverage began immediately, but complete multiemployer plan coverage was postponed until January 1, 1978—three years after the ERISA legislation was passed. Before the January start-up date, however, information began to accumulate indicating that many multiemployer plans (with billions of dollars worth of liabilities) were intending to terminate when PBGC insurance went into effect. The cost of providing benefits to workers of these plans would have had to be borne by nonterminating plans through very high insurance premium rates. Because of the financial equity issue involved in this situation and a desire not to encourage weak plans to terminate, Congress deferred PBGC coverage until PBGC had time to study the problem and recommend a redesigned system of insurance for multiemployer plans. In the meantime, PBGC has been exercising discretionary authority granted under ERISA to pay benefits to three multiemployer plans (in the printing, millinery, and milk industries) that have terminated without adequate funding.

*State and Local Pension Financing*    Pension plans established for state and local government employees are *not* covered by any provisions of the Employee Retirement Income Security Act of 1974. Substantial political pressure from various groups in the states caused the drafters of the legislation to exempt these plans—lest the resulting opposition to the bill endanger its chances of passage. The minimum funding provisions of the bill, which would have necessitated sizable tax increases in many states, were in large part responsible for the opposition. No doubt, opposition was also based on the tradition of state autonomy in the pension area and the fears of many government employees that compliance under the proposed law would be costly and ultimately result in their receiving smaller pensions.

There are over 7,000 state and local government pension plans. Unlike private pensions, these plans almost always require a contribution from the employee that is some percentage of salary. Most state and local plans are funded. The amount of funding varies greatly among the various plans but usually does not approach the extent of funding achieved by private plans.

Unfortunately, data on the actuarial status of the thousands of government plans (or even a representational sample of them) are difficult to obtain and also difficult to interpret when available. A study by James A. Maxwell (1975) of the pension plans in the twenty-nine largest cities "shows that many of them are in trouble." Using the ratio of current payments to assets as a rough indication of the financial strength or weakness of a fund, Maxwell also identifies four states where plan financing is weak: Delaware, Massachusetts, West Virginia, and Maine.

Another recent study by a Congressional Pension Task Force (U.S. House Committee on Education and Labor, 1978) surveyed plans covering 96 percent of all employees in public employee plans. The Pension Task Force reported serious deficiencies regarding the extent to which information is reported and disclosed to interested parties. They found that plans often did not operate in accordance with generally accepted financial and accounting procedures. And, most importantly, they found that "there is an incomplete assessment of true pension costs at all levels of government due to the lack of adequate **actuarial valuations** and standards."

The financial problems of public employee retirement systems are serious. The Pension Task Force reports that one-third of the plans did not have actuarial valuations over the five-year period investigated (1971–1975); 75 percent of the plans basing contribution rates at least in part on actuarial funding methods were found to understate current pension costs and unfunded accrued liabilities; and 40 percent of the total federal, state, and local pension systems fail to meet the funding test "which many pension experts consider a bare minimum."

Tilove's assessment of the current situation is that significant improvements have occurred in the funding situation of state and local plans but that funding is in fact poorest where it is most needed:

> The cases most in need of attention are the systems of the financially distressed urban centers and of the many smaller cities and counties that have no real assurance of future ability to pay. It is their fiscal difficulties that have kept many on pay-as-you-go, and that is precisely why they should begin to fund on an actuarial basis—so that they may confront the long-term implications of their pension decisions and, by the same policy, assure the ultimate security of their employees. [Tilove, 1976]

In many ways, state and local pension financing falls in between social security financing and private pension plans. Like the federal government, state and city governments are not likely ever to cease operations, and pensions are protected by law and the taxing powers of the government. But, like private business, states and cities are not assured of a continually growing financing base. Some states and cities may experience a net loss of businesses or population and/or their tax base. These shifts are difficult to predict and can cause serious problems if pension costs (based on past promises) are rising while the government's tax revenues are growing very slowly or falling.

Because pension benefits can be liberalized without any substantial increases in current costs, some people fear that pension plans will be liberalized without due regard to the future financing implications. It is argued that the political process is particularly susceptible to this problem because the conduct of state and local politicians is often "determined by relatively short-run considerations. The impact of failing to adhere to actuarial principles will frequently fall upon a different mayor and a different city council. In these circumstances, concessions that condemn a city to future impoverishment may not seem intolerable" (Wellington and Winter, 1971). Despite the large number of state and local funds, the magnitude of fund assets, the growth of benefit levels, and the fears of many professionals regarding state and local pension financing, very little attention has been given to the impact of these plans on the economic status of the current and future aged. Individuals covered by these plans, and relying on them for retirement security, should be aware of this gap in our knowledge. State and local taxpayers should probably be more sensitive to the long-term costs of these pensions and support an increase in the availability of information in this area. Currently Congress is considering federal pension legislation similar to ERISA for public employee plans.

## Suggested Readings

*1978 Annual Report of the Board of Trustees of the Federal Old-Age and Survivors Insurance and Disability Insurance Trust Funds.* House Document No. 95-336. Washington, D.C.: U.S. Government Printing Office.

This report summarizes the financial status of social security. Cost projections are presented and explained in a relatively nontechnical fashion. This report is issued yearly, and later reports should be consulted for the most recent information.

Fisher, Paul. "The Social Security Crisis: An International Dilemma." *Aging and Work* 1 (Winter 1978): 1–14.

Discusses the impact of the worldwide recession of the seventies on social security financing in various countries. The study reports on action taken by countries in the areas of migrant ("guest") workers, unemployment insurance, early retirement policies, and financing schemes.

*Funding Pensions: Issues and Implications for Financial Markets.* Conference Proceedings. Conference Series No. 16. Boston: The Federal Reserve Bank of Boston, 1976.

A highly technical but informative discussion covering the funding of social security, federal pensions, private plans, and state/local pension funds.

Leimer, Dean R., Ronald Hoffman, and Alan Freiden. *A Framework for Analyzing the Equity of the Social Security Benefit Structure.* Studies in Income Distribution No. 6. Washington, D.C.: Office of Research and Statistics, Social Security Administration.

A highly technical but insightful analysis of the equity implications of the social security benefit structures in both "the intracohort and intertemporal contexts."

Projector, Dorothy S. "Should the Payroll Tax Finance Higher Benefits Under OASDHI? A Review of the Issues." *Journal of Human Resources* 4 (Winter 1969): 60–75.

A somewhat dated but excellent discussion of some of the major issues.

Subcommittee on Fiscal Policy, U.S. Joint Economic Committee. "Issues in Financing Retirement Income." Paper No. 18 in *Studies in Public Welfare.* Washington, D.C.: U.S. Government Printing Office, 1974.

The best summary available of the financial history of social security and the issues as they have been discussed over the years. It also contains a comprehensive bibliography of congressional documents, monographs, and journal articles on social security financing.

Thompson, Lawrence H. *An Analysis of the Factors Currently Determining Benefit Level Adjustments in the Social Security Program.* Technical Analysis Paper

No. 1. Office of Income Security Policy, Office of the Assistant Secretary of Planning and Evaluation. Washington, D.C.: Department of Health, Education, and Welfare, 1974.

An explanation of the overadjustment (double adjustment or "decoupling") problem arising from the social security indexing mechanism adopted in 1972.

U.S. Senate Special Committee on Aging. *Women and Social Security: Adapting to a New Era.* A working paper prepared by the Task Force on Women and Social Security. Washington, D.C.: U.S. Government Printing Office, 1975.

An excellent summary of the various issues, including a discussion of various proposed changes in women's benefits.

# Chapter Nine

## *The Future: Prospects and Issues*

The last four chapters surveyed past pension developments and discussed some of the problems still to be resolved. Despite these problems we can look forward to continuing improvement in the economic condition of the elderly as a result of better public and private pension programs.

In addition to expanding pension coverage and higher benefit levels, there are a number of other specific factors operating to improve the future economic status of the elderly. First, there is the "demographic turnover" in the aged population. Every day approximately 5,000 Americans celebrate their sixty-fifth birthday and approximately 3,600 persons over age 64 die (Brotman, 1978). Those dying are usually the oldest and poorest part of the elderly population, while many of the new aged start this period of life with pension incomes that were undreamed of not many years ago. Quickly disappearing is the "no pension generation"—workers too old to have achieved regular pension status when social security or their employers' pension plans were initially established.

A second factor is the existence of a better welfare program for the aged—with higher benefit levels and better inflation protection. The Supplemental Security Income program—together with state supplementation —was launched in 1974 (see Chapter 6). It will take a few years to work out some of the problems connected with establishing this new program, but we can expect that gradually more people who are eligible will learn about and take advantage of the program.

Welfare expenditures have never been politically popular among legislators. Yet there have been some indications in recent years of a more favorable attitude developing in the United States toward government action

177

to eliminate poverty. This more favorable attitude seems to hold especially for the elderly. Certainly, as the nation's wealth grows over time, we find ourselves collectively better able to afford the expenditures needed to raise the incomes of the poor. Therefore, we can anticipate additional real increases in welfare benefits for the aged.

Third, as the long-run rise of 1 or 2 percent annually in real incomes of American families continues, there will be a greater potential for individual saving out of that income. While historically the data show (see Table 10, page 32) that few families have been able or willing to save much (beyond the equity in a home), we can probably expect some incremental improvements in this area.

### Social Security—How Much Is Enough?

Given rising social security costs and the improving economic situation of the older population, some people argue that we should be developing a pension policy that relies less heavily on the compulsory social security system for providing adequate income in retirement. For example, a much publicized report by the Consultant Panel on Social Security (1976), chaired by Professor William Hsaio, clearly opted for reducing the future role of social security by recommending price indexing of the earnings used to calculate benefits. Under that proposal, each succeeding generation's replacement rate of preretirement earnings from social security *would fall steadily over time*—unless Congress prevented the fall through a series of ad hoc decisions.

Economist Martin Feldstein (1977) has asserted that the high earnings replacement rates currently resulting at retirement from public and private pensions are "quite inappropriate for middle and higher income couples." Feldstein argues that retirement on social security now brings little decline in an average family's standard of living and that, furthermore, workers often receive additional income from private pensions. It is important to see how Feldstein reaches this debatable conclusion, since it is a view shared by others.

Feldstein and almost all recent discussants of social security reform focus on the replacement rate for a median (male) earner—that is, a hypothetical worker who earns the median annual wage *each year* of the working period. The social security benefit formula provides a retiring worker who has earned (each year) an amount equal to the median wage with a retirement benefit equal to about 46 percent of earnings just prior to retirement.*

---

*This figure appears in almost all recent reports and publications discussing social security benefit levels and is based on methodology and estimates developed by the Office of the Actuary, Social Security Administration.

But if the worker has a nonworking spouse, the replacement rate jumps to almost 70 percent as a result of the additional spouse benefit. Given estimates that 65–75 percent of gross earnings for nonpoor families allows these families to maintain their living standards in retirement, we see that social security has the *potential* of providing most of the normal retirement needs for *these* average workers.

We then must add the contribution to retirement living of private pensions for those who are eligible. A study of 1974 **defined benefit plan** formulas (Schulz, Leavitt, and Kelly, 1979) indicates, for example, that these formulas can provide 20 to 25 percent earnings replacement for hypothetical long-service workers.

Combining the replacement rates from social security with those from private pensions raises the average pension replacement rate for the "average" one-worker couple to over 90 percent. Can there be any doubt that we are overpensioning some workers today?

*Some Important Qualifications*    Well, like most generalizations the overpensioning characterization suffers from a number of major limitations. There is no doubt that severe economic deprivation faces far fewer retiring persons—at least as long as they stay well and avoid institutionalization. But the picture is not quite as rosy as the replacement rate percentages usually cited would suggest.

The median earnings before retirement selected by Feldstein and others for the hypothetical earnings calculations are an average for both part-time and full-time workers at *all* stages of their earnings career (i.e., for all age groups); that was about $8,800 for all male workers in 1976 covered by social security. In estimating pension replacement adequacy, do we really want to use the 1976 median earnings of men about thirty years of age as a measure of preretirement earnings for men *currently retiring?*—for that is what the $8,800 number is equivalent to. In contrast, men in their fifties, who were close to retirement, had 1976 median earnings of about $12,000. Using the median earnings level of this age group as a measure of preretirement earnings results in a replacement rate for a single worker of only 33 percent!

In addition, the couple replacement rates of 70 percent (social security alone) and 90 percent (with a private pension) are for a couple *with one worker, earning median wages, and retiring at age 65*. But not all those retiring fall into that particular category. To begin with, more than half of married women approaching retirement age are working in the labor force. The relevant replacement rates for many two-worker couples are very different from those for one worker; the higher earnings are not replaced proportionally by higher social security benefits. In fact, if the spouse doesn't earn enough to become entitled to a benefit greater than 50 percent of the other worker's benefit, there will be no increase in social security benefits. Thus, the pension replacement rate from social security for an "average" two-worker family will often be much lower.

An equally important consideration in the determination of actual (rather than potential) replacement rates is the age at retirement. The dramatic rise in the numbers of workers retiring before the usual retirement age of 65 has made early retirement almost the norm. Once again, because of the actuarial reduction provisions in social security (and reductions in most private pensions), the *actual* replacement rates of a great many retirees will be lower than the percentages originally cited.

While no individual is required to retire before age 65 and many retire early because they want to, numerous studies have shown that there is also a sizable group of early retirees without a meaningful option. These workers have little or no potential to engage in substantive employment activity because of poor health or structural unemployment problems.

Finally, as we discussed in Chapter 7, the private pension supplement that boosts the replacement rate for many is not available to all; many workers are never covered or lose pension credits before retiring. Failure to meet vesting requirements or plan terminations, for example, result in lost service credits for many workers, especially women (Thompson, 1978). Even those that are covered long enough to receive a pension do not achieve the long periods of service required for *large* private pension benefit amounts.

*Actual Replacement Rates*    An important new study by Alan Fox (1979) provides estimates of *actual* replacement rates for couples starting to receive social security benefits over the 1968–1974 period. This study shows that "hypothetical replacement rates for married couples—based on the dual assumptions that the husband's preretirement earnings match the median of all men and that the wife had no earnings—present a very inaccurate picture of the typical experience of retired couples." Analysis of the data shows that:

1. About half the wives had worked long enough to retire as workers rather than as dependent spouses—with earnings adding substantially to the couple's preretirement standard of living.
2. About nine couples in ten incurred permanent benefit reductions because of early retirement.
3. Wives were younger than their husbands and seldom retired in the same year or at the same age.
4. The social security replacement rate for the *hypothetical* couple (both age 65) retiring in 1973–74 was 63 percent, whereas the *actual* median rate was 43 percent for all couples in the survey population.
5. Only about half the survey couples received second pensions, with the

median total replacement rate being 62 percent, or 13 percentage points higher than the median replacement rate (49 percent) of couples without second pensions.

Table 31 shows the distribution of couple social security replacement rates for the 1968–1974 period. Couples with retired *worker*-wives had replacement rates 6–8 percentage points lower than couples with *dependent* wives. More importantly, few couples had replacement rates above 60 percent—the amount necessary to maintain living standards in retirement.

Table 32 shows the median replacement rates when second pensions are added. Among couples first receiving benefits in 1973–74, those with second pensions (private or public employee) had a median total replacement rate of 62 percent. Those without a second pension had a median replacement rate of 49 percent. Fox finds that this distinction between dual pension couples and those receiving social security only is also large at different earnings levels. For example, dual pension couples with preretirement earnings of $12,500 or more had a median replacement rate of 54 percent; in contrast, couples at the same earnings level without second pensions had only a 30 percent replacement rate.

*Thus, replacement rates as conventionally measured for most policy discussions do not realistically reflect actual benefits being paid to retiring workers.* For example, Robert Ball (1978a), former commissioner of Social Security, has recently written that "at average wages, the [social security] replacement rate for the couple *is approaching adequacy* [emphasis added]." Such an assertion—and similar ones by other pension experts (see Munnell, 1977, and Bassett, 1978)—is seriously misleading.

There remains, then, a considerable gap between a replacement rate goal of 60 to 80 percent and these *actual* social security replacement rates in the range of 25 to 45 percent for most aged families. This gap is too large to be ignored by individuals confronting retirement. In the absence of supplemental income, it means a large decline in living standards in retirement. Either personal saving will have to increase, social security benefits improve, or private pension coverage be expanded. Failure to act on one or more of those options will result in curtailed lifestyles for succeeding generations of Americans when they reach old age. At the time of writing, three major groups were studying this and other retirement issues: the 1978–79 Social Security Advisory Council, the National Commission on Social Security, and the President's Commission on Pension Policy.

Given the current political concern about rising social security costs, increased attention to the improvement of private pensions is likely. But, again, the problems associated with private pensions are not amenable to easy solution.

Table 31. Social Security Replacement Rates for Couples by Type of Wife's Benefit and Husband's Year of First Benefit Payment[a]

| Replacement Rate | 1968–1974 | | | 1973–1974 | | |
|---|---|---|---|---|---|---|
| | All Couples | Wife Retired Worker | Wife Dependent | All Couples | Wife Retired Worker | Wife Dependent |
| 0.1–19.9% | 6 | 6 | 4 | 2 | 2 | 0 |
| 20–39.9 | 43 | 50 | 36 | 35 | 38 | 32 |
| 40–59.9 | 37 | 34 | 41 | 47 | 47 | 47 |
| 60–79.9 | 11 | 7 | 15 | 13 | 9 | 18 |
| 80 and above | 4 | 4 | 4 | 3 | 4 | 3 |
| Total Percent[b] | 100 | 100 | 100 | 100 | 100 | 100 |
| Median Percent | 41 | 38 | 45 | 45 | 43 | 49 |

Source: Alan Fox, "Earnings Replacement Rates of Retired Couples: Findings from the Retirement History Study," Social Security Bulletin 42 (January 1979): 17–39.
[a]Combined social security benefits as a percent of combined estimated total earnings in the three highest years of the ten before the husband's first benefit payment. Restricted to couples in which the husband first received retired worker benefits between 1968 and 1974. Excludes couples whose combined earnings, social security benefits, or second pensions were unusable.
[b]May not add to 100 due to rounding.

Table 32. Median Total[a] Replacement Rates for Couples With and Without a Second Pension[b]

| Year of Husband's First Benefit Payment | Total | | | No Second Plan | | | Private Pension Plan | | |
|---|---|---|---|---|---|---|---|---|---|
| | Total | Wife Retired Worker | Wife Dependent | Total | Wife Retired Worker | Wife Dependent | Total | Wife Retired Worker | Wife Dependent |
| 1968–1974 | 52 | 50 | 55 | 46 | 44 | 50 | 59 | 57 | 61 |
| 1973–1974 only | 55 | 54 | 58 | 49 | 47 | 53 | 62 | 61 | 64 |

Source: Alan Fox, "Earnings Replacement Rates of Retired Couples: Findings from the Retirement History Study," *Social Security Bulletin* 42 (January 1979): 17–39.

[a] Social security plus, where applicable, income from a second pension (private or government employee).

[b] Restricted to workers first receiving benefits between 1973 and 1974. Preretirement earnings are estimated total earnings in the three highest years of the ten before initial benefit.

### The Future of Private Pensions

As we have indicated in preceding chapters, private pensions have been a major source of retirement income for many people. The amount of income ultimately received varies greatly—depending on an individual worker's employment experience, his preretirement earnings level, the size of the firms he works for, and the industry of employment (see Table 26 and Thompson, 1978). Coverage under a private plan and receipt of a pension are obviously no guarantee that a plan benefit will be adequate. There are plans that provide excellent benefits, and there are plans that provide very low benefits. Unlike social security, we cannot calculate one replacement rate for workers with a certain earnings history. Thousands of different plans produce thousands of different replacement rates.

Table 33 shows the levels of private pension benefits received in 1972 by a national sample of recipients. At the extremes, 16 percent of men and 41 percent of women received less than $1,000 per year. In contrast, 13 percent of men but only 2 percent of the women received benefits of $5,000 or more.

*Table 33.*   Income in 1972 from Private Pension Coverage on the Longest Job

| Income | Men | Women |
|---|---|---|
| Median | $2,230 | $1,200 |
| Less than $500 | 5 | 12 |
| $  500–999 | 11 | 29 |
| 1,000–1,499 | 12 | 19 |
| 1,500–1,999 | 16 | 13 |
| 2,000–2,499 | 11 | 10 |
| 2,500–2,999 | 10 | 6 |
| 3,000–3,999 | 13 | 4 |
| 4,000–4,999 | 8 | 4 |
| 5,000–5,999 | 5 | 1 |
| 6,000–7,499 | 4 | 0 |
| 7,500–9,999 | 2 | 0 |
| 10,000 or more | 2 | 1 |
| Total Percent[a] | 100 | 100 |

Source: Gayle B. Thompson, "Pension Coverage and Benefits, 1972: Findings from the Retirement History Study," *Social Security Bulletin* 41 (February 1978): 3–17.
[a]Does not add up to 100 due to rounding.

If private pensions are to become a truly effective supplement to social security, three problems must be solved: (a) coverage must be extended, (b) benefits receipt must become less risky, and (c) benefits must not be so vulnerable to inflation.

*Coverage*  ERISA did not obligate any employer without a pension plan to establish one. Thus, ERISA contained no provision beyond the tax incentives provided in the federal tax laws to encourage the expansion of existing private plan coverage. Rather, the principal focus of ERISA was on expanding the supervision and regulation of private plans by the federal government and creating tax exempt individual retirement accounts (IRAs).

This expanded regulation costs money. In addition to the costs to taxpayers for the federal supervisory agencies and their staffs, considerable new regulatory costs are imposed on the businesses with pension funds. These costs arise from the necessity of providing information to the government in order for it to carry out its various supervisory roles. Because of the complexity of the new regulations, business must often either develop staff or hire outside consultants to provide them with the expertise necessary to ensure compliance with the new complex law. Businesses have been complaining strongly before congressional committees about both the high costs of reporting required information to the government and the costs of simply understanding the law. Some plans have been terminated because of the increased administrative burdens and costs.

In addition to the impact of ERISA, the number of private plans has also been influenced by the serious economic downturn of recent years. Of the total number of plans that filed termination notices with the Pension Benefit Guaranty Corporation from fiscal 1975 through fiscal 1977, over 70 percent related plan termination to business conditions of the employer—either bankruptcy/liquidation or the deteriorating financial status of the plan. Together, these two factors (bankruptcy and deteriorating plan financial status) have accounted for a large part of the fluctuations in net plan formation occurring in recent years. Only 18 percent of terminating plans gave ERISA as the sole reason for doing so (Skopic, 1978).

Fluctuations in plan formation, however, have not had any major impact on the proportion of workers covered by private pensions. It is important to remember that while the number of plans approved and terminated every year is relatively large, almost all these individual plans are very small. In fiscal 1977, for example, the average terminating plan covered by PBGC had only twenty-three participants, and half of them had fewer than seven participants.

Thus, when we look at the coverage trend over the last couple of decades, we see a slowing down in coverage beginning *prior* to ERISA. This slowdown results primarily from the fact that almost all the workers in large, relatively affluent corporations have become covered. Noncoverage is now concentrated among small employer groups. A profile of these small employers would include the business proprietors found on any typical small-town Main Street or any large city neighborhood shopping center: the small retailer, the local restaurant, the service station, repair services, the barber and beauty shop, the doctor and dentist, the auto dealer—and many, many more small employers of wage and salary workers. The profile would likewise include partnership operations such as law firms, consulting engineers, accounting firms, and real estate firms, and small manufacturing plants operated as corporations or by self-employed owners.

The most recent attempt to extend coverage is new legislation passed as part of the Revenue Act of 1978 which allows the creation of "simplified pension plans." As we discussed in Chapter 7, IRA accounts may be set up by noncovered individuals, and tax-free contributions may be made annually up to 15 percent of earned income (a maximum of $1,500 or, with spouse, $1,750). The 1978 Revenue Act extends this provision in two ways: First, employers may now make tax deductible contributions to the IRA plan, with total contributions (employer and worker) limited to 15 percent of earned income. The maximum contribution for the employee is still $1,500, but the maximum for the two contributions combined is $7,500. Second, the simplified plan may be adopted even though the employee is a participant in a regular pension plan; eligibility only requires that regular plan contributions be under the maximum. As in the case of IRAs, reporting and disclosure requirements are minimal.

We will have to wait and see what impact this new legislation has on the coverage problem. In the meantime, large numbers of workers without private coverage will continue to rely primarily on their social security benefits for retirement protection.

*Pension Risk*   In August 1978 the Professional Drivers Council, a dissident Teamsters union group, charged that millions of dollars were being drained from the union's pension funds because of mismanagement and corrupt practices. The dissident group claimed that, among other abuses, multimillion dollar loans had been made to individuals and groups with questionable backgrounds or to entities running deficits when the loans were made (BNA, August 21, 1978). That same month a U.S. District Court ruled that a $20 million loan by pension trustees of Teamsters' Local 281 violated ERISA regulations; the money was loaned to finance a thousand-plus room hotel and gambling casino in Las Vegas. Earlier, a reform group called Miners for Democracy acted to displace the United Mine Workers' leadership—charged with illegal financial transactions and the use of union pension funds for personal gain. Although such abuse cases affect a minority of workers covered by private pensions, there has been a continuous history of such incidents. The result has been to depress the level of benefits in certain instances and threaten the actual financial viability of certain plans.

A more serious problem, because it affects even more workers, is the plight of individuals who think they have earned a right to a pension but at retirement suddenly discover they are mistaken. The most famous illustrative court case in recent years involved a Teamster, John B. Daniel. Daniel joined Teamsters' Local 705 in 1951 and worked as a truck driver for 22½ years, fully expecting a pension when he retired. In 1960–61, however, he was laid off involuntarily for four months, and for an additional three months of work no employer made payments for him because of a bookkeeper's embezzlement. When Daniel stopped driving at age 63 because of cataracts and applied for his pension, he was told that he had forfeited his pension twelve years before when payments were not made for those seven months. He was told his plan, prior to ERISA, only provided pensions to persons with twenty years of continuous service.

Daniel sued, basing his lawsuit on the antifraud provisions of the federal securities law—alleging his pension fund investment was no different from any other speculative investment in the capital markets. Both the federal district and appeals courts ruled in Daniel's favor, but on January 15, 1979, the Supreme Court ruled unanimously that the antifraud provisions did not apply (a month after Daniel died at the age of 68). Pension plan administrators breathed a big sigh of relief, claiming that a favorable decision for Daniel would have subjected them to massive retroactive liabilities.

Every year thousands of workers (or their spouses) are surprised to learn that they are not eligible for an expected pension or that the pension is much lower than anticipated. The Pension Rights Center in Washington, D.C., claims that it is deluged with complaints from individuals who misunderstood their pension plans or feel they have been mistreated.

The problem arises from the inherent complexity of *all* pensions, the large number of "ifs, ands, and buts" in private plans, and the general disinterest of many workers in pension matters until retirement. ERISA attempts to improve the flow of information to workers by mandating certain disclosure procedures, but uncertainty arising from fraud and misunderstanding are likely to continue.

Another major source of pension risk arises from vesting provisions. Since plans typically do not vest until ten years of credited service has been achieved, workers face unexpected pension losses arising from job terminations, alternative employment opportunities, and illness. An analysis of census data by Sommers and Eck (1977) found that less than half of those at work in 1970 were in the same occupation as they had been five years earlier; no age group (young or old) showed occupational continuity better than 60 percent. These data do not necessarily mean that all those who changed occupation also changed employers, but they do indicate that large numbers probably did.

A worker may join a company with an excellent pension plan that promises an adequate benefit after twenty to thirty years of service, but there is no way that the worker can be absolutely sure that either he or the company or the plan will be around when it is time to retire. As we indicated in Chapter 7, Thompson (1978) found in a 1972 survey that about one-quarter of the men and one-half of the women who were covered by a private pension on their longest job did not receive a private pension in retirement.

*Inflation*    Average life expectancy at age 65 is roughly fifteen years. After fifteen years of inflation at an annual rate of 5 percent, the real value of a private pension benefit would decline by about one-half. At 10 percent annual inflation, the value of the pension would be only 24 percent of its original value.

There are almost no private plans that automatically adjust pensions during retirement for increases in the Consumer Price Index. Some plans adjust benefits on an ad hoc basis every few years, but these adjustments usually lag far behind the rise in prices.

Some people have recommended "retiree bargaining" as a way of dealing with this problem. However, the Supreme Court ruled in 1971 *(Allied Chemical and Alkali Workers* v. *Pittsburgh Plate Glass)* that retirees are not "employees" within the meaning of the National Labor Relations Act and, therefore, that benefits for retirees are not mandatory subjects of union bargaining. This means that if a company does not want to discuss increases in retirees' pensions, there is no way a union can legally force them to do so. Thus, for example, major companies in the electrical manufacturing industry recently refused to bargain with unions seeking to improve what they saw as the serious financial plight of many retirees (Fitzgerald, 1978).

Deterioration of benefits by inflation represents one of the most serious problems confronting private pension plans. To date, however, no one has proposed a solution that has received significant support.

### Poverty Among Elderly Women

Perhaps most significant in the trend of poverty among the aged is the economic situation of aged women, especially widows. Poverty analyst Mollie Orshansky (1974) writes that "in our society, at every age and every stage, women are more vulnerable to poverty than men, especially if they must do double duty as both family head and homemaker." Table 34 shows that the largest number of such women are widowed (about 1½ million) and that the highest incidence of poverty occurs among separated women (42 percent).

Because of differences in life expectancies between men and women, most women can expect to become a widow during their lifetime—

*Table 34.*   Aged Women with Incomes Below the Poverty Index, 1976

| Marital Status | Number (thousands) | Percent |
|---|---|---|
| All Women | 2,326 | 17.9 |
| Single | 197 | 23.7 |
| Married, Spouse Present | 354 | 7.4 |
| Married, Spouse Absent | 91 | 39.0 |
| Separated | 57 | 42.3 |
| Other | 33 | 34.5 |
| Widowed | 1,572 | 23.3 |
| Divorced | 112 | 31.3 |

Source: U.S. Bureau of the Census, *Consumer Income,* Current Population Reports, Series P-60, No. 115 (Washington, D.C.: U.S. Government Printing Office, 1978).

especially during later life. Figures 23 and 24 show the contrasting marital status and living arrangements of men and women. Only one out of three women over age 64 is married and living with her husband. Over half of aged women are widowed, with about one-third living alone.

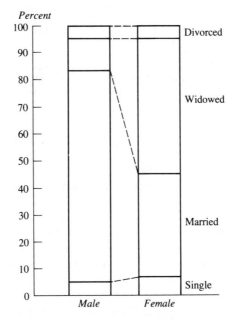

*Figure 23.   The Marital Status of Men and Women Age 65 and Over, 1975*

Source: Jacob S. Siegel, *Demographic Aspects of Aging and the Older Population in the United States,* Current Population Reports, Special Studies, Series P–23, No. 59 (Washington, D.C.: U.S. Government Printing Office, 1976).

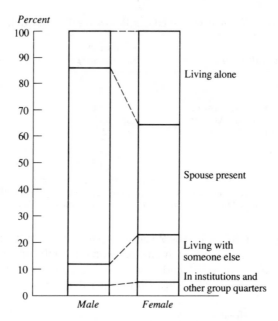

*Figure 24.    The Living Arrangements
of Men and Women Age 65 and Over, 1975*

Source: Jacob S. Siegel, *Demographic Aspects of Aging and the Older Population in the United States,* Current Population Reports, Special Studies, Series P–23, No. 59 (Washington, D.C.: U.S. Government Printing Office, 1976).

As we indicated previously, social security income drops sharply when a spouse dies. Typically, private pension income also drops when the worker-recipient dies and sometimes ceases entirely. Often pensions that were barely adequate become inadequate when one spouse dies. A large proportion of poverty among women can be traced to the inadequacy of mechanisms to provide sufficient financial support to survivors.

Women as workers also face many special problems that affect their ability to qualify for large pension benefits in their own right. Lower earnings and intermittent work histories are not uncommon among women. These two factors result in lower social security pensions (or in not qualifying for benefits at all).

Private pension coverage for women is lower than for men; in 1972 only 36 percent of full-time working women were covered, as compared to 52 percent for men. Vesting requirements of 10–15 years penalize women who move in and out of the labor force.

Until recently, relatively little attention was given to the economic status of women and their changing roles. Likewise, research to understand the changes in the economic situation of women in old age has been minimal. Both areas are now receiving quite a lot of attention (see Kahne, 1975). Moreover, changes in social security are under study, and there is evidence that many private pensions are improving those provisions that are important to women. How quickly the problems in this area will be solved, however, is still very unclear.

### The Nonsteady Worker

Just as women are at a relative disadvantage in accumulating pension rights because of intermittent labor force participation, there are both men and women who cannot achieve good pensions because of nonsteady employment. A significant number of workers are faced with one or more of the following problems that interfere with employment:

1. Health problems, ranging from total and complete disability to specific impairments that interfere with particular job functions.
2. Job discrimination.
3. Plant closedowns, which force older workers with experience, seniority, and special skills to compete for alternative opportunities.
4. Skill obsolescence, causing loss of jobs in declining industrial sectors and/or long-term unemployment due to the lack of demand for obsolete skills.
5. Recessional periods, when marginal workers are unable to find suitable employment.

As a result of such problems, some workers arrive at the retirement period with an intermittent employment record. When their gaps in employment are in the later years, these years of *potentially highest* earnings are lost for pension computation purposes.

Unemployable older workers usually "retire" at the first opportunity—taking early retirement benefits at significantly lower levels than those available at the regular retirement age. A 1969 survey by the Social Security Administration, for example, found that almost half of the men claiming social security benefits at age 62 had no private pension and did not want to retire when they had to leave their job. As Lenore E. Bixby (1970) has observed, "it appears . . . that the early retirement provisions of the OASDHI program often function as an intermediate disability program, providing benefits for older disabled workers who are unable to meet the eligibility requirements for disability insurance, are waiting to have a disability determination completed, or choose not to apply for disability benefits."

The circumstances faced by workers vary tremendously, however; some have few or no problems and some have very serious difficulties. The question is whether present policies and programs are adequate to deal with these differences. Various proposals have been made for improving unemployment, disability, and retraining programs. Before programmatic changes can be made, however, certain policy questions must be dealt with.

First, there is the question of whether the burden and solution of problems generated during the preretirement period are to be primarily the responsibility of the individual. If so, actuarially reduced private and public pensions are examples of program development that give the individual flexibility in deciding when the pension should start but do not add to program costs. That is, persons forced into early retirement by certain problems can collect a reduced pension, but if they want to maintain their income at a higher level, they must do so through supplemental income sources.

Alternatively, if it is decided to develop a national policy to better assist workers with special problems, should the policy be to maintain the income level for the affected families at or close to their previous living standard or should the policy simply guarantee that a family should not fall below a designated minimum?

What should be the basic mechanism for any public program in this area—an insurance-type program, a welfare program, or another mechanism? Several countries in Europe have established a variety of special mechanisms for assisting older workers who have employment problems but are too young to receive regular pensions. West Germany, for example, permits older workers with long-term unemployment to qualify for retirement pensions before the regular retirement age and also promotes work-sharing (Fisher, 1978).

In the United States, there are a number of programs to help workers with employment problems. These include disability insurance, Workmen's Compensation, the Vocational Rehabilitation Program, and the Comprehensive Employment and Training Act. In addition, there are some special vehicles for older workers: (a) the Age Discrimination in Employment Act, (b) special programs (VISTA, SCORE, RSVP, and Foster Grandparent) under the Domestic Volunteer Service Act, and (c) the Older Americans Community Service Employment Program.

All these programs in the United States are very limited in scope and fail to deal adequately with the magnitude and variety of the older worker problems listed above. Two basic questions remain: How much more in this problem area does the nation desire to do, and what mechanisms will be used?

### Rising Medical Costs and Long-Term Care

Even with Medicare, the elderly have had to make sizable expenditures for health care. Medicare, however, has helped to regularize and level off these expenditures, while removing much of the insecurity caused by large medical bills arising from "medium-term" illness.

Figure 25 shows what percentage of various types of health care

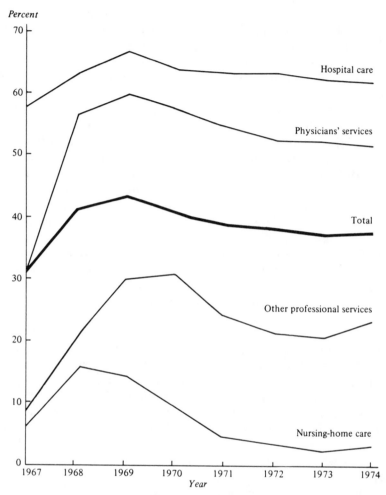

*Figure 25. Percent of Aged*[a] *Personal Health Care Expenditures Paid by Medicare, 1967–1974*[b]

Source: Errata to Marjorie Smith Mueller and Robert M. Gibson, "Age Differences in Health Care Spending, Fiscal Year 1974," *Social Security Bulletin* 38 (June 1975): 3–16.
[a] Persons aged 65 and over.
[b] Fiscal years.

expenditures were paid for by Medicare over the 1967–1974 period. In 1974, for example, over 60 percent of hospital care and over 50 percent of physicians' services were covered. In contrast, the fact that only about 3 percent of expenses of nursing home care were paid for by Medicare illustrates a major problem. Gaps still exist in health care economic security.

The two problems most often cited are the dangers of progressive impoverishment and the financial drain of expenses not covered by health insurance. The former problem usually results when an illness extends over a very long period of time or the person's state of health requires nonhospital institutionalization. Medicare provides benefits for inpatient hospital services up to 90 days in each benefit period* and up to 60 consecutive days in a skilled nursing facility. Care in a posthospital care service or convalescent section of a hospital is available up to 100 days, but qualification for these benefits is difficult because of stringent rules of eligibility. Nursing home care is authorized under Medicare but only in very limited circumstances.

All these limits on insurance protection are a problem for older people. "The fear of a long and costly final illness haunts many old people. To end one's life as a ward of the state, or to drain the resources of one's children, is an all-too-frequent prospect for old persons in America" (Brown, 1972).

When Medicare coverage runs out, older persons must either have supplemental private coverage or finance the health costs themselves. Once they draw down their assets sufficiently, they may become eligible for means-tested Medicaid benefits; eligibility requirements vary from state to state. This pauperization process is not only demeaning but also causes the elderly, in order to avoid it, to hold onto income and assets—economic resources that could otherwise contribute to their improved living standards.

Political efforts to liberalize medical cost protection for the elderly (and others) are hampered by the spiraling costs of medical care in general. The nation spent $163 billion for health care in 1977 (or $737 per person). This represents almost 10 percent of the nation's gross national product (Gibson and Fisher, 1978). Per capita personal health expenditures for the elderly alone were $1,745.

But what is most worrisome is the rapid escalation of these costs in recent years. For example, between 1976 and 1978, the cost of Medicare and Medicaid rose 40 percent—with very little increase in the numbers covered or in benefits (Iglehart, 1978). Between 1965 and 1976, Medicaid expenditures for nursing home care increased more than fourfold. And the Department of Health, Education, and Welfare projects that between 1978 and 2025, Medicare and Medicaid costs will increase, in real terms, more than ten times—at twice as fast a pace as increases in social security (Califano, 1978b).

Financing health care costs associated with chronic illness and long-term care is one of the most important economic issues confronting the el-

---

*A benefit period begins when the individual is admitted to a hospital and when he has not received inpatient hospital or skilled nursing facility services for 60 consecutive days. After the 90 days are exhausted, each person has a lifetime reserve of 60 days of hospital care for his optional use at a shared cost.

derly. According to the National Center for Health Statistics, almost 30 million people in the United States are limited in activity due to chronic disease or impairment, many of them aged. There are currently more than 1.2 million aged in long-term care institutions (Congressional Budget Office, 1977a). The economic cost of illness, disability, and death due to chronic diseases is very large, estimated by the Social Security Administration to be almost $50 billion in 1974.

In developing long-term care policy we are not only confronted with cost problems but also with a lack of clear knowledge and information about what should be done. In a review of research in this area, Sager (1978) concludes that there are three major gaps in our understanding:

1. We do not know how many elderly are dependent—requiring the assistance of other persons in living from day to day.
2. We do not know with any real certainty the desirable types, quantities, or providers of services to compensate for dependence.
3. We do not know the cost or effect of providing these services.

There is no doubt, however, that the need for long-term care services will continue to grow. Currently this care is provided by hospitals, nursing homes, day care and home care programs, and families. HEW Secretary Joseph Califano (1978a) describes the present situation as "a confusing and expensive patchwork of financing systems that spawn an ever more inadequate delivery system" and calls for a "more rational, comprehensive, efficient, and human system for delivering health services." Few would question that goal, but all would also agree on the difficulty of the task.

### Money Can't Buy Everything

Even with the expansion of income in retirement, the elderly are still faced with some important problems. While adequate income goes most of the way toward solving the economic problems of the aged, there are some things money can't buy.

As Robert Atchley (1972) points out, "aging and dependency are linked by the fact that as we grow older, we become increasingly susceptible to a loss of independence." Many older people require—or would find life much more enjoyable with—a different type of housing. Their mobility is threatened when they can no longer drive a car, and they often find that public transportation is either unavailable or inadequate. Illness and disability often make the ordinary tasks of dressing, eating, and shopping a major problem.

In Senate testimony, Dr. Wilma Donahue, Director of the International Center for Social Gerontology, discussed one of the unmet special needs that arises as people grow older:

> *Senator Williams, my purpose in appearing before your subcommittee this morning is to support the position of the Congress and of increasing numbers of researchers and practitioners in the field of aging that the time, knowledge, and resources are at hand to fill a glaring gap in the continuum of housing that the United States should be making available to its older population. Specifically, it has been amply demonstrated that there is need for specially designed housing with a variety of associated services ["congregate housing"]\* for scores, if not hundreds, of thousands of older people who must now live under growing apprehension of having too soon to seek refuge in long-term medical care facilities as they progress through the later years of their lives. These are the impaired but not ill, noninstitutionalized, often low-income older people who must struggle against rising odds to maintain themselves in the community. [U.S. Subcommittee on Housing for the Elderly, 1975]*

Increasing attention is currently focused on the various services required or desired by the elderly that are either not offered in the marketplace or not offered in sufficient quantity and quality. One of the major goals of the U.S. Administration on Aging, for example, is to promote comprehensive coordinated services for older persons. But action in this area is still very experimental; programs are widely scattered and unavailable to most of the aged. It will be many years before we know exactly what are the best services to offer, how these services should be provided, and what mechanisms should be used to finance them.

### Planning for Retirement

President John F. Kennedy once remarked that "it is not enough for a great nation merely to have added new years to life—our objective must also be to add new life to years." For those approaching retirement, the challenge is to take advantage of those years in a creative and fulfilling manner. And there is little doubt that preretirement planning by individuals can help many achieve this end.

As we have seen in the preceding chapters of this book, however, the problems involved in preretirement planning are very complex. Hence, most people, having a natural inclination to live for today and avoid thinking about old age and death, give very little systematic thought to the problems until they come face to face with them—which is usually too late. The flood of criticism about the adequacy, financial viability, and equity of social security and private pensions (regardless of their merits) creates confusion and

---

\*Congregate housing is defined by Donahue as "a residential environment which incorporates shelter and service, needed by the functionally impaired and socially deprived but not ill elderly, to enable them to maintain or return to a semi-independent life-style and avoid institutionalization as they grow older."

distrust among workers—further discouraging early thinking about retirement preparation.

In recent years, the major efforts to deal with this problem have shifted from the individual to private and public collective efforts. Businessmen, labor leaders, and gerontologists all bring different perspectives to their efforts to deal with and improve preretirement planning. Their goal, however, is similar: to generate a greater awareness among workers and their spouses of the problems and potentials of approaching old age and to assist where appropriate in the preparation for successful retirement.

Studies by Reich (1977) show a significant growth in group preretirement education and the range of institutions offering programs: community colleges, adult education schools, social service agencies, chambers of commerce, religious institutions, universities, unions, private companies, government, senior citizen organizations, and profit making organizations.

The development of preretirement programs is still in a very early stage. Significant numbers of workers do not have access to a program. Moreover, there is still disagreement over the need for such programs and whose responsibility it is to provide them. A number of studies have argued that many programs are neither suitably designed nor well implemented (see Kasschau, 1974, in Suggested Readings for this chapter). Many employers, for example, offer little more than fringe benefit information, and many are skeptical about the worth of preretirement programs.

One major effort in retirement planning is currently being developed by the National Council on Aging in cooperation with a consortium of nine major corporations and four large unions (Fitzpatrick, 1978 and 1979). The program is designed to reach employees early—in their forties and fifties. Another large program is Action for Independent Maturity conducted in association with the American Association of Retired Persons. This program trains industry officials to be discussion leaders and provides materials for the retirement-planning seminars.

The challenge is (a) to increase the availability of preretirement education to persons seeking such information, (b) to improve the quality of available programs, and (c) to encourage people to begin preparing for retirement at a relatively early age.

### Will We Pay the Price of Economic Adequacy?

Providing adequately for the retirement period is an expensive proposition. As the retirement age declines, we face the prospect of providing individuals with income and services for a twenty to thirty-year period outside the labor force. Increasingly, people are developing expectations that retirement can and should be an enjoyable period of life and that economic resources should be sufficient to avoid the limitations imposed on retirement living by financial stringency. Unfortunately, if individuals only begin to worry and seriously plan for their own retirement shortly before the event, the magnitude of the financing problem becomes insuperable for most. The best and easiest way of accumulating the resources necessary for retirement is to begin very early. But historically most people have shown a reluctance to think about retirement until it is *almost* a reality or until it *is* a reality. The result has been a great deal of poverty among the aged.

Pension systems and, before them, families have stepped in to provide needed economic support for many of these people—often preventing destitution. But the level of support was often very low. Yet (as we discussed in Chapter 8) the financial burden imposed on the working population, even at these low levels of support, has created political concern, and there is particular concern regarding the future burden.

How willing are people to finance higher levels of support? It seems to me that one of the best answers is provided by the individuals *now covered* by good private pensions and social security. The combined reduction in their take-home pay to provide social security and a good private pension is quite large (about 16–20 percent). Yet there is little complaining from this group, probably in large part because these costs are taken out before they ever get their earnings check. We can also look at the European experience (Wander, 1978). Other industrialized countries have payroll taxes that range between 16 and 20 percent. Again, we see very little political opposition in these countries to this level of taxation for pension purposes.

Recent data indicate, in fact, a willingness of American workers to pay for better benefits. A 1977 survey by the University of Michigan Survey Research Center found that a great many wage and salary workers expressed a willingness to trade increments in pay for better retirement benefits. In the survey, 54 percent of workers preferred an improvement in retirement benefits over a pay increase (Staines and Quinn, 1979).

Certainly we must be sensitive to the political realities of rising pension costs in the United States, but it is foolish to think we can escape the cost of providing an individual with an adequate retirement income by keeping the cost of social security down. If we do not provide for older Americans through taxation, then we will do so by other but less visible means—for example, by reducing a worker's take-home pay to finance private pensions or by transferring income within the family from the young to the old. Older people are no longer willing to live as paupers in their retirement. They expect to be provided for, one way or another.

Certainly the days of cheap social security, like the days of cheap gasoline, are gone forever. We will have to do some very hard thinking and some belt-tightening. But there is no rational justification for the hysteria that is being promoted today by some people who are attacking social security. They make emotional statements that our system is going bankrupt; it is not. They say that the burdens of funding pensions into the future will be unbearable; they will not be.

In 1961, then Secretary of Health, Education, and Welfare Abraham Ribicoff stated that he thought the limit to public acceptance of the social security payroll tax was 10 percent. We have passed through that ceiling without difficulty. Now people worry about the high rates in the year 2010 or 2020. But as economist Martin Feldstein (1975) has pointed out:

> *An increase in the social security tax rate to 16 or 20 percent would be a substantial increase. . . . There are some who believe that such high rates would create an intolerable burden on low-income and middle-income families. This is a false argument that ignores the substantial increase in real earnings that these families will enjoy at the same time that tax rates rise. Even a tax rate increase of 10 percentage points over the next 50 years is only an increase of 0.2 percent per year. The higher tax would absorb only one tenth of the annual real wage growth of 2 percent. Stated somewhat differently, with a 2 percent annual rate of growth, real wages would rise by 200 percent between now and 2030, and the higher social security tax would absorb no more than 10 percentage points of this 200 percentage point increase in real wages.*

Thus, it is important to remember the political acceptability of gradual increases in tax rates. This suggests that better pensions should be phased in over a period of years—similar to the way many other countries have introduced the major improvements in their programs. And it is probably wise to anticipate the demographic bulge and consequent sharp rise in costs beginning around the year 2010 as a result of the World War II baby boom.

Also, there is a need for a greater awareness of the intra- and intergenerational equity issues. As the costs of aged retirement living increase, more attention should be given to these issues in order both to maintain public confidence in and support for the programs and to use with maximum effectiveness the money allocated.

One of the most important issues we must deal with is the trend toward increasingly early retirement. It is certainly natural for many people to want to retire as early as possible. The evidence shows that as one gets older, the desire to continue working is clearly not as strong as it was once thought to be by many sociologists (see Chapter 3). There are many people who enjoy the new lifestyle retirement provides. But as society responds to the pressure for bigger pensions at earlier ages, pension costs rise at dramatic and staggering rates. For example, actuaries point out that pension costs increase by about 50 percent once the *normal* age of retirement is reduced from age 65 to age 60. Some private pension plans today allow people to retire below the age of 60 with no serious penalty. The cost of earlier retirement is measured not only by the costs of the pension benefits paid out, but also by the reduced economic output resulting when fewer workers remain in the work force.

Apart from the natural desire of many people to retire at an earlier age, there has also been a systematic, institutionalized pressure in this country to encourage older workers to leave the labor force. The Social Security Act itself imposes a severe retirement test on workers. More recently, private pension systems and early retirement policies have been instrumental in encouraging, and even forcing, workers to retire at increasingly earlier ages. Unions and management have responded to chronic unemployment in this country by devising pension systems that encourage one part of the labor force, the older workers, to leave in order to make room for another part, the younger workers.

What economists call "the lump of labor fallacy" is at the heart of this kind of thinking. There are those who believe there is a fixed number of jobs in the economy; so if younger people enter the labor force, older people must leave it. We do not need to accept such reasoning, however; the number of jobs in the economy is not fixed. We can provide jobs for younger and older people if we are willing to undertake the policies necessary to promote and ensure full employment while restraining prices. Full employment policies would reverse the trend toward early retirement.

Unfortunately, however, this solution does not appear to be a politically viable one—at least not in the near future; the political record of equivocation speaks for itself. Full employment without high inflation probably requires some major changes in the structure of the American economy and the rules under which it operates. Such changes are unlikely to occur in the near future, given "the privileged position of business" and the insecure position of unions (Lindblom, 1977).

Instead, we must look at more marginal, less effective solutions. Stopgap measures such as offering bonuses for delayed retirement, abolishing mandatory retirement policies, liberalizing the social security retirement test, and promoting full-time and part-time work among older people are being tried. But these attempts alone *will not have a major effect* on the trend toward early retirement.

We may have to do something more dramatic; we may have to regulate the early retirement policies of private pensions. As unattractive as government regulation is, it may be necessary in order to combat the very serious alternative of increasing early retirement. In this country the large and very prosperous corporations cover most of the workers with private pensions. When these large companies introduce an early retirement policy, competitive pressures force other less prosperous companies to follow suit.

As an alternative, some advocate that we gradually raise the social security retirement age. To raise the retirement age above 65, however, would be to renege on a national promise and seriously undermine public confidence in other social security promises. Yet this is an option that will have to be seriously debated in the years to come.

One thing is clear about future costs. The major economic issue is not whether—in the face of other public expenditure problems such as urban blight, national defense, and pollution—we can have better pensions and services for the aged. The issue is whether we want a higher standard of living in our retirement years at the expense of a lower standard in our younger years. While trade-offs must be continually made in the short run, rising incomes in retirement are closely related over the long run to sacrifices in consumption made in the earlier years. Whether we like it or not, the "economics of aging" begins for most of us quite early in life.

## Suggested Readings

Clark, Robert, Juanita Kreps, and Joseph Spengler. "Economics of Aging: A Survey." *Journal of Economic Literature* 16 (September 1978): 919–962.

  An excellent article for those who want a somewhat more technical overview. It contains an especially good section on "population aging—its sources and impact on dependency."

Derthick, Martha. "No Easy Votes on Social Security." *The Public Interest* 54 (Winter 1979): 94–105.

  Derthick argues that we do not know how popular social security really is because the costs were "initially deceptively low"; she foresees a shift to general revenues.

Doherty, Neville, Joan Segul, and Barbara Hicks. "Alternatives to Institutionalization for the Aged: Viability and Cost Effectiveness." *Aged Care and Services Review* 1 (January–February 1978): 1, 3–16.

  An up-to-date review of alternatives to hospital and nursing home care for the elderly. The authors conclude that existing information on the relative cost effectiveness of alternative programs is conflicting and inadequate as a base for policy decisions.

Hudson, Robert B., and Robert H. Binstock. "Political Systems and Aging." In Robert H. Binstock and Ethel Shanas, eds., *The Handbook of Aging and the Social Sciences.* New York: Van Nostrand Reinhold, 1976.

  A survey of what we know about the political attitudes and behavior of aging persons. The chapter has an excellent discussion of "aging power" and its organizations, with insightful analysis of the political realities involved in improving the social and economic status of the elderly through government action.

International Social Security Association. *Social Security Provisions in Case of Divorce.* Studies and Research No. 11. Geneva: 1978.

  Conference proceedings and country studies that provide an overview of alternative approaches to legislation in this area.

Kasschau, Patricia L. "Reevaluating the Need for Retirement Preparation Programs," *Industrial Gerontology,* new series 1 (Winter 1974): 42–59.

  A good overview of preretirement planning issues.

Kleiler, Frank M. *Can We Afford Retirement?* Baltimore: The Johns Hopkins University Press, 1978.

  A very readable overview of issues and data bearing on this important question.

Subcommittee on Aging of the Senate Committee on Labor and Public Welfare and
U.S. Senate Special Committee on Aging. *Post-White House Conference on
Aging Reports, 1973.* Washington, D.C.: U.S. Government Printing Office,
1973.

The recommendations of the White House Conference, the reaction of,
or action taken by, the Nixon Administration to the recommendations, and
an analysis prepared by study panels of the Post-Conference Board of the
White House Conference on Aging.

U.S. Senate Special Committee on Aging. *Future Directions in Social Security.* Parts
1–11. Washington, D.C.: U.S. Government Printing Office, 1974, 1975.

A series of hearings held by the committee during 1973 to 1976, explor-
ing various aspects of social security and seeking to develop information on
recommended changes.

# Glossary

**Actuarial valuation** Cost projections that take into account (for pensions) the number of employees retiring and dying each year, labor force turnover, the benefit formula, plan expenses, and investment income.

**Deferred profit sharing plan** A plan in which the company's contributions are based upon business profits. Profits are credited to employee accounts to be paid at retirement or other stated dates or circumstances (for example, disability or death).

**Defined benefit plans** Pension plans that state *before* retirement how much they will pay in benefits at retirement, benefits usually varying by years of service and/or earnings. These plans contrast with defined contribution plans that specify certain contributions to be made on an employee's behalf; the benefit is then determined at retirement on the basis of the total contribution accumulated.

**Depreciation allowance** A charge against the current income of a business to reflect the using up or "wear and tear" on a certain amount of its assets—primarily buildings and equipment. This charge is not paid out to other businesses but is retained within the firm as a bookkeeping entry.

**Depression** The recurrent ups and downs in the level of economic activity that extend over a period of years are referred to as the "business cycle." Depression usually refers to extreme low levels of economic activity extending over a long period (not seasonally). The Great Depression of the 1930s extended over almost a decade and resulted, at one point, in about a quarter of the work force being unemployed.

**Disregard** A term used to refer to provisions in means-tested financial support programs that exempt certain amounts of financial resources in determining benefit eligibility. For example, in the SSI program, $20 of social security benefits is disregarded in determining whether an applicant's total income falls below the level specified for payment of benefits.

**ERISA**   Employee Retirement Income Security Act of 1974. Federal legislation establishing participation, vesting, funding standards, plan-termination insurance, disclosure requirements, and Individual Retirement Accounts (IRAs).

**Federal Reserve**   The Federal Reserve is a central banking system for the United States established in 1913. There are twelve district banks and a coordinating seven-member Federal Reserve Board of Governors in Washington. Appointed to the Board of Governors for fourteen-year terms, members constitute a body that has been purposely established as an independent monetary authority.

**Fertility rate**   The total fertility rate is the number of births that 1,000 women would have in their lifetime if, at each year of age, they experienced the birth rates occurring in the specified calendar year. The fertility rate is an annual (or percentage) measure, even though it is expressed as a hypothetical lifetime (or cohort) measure.

**Fiscal policy**   Action by the government to influence the economy (especially to promote employment and decrease inflation) through changing tax rates and expenditure levels.

**Gross national product (GNP)**   The dollar value of the total annual output of final goods and services in the nation.

**Index(ing)**   The use of mathematical ratios to make comparisons between two different periods of time (or comparisons between different locations, industries, nationalities, etc.). The Consumer Price Index is probably the most well-known index, comparing "average" prices in a given year with those in a predetermined base year.

**Individual Retirement Account (IRA)**   Workers not covered by a retirement plan where they are employed may make tax deferrable contributions of 15 percent of earned income up to $1,500 per year to an individual account or annuity. Beginning in 1977, if there is a nonemployed spouse, the maximum is increased to $1,750. Funds in IRAs may be placed in a life insurance company, a bank, a mutual fund, or in certain special government bonds. There are penalties and immediate tax liability if funds are withdrawn prematurely.

**Inflation**   A substantial and sustained increase in the general level of prices. The result is a loss in the purchasing power of money which is customarily measured by various price indexes.

**Investment**   *Economic* investment is an activity (usually by businesses) that uses the resources of a nation to maintain or add to its stock of physical capital (i.e., buildings and equipment). The main source of investment expenditure is the retained earnings and depreciation allowances of business. Expenditures, however, are also made possible by savings from households by (a) direct borrowing or by sale of new stock issues or (b) indirectly via financial institutions.

**Joint and survivor option**   A type of pension benefit that provides income to the surviving spouse in an amount equal to some percentage of the income payable during the time that the employee and spouse were alive. Typically the percentage is 50 or 100 percent. In the absence of this provision, the spouse often loses his or her interest in the pension benefit.

**Life expectancy** A statistical measure of the average number of years persons born in a given year can be expected to live under the conditions prevailing in that year. Life expectancy is measured both at birth and at other stages of life.

**Lifetime rate of return** The interest rate that equalizes the compounded value of total taxes paid over a lifetime and the "present value" of the expected stream of benefits. A less technical definition is the rate at which the total value of accumulated payroll taxes (increased for interest) is equated to the value of benefits (decreased for interest). The present value of a sum of money due at a future date is the amount which, put at compound interest at a given rate, will amount to the sum specified at the stated date. The present value of, say, $1,000 at 5 percent is $746.30, since that sum compounded at 5 percent equals $1,000.

**Means test** A regulation stipulating that eligibility for aid and the amount of aid provided depend not, for example, on past employment or earnings but on specified amounts of income and/or assets of the person (family) requesting assistance.

**Median** A statistical measure that is often used instead of the mean to describe the center, middle, or average of a set of data. It is the value of the middle data item when the items are arranged in an increasing or decreasing order of magnitude. For example, the median of the data set 13 16 18 20 40 is 18.

**Monetary policy** Action by the government to influence the economy by changing the demand for, and supply of, money.

**Pension** A fixed dollar amount that is paid regularly by a former employer or government to a retired, disabled, or deserving person (or his dependents).

**Portability** A type of *vesting* (defined below) mechanism that allows employees to take their pension credits with them when they change jobs. For credits to be portable they must be vested, that is, nonforfeitable. ERISA permits portability but only if both employees and the involved employers mutually agree.

**Private pensions** These are pensions obtained through employment in the nongovernment sector of the economy. See **pension.**

**Productivity** An economic concept defined as the total output of a good or service divided by the total number of man-hours expended in producing the goods. Productivity is influenced by the level of technology, changes in capital plant and equipment, and the quality of the labor force.

**Profit sharing plan** See **deferred profit sharing plan.**

**Recession** A "mild" depression (defined above).

**Retained earnings** Business income after expenses that is not paid out in dividends or government taxes.

**Transfer income** Income that results from government disbursements for which no products or services are received. Most government welfare expenditures fall into this classification—social security payments, unemployment compensation, etc. Transfer payments, in a sense, rechannel tax revenues of the public sector back into the hands of individuals and groups in the private sector.

**Vesting**  The pension rights of a terminating employee depend on the plan provisions. Vesting refers to the provision that gives a participant the right to receive an accrued benefit at a designated age, regardless of whether the employee is still employed at that time. Thus, vesting removes the obligation of the participant to remain in the pension plan until the date of early or normal retirement.

**Wage index**  A measure of the change in general wage levels. Such an index is used in the social security program to adjust recorded wages of workers before calculating benefits. Thus, if a worker earned $3,000 in 1956, retired at age 65 in 1984, and wage levels were, say, two and one-half times higher than in 1956, the indexing factor of 2½ would be applied to the $3,000 and the index earnings would be $7,500 (see also **indexing**).

# References

Aaron, Henry J. 1977. "Demographic Effects on the Equity of Social Security Benefits." In M. S. Feldstein and R. P. Inman, eds., *The Economics of Public Service.* New York: Macmillan, pp. 151–173.

Aaron, Henry J.; John A. Brittain; Joseph A. Pechman; Alice Rivlin; Charles Schultze; and Nancy H. Teeters. 1972. *Washington Post* (October 4).

Abbott, Julian. 1977. "Socioeconomic Characteristics of the Elderly: Some Black-White Differences." *Social Security* 40 (July): 16–42.

Ad Hoc Advisory Committee. 1975. "Social Security: A Sound and Durable Institution of Great Value." In U.S. Senate Special Committee on Aging. *Future Directions in Social Security—Unresolved Issues: An Interim Staff Report.* Washington, D.C.: U.S. Government Printing Office.

Advisory Council on Social Security. 1975. Reports. Washington, D.C.: mimeographed.

Ahart, Gregory J. 1978. Testimony. In Subcommittee on Social Security, U.S. House Committee on Ways and Means, *Disability Insurance Program: 1978.* Washington, D.C.: U.S. Government Printing Office, pp. 2–9.

Andrisani, Paul J. 1977. "Effects of Health Problems on the Work Experience of Middle-aged Men." *Industrial Gerontology* 4 (Spring): 97–112.

Aspin, Les. 1976. "The Burden of Generosity." *Harper's* 253 (December): 22–24.

Atchley, Robert. 1971. "Retirement and Leisure Participation: Continuity or Crisis?" *The Gerontologist* 11 (Spring Part I): 13–17.

———. 1972. *The Social Forces in Later Life.* Belmont, Calif.: Wadsworth.

———. 1976. *The Sociology of Retirement.* New York: Wiley/Schenkman.

Ball, Robert. 1978a. "Income Security for the Elderly." In *The Economics of Aging.* A National Journal Issues Book. Washington, D.C.: The Government Research Corporation, pp. 1748–1753.

————. 1978b. *Social Security Today and Tomorrow*. New York: Columbia University Press.

Bankers Trust. 1977. *Study of Employee Savings and Thrift Plans*. New York: Bankers Trust.

Barfield, Richard E., and James N. Morgan. 1978a. "Trends in Planned Early Retirement." *The Gerontologist* 18 (February): 13–18.

————. 1978b. "Trends in Satisfaction with Retirement." *The Gerontologist* 18 (February): 19–23.

Barro, Robert J. 1978. *The Impact of Social Security on Private Saving—Evidence from the U.S. Time Series*. Washington, D.C.: American Enterprise Institute.

Bassett, Preston C. 1978. "Future Pension Policy and the President's Commission." *Employee Benefit Plan Review* 33 (December): 28, 30, 91.

Batten, Michael D. 1973. "Application of a Unique Industrial Health System." *Industrial Gerontology* (Fall): 38–48.

Baugher, Dan. 1978. "Is the Older Worker Inherently Incompetent?" *Aging and Work* 1 (Fall): 243–250.

Berkowitz, Monroe. 1979. "The Search for a Health Variable." In *Proceedings of the Workshop on Policy Analysis with Social Security Research Files*. Washington, D.C.: Social Security Administration.

Berkowitz, Monroe; William G. Johnson; and Edward H. Murphy. 1976. *Public Policy Toward Disability*. New York: Praeger.

Bernstein, Merton. 1973. "Rehabilitating Workmen's Compensation: Alternatives for the Future." In Philip Booth, ed., *Social Security: Policy for the Seventies*. Ann Arbor: Institute of Labor and Industrial Relations, University of Michigan and Wayne State University, pp. 132–172.

Bernstein, Peter L. 1975. "Capital Shortage: Cyclical or Secular?" *Challenge* 17 (November–December): 6–11.

Bixby, Lenore E. 1970. "Income of People Aged 65 and Over." *Social Security Bulletin* 33 (April): 3–34.

————. 1976. "Retirement Patterns in the United States: Research and Policy Interaction." *Social Security Bulletin* 39 (August): 3–19.

BNA. 1978. *Pension Reporter* 202 (August 21): A-9.

————. 1979a. *Pension Reporter* 220 (January 1): A–14 and A–15.

————. 1979b. *Pension Reporter* 238 (May 7): A–10.

Borzilleri, Thomas C. 1978. "The Need for a Separate Consumer Index for Older Persons." *The Gerontologist* 18 (June): 230–236.

Bosworth, Barry; James S. Duesenberry; and Andrew S. Carron. 1975. *Capital Needs in the Seventies*. Washington, D.C.: The Brookings Institution.

Boulding, Kenneth. 1958. *Principles of Economic Policy*. Englewood Cliffs, N.J.: Prentice-Hall.

Brittain, John A. 1972. *The Payroll Tax for Social Security*. Washington, D.C.: The Brookings Institution.

Broder, David S. 1973. "Budget Funds for Elderly Grow Rapidly." *Washington Post* (January 30, 1973): A-16.

Brotman, Herman B. 1978. "The Aging of America: A Demographic Profile." In *The Economics of Aging.* A National Journal Issues Book. Washington, D.C.: The Government Research Corporation, pp. 1622–1627.

Brown, J. Douglas. 1972. *An American Philosophy of Social Security.* Princeton, N.J.: Princeton University Press.

———. 1973. Memorandum. In U.S. Senate Special Committee on Aging, *Future Directions in Social Security.* Part 3. Washington, D.C.: U.S. Government Printing Office, pp. 220–221.

Browning, Edgar K. 1973. "Social Insurance and Intergenerational Transfers." *Journal of Law and Economics* (October): 215–237.

Buchanan, James M. 1968. "Social Insurance in a Growing Economy: A Proposal for Radical Reform." *National Tax Journal* (December): 386–395.

*Business Week.* 1977. "Unfunded Pension Liabilities: A Growing Worry for Companies." (July 18): 86–88.

Califano, Joseph A., Jr. 1978a. "U.S. Policy for the Aging—A Commitment to Ourselves." In *The Economics of Aging.* A National Journal Issues Book. Washington, D.C.: The Government Research Corporation, pp. 1575–1581.

———. 1978b. "The Aging of America: Questions for the Four Generation Society." *Annals of the American Academy of Political and Social Science* (July): 96–107.

———. 1979. Testimony. In U.S. Senate Special Committee on Aging, *Retirement, Work, and Lifelong Learning.* Washington, D.C.: U.S. Government Printing Office.

Campbell, Colin D., and Rosemary G. Campbell. 1976. "Conflicting Views on the Effect of Old-Age and Survivors Insurance on Retirement." *Economic Inquiry* 14 (September): 369–388.

Campbell, Rita Ricardo. 1975. Supplementary Statement. In *Reports of the Quadrennial Advisory Council on Social Security.* Washington, D.C.: U.S. Government Printing Office.

Cardwell, James B. 1976. Testimony. In Subcommittee on Social Security, U.S. House Committee on Ways and Means, *Disability Insurance Program.* Washington, D.C.: U.S. Government Printing Office, pp. 273–281.

Caswell, Jerry. 1974. "Economic Efficiency in Pension Plan Administration: A Study of the Construction Industry." Ph.D. dissertation, University of Pennsylvania.

Chen, Yung-Ping, and Kwang-Wen Chu. 1974. "Tax-benefit Ratios and Rates of Return Under OASI: 1974 Retirees and Entrants." *The Journal of Risk and Insurance* 41 (June): 189–206.

———. 1977. "Total Dependency Burden and Social Security Solvency." In Industrial Relations Research Association, *Proceedings of the 29th Annual Meeting.* Madison, Wisconsin: pp. 43–51.

Clark, Robert; Juanita Kreps; and Joseph Spengler. 1978. "Economics of Aging: A Survey." *Journal of Economic Literature* 16 (September): 919–962.

Clark, Robert, and Joseph Spengler. 1978. "The Implications of Future Dependency Ratios and Their Composition." In Barbara Pieman Herzog, ed., *Aging and Income.* New York: Human Sciences Press, pp. 55–89.

Cohen, Wilbur J. 1957. *Retirement Policies Under Social Security*. Berkeley: University of California Press.

Cohen, Wilbur J., and Milton Friedman. 1972. *Social Security: Universal or Selective?* Rational Debate Seminars. Washington, D.C.: American Enterprise Institute for Public Policy Research.

Colberg, Marshall R. 1978. *The Social Security Retirement Test—Right or Wrong?* Washington, D.C.: American Enterprise Institute for Public Policy Research.

Congressional Budget Office. 1977a. *Long-Term Care for the Elderly and Disabled*. Washington, D.C.: U.S. Government Printing Office.

———. 1977b. *Poverty Status of Families Under Alternative Definitions of Income*. Background Paper No. 17. Washington, D.C.: U.S. Congress.

Consultant Panel on Social Security. 1976. *Report on Social Security to the Congressional Research Service*. Washington, D.C.: U.S. Government Printing Office.

Cottrell, Fred, and Robert C. Atchley. 1969. *Women in Retirement: A Preliminary Report*. Oxford, Ohio: Scripps Foundation.

Cutler, Neal E., and Robert A. Harootyan. 1975. "Demography of the Aged." In Diana S. Woodruff and James E. Birren, eds., *Aging*. New York: Van Nostrand, pp. 31–69.

Dale, Edwin L., Jr. 1973. "The Young Pay for the Old." *New York Times Magazine* (January 14): 8ff.

Diamond, P. A. 1977. "A Framework for Social Security Analysis." *Journal of Public Economics* 8 (December): 275–298.

Donahue, Wilma; Harold L. Orbach; and Otto Pollak. 1960. "Retirement: The Emerging Social Pattern." In Clark Tibbitts, ed., *Handbook of Social Gerontology*. Chicago: University of Chicago Press, pp. 330–406.

Dowd, James J., and Vern Bengtson. 1978. "Aging in Minority Populations." *Journal of Gerontology* 33 (May): 427–436.

Ehrbar, A. F. 1977. "Those Pension Plans Are Even Weaker Than You Think." *Fortune* 96 (November): 104–114.

Epstein, Lenore A., and Janet H. Murray. 1967. *The Aged Population of the United States*. Office of Research and Statistics, Social Security Administration. Report No. 19. Washington, D.C.: U.S. Government Printing Office.

Fairholm, Gilbert W. 1978. *Property Tax Relief Programs for the Elderly: A Review of Current Literature and Policy Implications for Virginia*. Richmond: Virginia Center on Aging, Virginia Commonwealth University, mimeographed.

Federal Council on Aging. 1975. *Study of Interrelationships of Benefit Programs for the Elderly*. Appendix I: "Handbook of Federal Programs Benefiting Older Americans." Prepared for the Federal Council on Aging by the Human Resources and Income Security Project, The Urban Institute. Washington, D.C.: mimeographed.

Feldstein, Martin S. 1972. "The Incidence of the Social Security Payroll Tax: Comment." *The American Economic Review* 42 (September): 735–742.

———. 1974. "Social Security, Induced Retirement, and Aggregate Capital Accumulation." *Journal of Political Economy* 82 (September–October): 905–926.

————. 1975. "Toward a Reform of Social Security." *The Public Interest* 40 (Summer): 80–81.

————. 1977. "Facing the Social Security Crisis." *The Public Interest* 47 (Spring): 88–100.

Fisher, Paul. 1978. *Work Sharing in the Federal Republic of Germany.* Report to the U.S. Department of Labor. Washington, D.C.: mimeographed.

Fitzgerald, Albert J. 1978. Testimony. In Subcommittee on Retirement Income and Employment, U.S. House Select Committee on Aging, *National Pension Policies: Private Pension Plans.* Washington, D.C.: U.S. Government Printing Office, pp. 486–494.

Fitzpatrick, Edmund W. 1978. "An Industry Consortium Approach to Retirement Planning—A New Program." *Aging and Work* 1 (Summer): 181–188.

————. 1979. "Evaluating a New Retirement Planning Program—Results with Hourly Workers." *Aging and Work* (Spring): 87–94.

Flint, Jerry. 1977. "Early Retirement Is Growing in U.S." *New York Times* (July 10): 1.

Flowers, Marilyn R. 1977. *Women and Social Security: An Institutional Dilemma.* Washington, D.C.: American Enterprise Institute for Public Policy Research.

Fox, Alan. 1979. "Earnings Replacement Rates of Retired Couples: Findings from the Retirement History Study." *Social Security Bulletin* 42 (January): 17–39.

Freiden, Alan; Dean Leimer; and Ronald Hoffman. 1976. *Internal Rates of Return to Retired Worker-Only Beneficiaries Under Social Security, 1967–70.* Studies in Income Distribution No. 5. Washington, D.C.: Office of Research and Statistics, Social Security Administration.

Friedman, Eugene A., and Harold L. Orbach. 1974. "Adjustment to Retirement." In Silvano Arieti, ed., *The Foundations of Psychiatry.* Vol. 1, *American Handbook of Psychiatry,* 2nd ed. New York: Basic Books, pp. 609–645.

Friedman, Milton. 1962. *Capitalism and Freedom.* Chicago: University of Chicago Press.

————. 1971. "Purchasing Power Bonds." *Newsweek* (April 12): 86.

————. 1972. "Second Lecture." In Wilbur J. Cohen and Milton Friedman, *Social Security: Universal or Selective?* Rational Debate Seminars. Washington, D.C.: American Enterprise Institute.

Frumpkin, Robert, and Donald Schmitt. 1979. "Pension Improvements Since 1974 Reflect Inflation—New U.S. Law." *Monthly Labor Review* 102 (March): 32–37.

Galbraith, John Kenneth. 1967. *The New Industrial State.* New York: New American Library.

Gibson, Robert M., and Charles R. Fisher. 1978. "National Health Expenditures, Fiscal Year 1977." *Social Security Bulletin* 41 (July): 3–20.

Gibson, Robert M.; Marjorie Smith Mueller; and Charles R. Fisher. 1977. "Age Differences in Health Care Spending, Fiscal Year 1976." *Social Security Bulletin* 40 (August): 3–14.

Griffin, Frank L., and C. L. Trowbridge. 1969. *Status of Funding Under Private Pension Plans.* Homewood, Ill.: Irwin.

Hauser, Philip M. 1976. "Aging and World-Wide Population Change." In R. H. Binstock and E. Shanas, eds., *Handbook of Aging and the Social Sciences.* New York: Van Nostrand Reinhold, pp. 59–86.

Hayghe, Howard. 1978. "Marital and Family Characteristics of Workers, March 1977." *Monthly Labor Review* 101 (February): 51–54.

HEW Task Force (on the Treatment of Women Under Social Security). 1978. *Report.* Washington, D.C.: U.S. Department of Health, Education and Welfare.

Hewitt, Edwin S. 1970. Testimony. In U.S. Senate Special Committee on Aging, *Economics of Aging: Toward a Full Share in Abundance,* Part 10B. Washington, D.C.: U.S. Government Printing Office.

Hollister, Robinson G., and John L. Palmer. 1972. "The Impact of Inflation on the Poor." In Kenneth Boulding and M. Pfaff, eds., *Redistribution to the Rich and Poor: The Grants Economics of Income Distribution.* Belmont, Calif: Wadsworth, pp. 240–270.

Hudson, Robert. 1978. "The 'Graying' of the Federal Budget and Its Consequences for Old-Age Policy." *The Gerontologist* 18 (October): 428–440.

Iglehart, John K. 1978. "The Cost of Keeping the Elderly Well." In *The Economics of Aging.* A National Journal Issues Book. Washington, D.C.: The Government Research Corporation, pp. 1728–1731.

Irelan, Lola M., and K. Bond. 1976. "Retirees of the 1970's." In Gary S. Kart and Barbara B. Manard, *Aging in America—Readings in Social Gerontology.* Port Washington: Alfred, pp. 231–251.

Jackson, J. J. 1970. "Aged Negroes: Their Cultural Departures from Statistical Stereotypes and Rural-Urban Differences." *Gerontologist* 10 (Summer): 140–145.

Kahne, Hilda. 1975. "Economic Perspectives on the Roles of Women in the American Economy." *The Journal of Economic Literature* 13 (December): 1249–1292.

King, Jill. 1976. *The Consumer Price Index.* Technical Paper V. The Measure of Poverty reports. Washington, D.C.: U.S. Department of Health, Education, and Welfare.

Kingson, Eric R. 1979. "Men Who Leave Work Before Age 62: A Study of Advantaged and Disadvantaged Very Early Labor Force Withdrawal." Ph.D. dissertation, Florence Heller Graduate School, Brandeis University.

Kreps, Juanita M. 1971. *Lifetime Allocation of Work and Income.* Durham, N.C.: Duke University Press.

——. 1977. "Age, Work, and Income." *Southern Economic Journal* 43 (April): 1423–1437.

Kreps, Juanita M., and Joseph J. Spengler. 1966. "The Leisure Component of Economic Growth." In National Commission on Technology, Automation, and Economic Progress. *Technology and the Economy.* Appendix 2: The Employment Impact of Technological Change. Washington, D.C.: U.S. Government Printing Office.

Krute, Aaron, and Mary Ellen Burdette. 1978. "1972 Survey of Disabled and Non-disabled Adults: Chronic Disease, Injury, and Work Disability." *Social Security Bulletin* 41 (April): 3–17.

Leimer, Dean R. 1979. "Projected Rates of Return to Future Social Security Retirees Under Alternative Benefit Structures." In *Proceedings of the Workshop on Policy Analysis with Social Security Record Files.* Washington, D.C.: Social Security Administration.

Leuthold, Jane H. 1975. "The Incidence of the Payroll Tax in the United States." *Public Finance Quarterly* 3 (January): 3–13.

Liang, J., and T. J. Fairchild. 1979. "Relative Deprivation and Perception of Financial Adequacy Among the Aged." *Gerontology* 34 (September): 747–760.

Lindblom, Charles E. 1977. *Politics and Markets—The World's Political–Economic Systems.* New York: Basic Books.

Lingg, Barbara A. 1977. "Beneficiaries Affected by Annual Earnings Test in 1973." *Social Security Bulletin* 40 (September): 3–14.

Lopata, Helena. 1977. "Widows and Widowers." *The Humanist* 37 (September–October): 25–28.

Loren, Eugene, and Thomas Barker. 1968. *Survivor Benefits.* Detroit: Michigan Health and Social Security Research Institute.

McGill, Dan M. 1975. *Fundamentals of Private Pensions,* 3rd ed. Homewood, Ill.: Irwin.

Mallan, Lucy B. 1975. "Young Widows and Their Children: A Comparative Report." *Social Security Bulletin* 38 (May): 3–21.

Marcou, Ross A. 1978. "Comparing Federal and Private Employee Benefits." *Civil Service Journal* (October–December): 12–18.

Maxwell, James A. 1975. "Characteristics of State and Local Trust Funds." In David J. Ott, Attiat F. Ott, James A. Maxwell, and J. Richard Aronson, *State-Local Finances in the Last Half of the 1970's.* Washington, D.C.: The American Enterprise Institute, pp. 35–62.

Meier, Elizabeth. 1975. "Over 65: Expectations and Realities of Work and Retirement." *Industrial Gerontology* (Spring): 95–109.

Michael, Robert T. 1979. "Variations Across Households in the Rate of Inflation." *Journal of Money, Credit, and Banking* 2 (February): 32–46.

Mirer, Thad W. 1974. "The Distributional Impact of Inflation and Anti-inflation Policy." Discussion Paper 231-74. Madison: Institute for Research on Poverty, University of Wisconsin-Madison.

Moeller, Charles. 1972. "The Role of Private Pension Plans in the Economy." In *Financing Retirement: Public and Private.* Conference Proceedings. New York: The Tax Foundation, Inc.

Moon, Marilyn. 1977. *The Measurement of Economic Welfare—Its Application to the Aged Poor.* New York: Academic Press.

Morgan, James N. 1977. "An Economic Theory of the Social Security System and Its Relation to Fiscal Policy." In G. S. Tolley and Richard V. Burkhauser, eds.,

*Income Support Policies for the Aged.* Cambridge, Mass.: Ballinger, pp. 107–126.

Morgan, James N.; Katherine Dickinson; Jonathan Dickinson; Jacob Benus; and Greg Duncan. 1974. *Five Thousand American Families—Patterns of Economic Progress.* Ann Arbor, Michigan: Survey Research Center, Institute for Social Research, University of Michigan.

Morris, George B. 1977. Testimony. In U.S. House Select Committee on Aging, *Retirement Age Policies, Part I.* Hearings. Washington, D.C.: U.S. Government Printing Office, pp. 13–30.

Motley, Dena K. 1978. "Availability of Retired Persons for Work: Findings from the Retirement History Study." *Social Security Bulletin* 41 (April): 18–29.

Munnell, Alicia H. 1974. *The Impact of Social Security on Personal Saving.* Cambridge, Mass.: Ballinger.

———. 1977. *The Future of Social Security.* Washington, D.C.: The Brookings Institution.

———. 1979. "Are Private Pensions Doomed?" *New England Economic Review* (March/April): 5–20.

Musgrave, Richard. 1968. "The Role of Social Insurance in an Overall Program for Social Welfare." In Bowen et al., *The American System of Social Insurance.* New York: McGraw-Hill, pp. 23–45.

Myers, Robert J. 1970. "Government and Pension." In *Private Pensions and the Public Interest.* Washington, D.C.: The American Enterprise Institute.

———. 1975a. *Social Security.* Homewood, Ill.: Irwin.

———. 1975b. "Social Security and Private Pensions—Where Do We Go from Here?" *Industrial Gerontology* 2 (Spring): 158–163.

———. 1978. "The New Social Security Amendments: How They Affect Private Pension Plans." *Pension World* (March): 14–18.

Myrdal, Gunnar. 1963. *Challenge to Affluence.* New York: Pantheon Books.

National Council on the Aging. 1975. *The Myth and Reality of Aging in America.* Washington, D.C.

National Survey of the Black Aged. 1978. Summary Report. *Social Security Bulletin* 41 (July): 33–35.

Nordhaus, W., and J. Tobin. 1973. "Is Growth Obsolete?" In *The Measurement of Economic and Social Performance.* New York: National Bureau of Economic Research, pp. 509–532.

Okonkwo, Ubadigbo. 1975. "Intragenerational Equity Under Social Security." Washington, D.C.: mimeographed.

Okun, Arthur. 1975. *Equality and Efficiency—The Big Trade-Off.* Washington, D.C.: The Brookings Institution.

Orshansky, Mollie. 1974. *Federal Welfare Reform and the Economic Status of the Aged Poor.* Staff Paper No. 17. Washington, D.C.: Office of Research and Statistics, U.S. Social Security Administration.

———. 1978. Testimony. In U.S. House Select Committee on Aging, *Poverty Among America's Aged.* Washington, D.C.: U.S. Government Printing Office.

Palmore, Erdman. 1977. "Facts on Aging—A Short Quiz." *The Gerontologist* 17 (July): 315–320.

Parnes, Herbert S. et al. 1974. *The Pre-retirement Years.* Vol. 4. Columbus, Ohio: Center for Human Resource Research, Ohio State University.

Pechman, Joseph A.; Henry J. Aaron; and Michael K. Taussig. 1968. *Social Security: Perspectives for Reform.* Washington, D.C.: The Brookings Institution.

Poverty Studies Task Force. 1976. *The Measure of Poverty.* A Report to Congress as Mandated by the Education Amendments of 1974. Washington, D.C.: U.S. Department of Health, Education, and Welfare.

Profit Sharing Research Foundation. 1978. *Profit Sharing in 38 Large Companies.* Evanston, Ill.

Pursell, Donald E., and William D. Torrence. 1979. "Age and the Jobhunting Methods of the Unemployed." *Monthly Labor Review* 102 (January): 68–69.

Quinn, Joseph F. 1975. "The Microeconomics of Early Retirement: A Cross-Section View of White Married Men." *Journal of Human Resources* 12 (Summer): 329–346.

Reich, Murray H. 1977. "Group Preretirement Education Programs: Whither the Proliferation?" *Industrial Gerontology* 4 (Winter): 29–43.

Rejda, George E., and Richard J. Shepler. 1973. "The Impact of Zero Population Growth on the OASDHI Program." *The Journal of Risk and Insurance* 40 (September): 313–325.

Reno, Virginia. 1971. "Why Men Stop Working At or Before Age 65: Findings from the Survey of New Beneficiaries." *Social Security Bulletin* (June): 3–11.

Riley, Matilda White, and Anne Foner. 1968. *Aging and Society,* Vol. 1. New York: Russell Sage Foundation.

Robertson, A. Haeworth. 1977. "OASDI: Fiscal Basis and Long-Range Cost Projections." *Social Security Bulletin* 40 (January): 1–9.

————. 1978. "Financial Status of Social Security Program After the Social Security Amendments of 1977." *Social Security Bulletin* 41 (March): 21–30.

Rones, Philip L. 1978. "Older Men—The Choice Between Work and Retirement." *Monthly Labor Review* 101 (November): 3–10.

Ross, Irwin. 1978. "Retirement at Seventy: A New Trauma for Management." *Fortune* 97 (May 8): 106–112.

Rosset, E. 1964. *Aging Process of Populations.* New York: Macmillan.

Rowen, Hobart. 1978. "Rethinking That Bite in Social Security." *Washington Post* (February 16): A19.

Sager, Alan. 1978. *Improving the Provisions of Non-Institutional Long-Term Care to the Elderly.* Waltham: Levinson Policy Institute, mimeographed.

Samuelson, Paul. 1958. "An Exact Consumption-Loan Model of Interest With or Without the Social Contrivance of Money." *Journal of Political Economy* 66 (December): 467–482.

Samuelson, Robert J. 1978. "The Withering Freedom to Govern—Soaring Costs for Elderly Curb President's Choices." *Washington Post* (March 5): C1 and C5.

Schieber, Sylvester J. 1978. "First Year Impact of SSI on Economic Status of 1973 Adult Assistance Populations." *Social Security Bulletin* 41 (February): 18–51.

Schmundt, M.; E. Smolensky; and L. Stiefel. 1975. "The Evaluation of Recipients of In-Kind Transfers." In I. Laurie, ed., *Integrating Income Maintenance Programs.* New York: Academic Press, pp. 189–207.

Schulz, James H. 1977. "The Social Security Retirement Test: Time for a Change?" *The Urban and Social Change Review* 10 (Summer): 14–18.

———. 1978. "Liberalizing the Social Security Retirement Test—Who Would Receive the Increased Pension Benefits?" *Journal of Gerontology* 33 (March): 262–268.

Schulz, James H., and Guy Carrin. 1972. "The Role of Savings and Pension Systems in Maintaining Living Standards in Retirement." *Journal of Human Resources* 7 (Summer): 343–365.

Schulz, James; Guy Carrin; Hans Krupp; Manfred Peschke; Elliott Sclar; and J. Van Steenberge. 1974. *Providing Adequate Retirement Income—Pension Reform in the United States and Abroad.* Hanover, N.H.: New England Press for Brandeis University Press.

Schulz, James H.; Thomas Leavitt; and Leslie Kelly. 1979. "Private Pensions Fall Far Short of Preretirement Income Levels." *Monthly Labor Review* 102 (February): 28–32.

Schwab, Karen. 1976. "Early Labor-Force Withdrawal of Men: Participants and Nonparticipants Aged 58–63." In Social Security Administration, *Almost 65: Baseline Data from the Retirement History Study.* Washington, D.C.: Office of Research and Statistics, pp. 43–56.

Shanas, Ethel, and Philip M. Hauser. 1974. "Zero Population Growth and the Family Life of Old People." *Journal of Social Issues* 30: 79–92.

Shanas, Ethel; Peter Townsend; Dorothy Wedderburn; Henning Friis; Poul Milhoj; and Jan Stehouwer. 1968. *Old People in Three Industrial Societies.* New York: Atherton.

Sheppard, Harold L. 1978. "The Economics of Population, Mortality, and Retirement." In *The Economics of Aging.* A National Journal Issues Book. Washington, D.C.: The Government Research Corporation, pp. 1880–1883.

Sheppard, Harold L., and A. Harvey Belitsky. 1966. *The Job Hunt.* Baltimore, Md.: Johns Hopkins Press.

Sheppard, Harold L., and Sara E. Rix. 1977. *The Graying of Working America—The Coming Crisis in Retirement-Age Policy.* New York: The Free Press.

Shishkin, Julius. 1974. "Updating the Consumer Price Index—An Overview." *Monthly Labor Review* 97 (July): 3–20.

Siegel, Jacob S. 1976. *Demographic Aspects of Aging and the Older Population in the United States.* Current Population Reports, Special Studies. Series P-23, No. 59. Washington, D.C.: U.S. Government Printing Office.

Siegfried, Charles A. 1970. "The Role of Private Pensions." In *Private Pensions and the Public Interest.* Washington, D.C.: The American Enterprise Institute.

Skolnik, Alfred M. 1975. "Restructuring the Railroad Retirement System." *Social Security Bulletin* 38 (April): 23–29.

Skopic, Charles. 1978. Testimony. In Subcommittee on Retirement Income and Employment, U.S. House Select Committee on Aging, *National Pension Policies: Private Pension Plans*. Washington, D.C.: U.S. Government Printing Office, pp. 216–227.

Slavick, Fred. 1966. *Compulsory and Flexible Retirement in the American Economy*. Ithaca, N.Y.: Cornell University Press.

Sobel, Irvin, and Richard C. Wilcock. 1963. "Job Placement Services for Older Workers in the United States." *International Labor Review* 88: 129–156.

Social Security Administration. 1976. *Almost 65: Baseline Data from the Retirement History Study*. Washington, D.C.: Office of Research and Statistics.

———. 1978. "Benefits and Beneficiaries Under Public Employee Retirement Systems, Calendar Year 1976." *Research and Statistics Note* No. 8 (July).

Solow, Robert M. 1975. "The Intelligent Citizen's Guide to Inflation." *The Public Interest* 38 (Winter): 30–66.

Sommers, Dixie, and Alan Eck. 1977. "Occupational Mobility in the American Labor Force." *Monthly Labor Review* 3 (January): 3–19.

Staines, Graham L., and Robert P. Quinn. 1979. "American Workers Evaluate the Quality of Their Jobs." *Monthly Labor Review* 102 (January): 3–12.

Storey, James R. 1973. *Public Income Transfer Programs: The Incidence of Multiple Benefits and the Issues Raised by Their Receipt*. Subcommittee on Fiscal Policy, U.S. Joint Economic Committee. Studies in Public Welfare No. 1. Washington, D.C.: U.S. Government Printing Office.

Streib, Gordon F., and Clement J. Schneider. 1971. *Retirement in American Society*. Ithaca, N.Y.: Cornell University Press.

Subcommittee on Social Security, U.S. House Committee on Ways and Means. 1978a. *Disability Insurance—Possible Areas of Subcommittee Action*. Washington, D.C.: U.S. Government Printing Office.

———. 1978b. *Proposed Disability Insurance Amendments of 1978 (H.R. 14084)*. Washington, D.C.: U.S. Government Printing Office.

Surrey, Stanley. 1973. *Pathways to Tax Reform—The Concept of Tax Expenditures*. Cambridge, Mass.: Harvard University Press.

Taggart, Robert. 1973. *The Labor Market Impacts of the Private Retirement System*. U.S. Subcommittee on Fiscal Policy, U.S. Joint Economic Committee. Studies in Public Welfare No. 11. Washington, D.C.: U.S. Government Printing Office.

Task Force on Women and Social Security. 1975. *Women and Social Security: Adapting to a New Era*. Prepared for the Special Senate Committee on Aging. Washington, D.C.: U.S. Government Printing Office.

The Tax Foundation, Inc. 1969. *State and Local Employee Pension Systems*. New York: The Tax Foundation, Inc.

Thompson, Gayle B. 1978. "Pension Coverage and Benefits, 1972: Findings from the Retirement History Study." *Social Security Bulletin* 41 (February): 3–17.

Thurow, Lester. 1976. "Tax Wealth, Not Income." *New York Times Magazine* (April 11): 32.

Tibbits, Clark. 1977. "Older Americans in the Family Context." *Aging* 270–271 (April–May): 6–11.

Tilove, Robert. 1976. *Public Employee Pension Funds.* Twentieth Century Fund. New York: Columbia University Press.

Tissue, Thomas. 1978. "Response to Recipiency Under Public Assistance and SSI." *Social Security Bulletin* 41 (November): 3–15.

Torda, Theodore S. 1972. "The Impact of Inflation on the Elderly." *Federal Reserve Bank of Cleveland Monthly Review* (October–November): 3–19.

Trowbridge, Charles L. 1970. "Private Pension Funding and Vesting—Where Do They Stand Today?" In *Private Pensions and the Public Interest.* Washington, D.C.: The American Enterprise Institute, pp. 139–158.

Turnbull, John G.; C. Arthur Williams, Jr.; and Earl F. Cheit. 1967. *Economic and Social Security,* 3rd ed. New York: Ronald Press.

U.S. Bureau of the Census. 1976. *Consumer Income.* Current Population Reports, Series P-60, No. 101. Washington, D.C.: U.S. Government Printing Office.

———. 1978. *Consumer Income.* Current Population Reports, Series P-60, No. 116. Washington, D.C.: U.S. Government Printing Office.

U.S. Bureau of Labor Statistics. 1966. *Retired Couple's Budget for a Moderate Living Standard.* Bulletin No. 1570-4. Washington, D.C.: U.S. Government Printing Office.

———. 1967. *Three Standards of Living for an Urban Family of Four Persons.* Bulletin No. 1570-5. Washington, D.C.: U.S. Government Printing Office.

———. 1978. "Three Budgets for a Retired Couple, Autumn 1977." *News.* Washington, D.C.: Department of Labor news release, August 13.

U.S. Department of Health, Education, and Welfare. 1979. *Social Security and the Changing Roles of Men and Women.* Report to Congress. Washington, D.C.: U.S. Department of Health, Education, and Welfare.

U.S. Department of Labor. 1965. *The Older American Worker.* Washington, D.C.: U.S. Department of Labor.

U.S. House Committee on Education and Labor. 1972. *Interim Staff Report of Activities of the Pension Study Task Force.* Washington, D.C.: U.S. Government Printing Office.

———. 1978. *Pension Task Force Report on Public Employee Retirement Systems.* Washington, D.C.: U.S. Government Printing Office.

U.S. House Committee on Ways and Means. 1967a. *President's Proposals for Revision in the Social Security System.* Hearings, Part 1. Washington, D.C.: U.S. Government Printing Office.

———. 1967b. *Social Security Amendments of 1967.* Report on H.R. 12080. Washington, D.C.: U.S. Government Printing Office.

U.S. House Select Committee on Aging Staff. 1978. *Poverty Among America's Aged—A Staff Review.* In U.S. House Select Committee on Aging, *Poverty Among America's Aged.* Hearings. Washington, D.C.: U.S. Government Printing Office.

U.S. Joint Economic Committee. 1972. *Studies in Public Welfare.* Paper No. 2. Washington, D.C.: U.S. Government Printing Office.

U.S. Manpower Administration. 1970. *The Pre-retirement Years.* Vol. 1. Manpower Research Monograph No. 15. Washington, D.C.: U.S. Department of Labor.

U.S. Senate Committee on Finance. 1975. *Report of the Panel on Social Security Financing.* Washington, D.C.: U.S. Government Printing Office.

————. 1977. *The Supplemental Security Income Program.* Report of the staff. Washington, D.C.: U.S. Government Printing Office.

U.S. Senate Special Committee on Aging. 1970. *The Stake of Today's Workers in Retirement Security.* Washington, D.C.: U.S. Government Printing Office.

U.S. Subcommittee on Housing for the Elderly, U.S. Senate Special Committee on Aging. 1975. *Adequacy of Federal Response to Housing Needs of Older Americans.* Part 13. Washington, D.C.: U.S. Government Printing Office.

Van De Water, Paul N. 1979. "Disability Insurance." *American Economic Review* 69 (May): 275–278.

Viscusi, W. Kip. 1979. *Welfare of the Elderly.* New York: Wiley-Interscience.

Walker, James W., and Daniel E. Lupton. 1978. "Performance Appraisal Programs and Age Discrimination Law." *Aging and Work* 1 (Spring): 73–83.

Wallich, Henry. 1969. "Adjustable Bonds: Purchasing Power Bonds." *Newsweek* (November 24).

Wander, Hilde. 1978. "ZPG Now: The Lesson from Europe." In Thomas Espenshade and William Serow, eds., *The Economic Consequences of Slowing Population Growth.* New York: Academic Press.

Watts, Harold, and Felicity Skidmore. 1977. "An Update of the Poverty Picture Plus a New Look at Relative Tax Burdens." *Focus* (University of Wisconsin Institute for Research on Poverty Newsletter) 2 (Fall): 5–7, 10.

Weisbrod, Burton A., and W. Lee Hansen. 1968. "An Income-Net Worth Approach to Measuring Economic Welfare." *The American Economic Review* 58 (December): 1313–1329.

Weise, Robert W., Jr. 1976. "Housewives and Pensions: Foreign Experience." *Social Security Bulletin* 39 (September): 37–44, 50.

Weiss, Randall D. 1976. "Private Pensions: The Impact of ERISA on the Growth of Retirement Funds." In *Funding Pensions: Issues and Implications for Financial Markets.* Federal Reserve Bank of Boston Conference Series, Vol. 16. Boston: Federal Reserve Bank of Boston, pp. 137–151.

Wellington, H. H., and Ralph K. Winter, Jr. 1971. *The Unions and the Cities.* Washington, D.C.: The Brookings Institution.

Wortman, Don I. 1978. Testimony. In Subcommittee on Social Security, U.S. House Committee on Ways and Means, *Disability Insurance Program: 1978.* Serial 95-64. Washington, D.C.: U.S. Government Printing Office, pp. 50–55.

# Index